The Printed Reader

TRANSITS:
LITERATURE, THOUGHT & CULTURE, 1650–1850

Series Editors
Greg Clingham, Bucknell University
Kathryn Parker, University of Wisconsin—La Crosse
Miriam Wallace, New College of Florida

Transits is a series of scholarly monographs and edited volumes publishing beautiful and surprising work. Without ideological bias the series seeks transformative readings of the literary, artistic, cultural, and historical interconnections between Britain, Europe, the Far East, Oceania, and the Americas during the years 1650 and 1850, and as their implications extend down to the present time. In addition to literature, art, and history, such "global" perspectives might entail considerations of time, space, nature, economics, politics, environment, gender, sex, race, bodies, and material culture, and might necessitate the development of new modes of critical imagination. At the same time, the series welcomes considerations of the local and the national, for original new work on particular writers and readers in particular places in time continues to be foundational to the discipline.

Since 2011, sixty-five *Transits* titles have been published or are in production. For a list of recent titles in the series, see the last page in the book.

TRANSITS

The Printed Reader

GENDER, QUIXOTISM, AND
TEXTUAL BODIES IN
EIGHTEENTH-CENTURY BRITAIN

AMELIA DALE

Bucknell | UNIVERSITY
UNIVERSITY | PRESS
LEWISBURG, PENNSYLVANIA

Library of Congress Cataloging-in-Publication Data

Names: Dale, Amelia, author.
Title: The printed reader : gender, quixotism, and textual bodies in
    eighteenth-century Britain / Amelia Dale.
Description: Lewisburg, PA : Bucknell University Press, [2019] |
    Series: Transits : literature, thought & culture 1650–1850 |
    Includes bibliographical references and index.
Identifiers: LCCN 2018057846 | ISBN 9781684481026 (paperback) |
    ISBN 9781684481033 (cloth)
Subjects: LCSH: English literature—18th century—History and
    criticism. | Cervantes Saavedra, Miguel de, 1547–1616—Influence. |
    Quixote, Don (Fictitious character) | Books and reading—Great
    Britain—History—18th century.
Classification: LCC PR441 .D35 2019 | DDC 820.9/005—dc23
LC record available at https://lccn.loc.gov/2018057846

A British Cataloging-in-Publication record for this book is available
from the British Library.

♾ The paper used in this publication meets the requirements of
the American National Standard for Information Sciences—
Permanence of Paper for Printed Library Materials,
ANSI Z39.48-1992.

www.bucknell.edu/UniversityPress

Distributed worldwide by Rutgers University Press

Manufactured in the United States of America

CONTENTS

FQ   Charlotte Lennox, *The Female Quixote, or, The Adventures of Arabella*, edited by Margaret Dalziel, introduction by Margaret Anne Doody, chronology and appendix by Duncan Isles (1989; repr., Oxford: Oxford University Press, 2008).

MP   Elizabeth Hamilton, *Memoirs of Modern Philosophers*, edited by Claire Grogan (Peterborough, Ontario: Broadview Press, 2000).

PH   George Colman the Elder, *Polly Honeycombe*, in *The Rivals and Polly Honeycombe*, by Richard Brinsley Sheridan and George Colman the Elder, edited by David A. Brewer (Peterborough, Ontario: Broadview Press, 2012), 59–110.

SQ   Richard Graves, *The Spiritual Quixote, or The Summer's Ramble of Mr. Geoffry Wildgoose, a Comic Romance*, edited by Clarence Tracy (London: Oxford University Press, 1967).

TS   Laurence Sterne, *The Life and Opinions of Tristram Shandy, Gentleman*, vols. 1 and 2 of *The Florida Edition of the Works of Laurence Sterne*, edited by Melvyn New and Joan New (Gainesville: University Presses of Florida, 1978). In-text references provide book, chapter, and page numbers for this edition.

The Printed Reader

Impressions and the Quixotic Reader

I N RICHARD ALLESTREE'S CONDUCT BOOK *The Ladies Calling* (1673), which remained in print until 1787, Allestree observes that romances mark their readers with "ill impressions":

> I fear they [romances] often leave ill impressions behind them. Those amo-
> rous Passions, which 'tis their design to paint to the utmost Life, are apt
> to insinuate themselves into their unwary Readers, and by an unhappy
> inversion a Copy shall produce an Original. When a poor young Crea-
> ture shall read there of som triumphant Beauty, that has I know not how
> many captiv'd Knights prostrate at her feet, she will probably be temted
> to think it a fine thing.[1]

Allestree uses "impressions" to describe a devious and quasi-textual reproduction. The female reader of romance is so captivated, so tempted by her reading,
that not only does she imitate "some triumphant Beauty" from the pages of
romance, she becomes a paradoxical "Original" to the text's mimetic imitation
of "Life" in a perverse or "unhappy inversion" of the way books are produced
and reproduced.

The central preoccupation of Allestree here is a critical problem that structures literary studies in general and quixotic studies in particular: the interrelation between two bodies in history, the book, a body of paper and print, and the
reader, a fleshly body. Allestree is one among countless writers in the long eighteenth century who refer to "impressions" when trying to describe what it is books
do to their readers, or what happens when texts touch reading minds, and, when
the reader eventually ceases reading, closes the book, what it is that remains or
lingers. Eighteenth-century writers describe romances, novels, theatrical works, sermons, and other media as altering, marking, impressing, and imprinting their
readers and viewers in variously gendered ways. In Britain, alongside both the
expansion of the reading public and the rapid growth in the publication of prose
fiction, there was a well-documented fascination with and anxiety around reading's effect on readers. Turning an eye to quixotic narratives, this book examines

how the relation between reader and text was conceptualized in mid- to late eighteenth-century British literary cultures. I claim that literature was envisaged as *imprinting*—in crucially gendered terms—readers' minds, characters, and bodies. Representations of impressionable quixotic readers were inextricable from eighteenth-century anxieties around subjectivity and gender, as much as literary consumption and production. To examine representations of impressionable readers will be to examine tentative, equivocal and shifting formulations of eighteenth-century selves.

IMPRESSIONS

Descriptions of experience impressing or imprinting the individual have a long history closely bound to histories of media. For instance, in the Platonic dialogues, Socrates tells Theaetetus to imagine that our minds contain a wax block: "We make impressions upon this of everything we wish to remember among the things we have seen or heard or thought of ourselves; we hold the wax under our perceptions and thoughts and take a stamp from them, in the way in which we take the imprints of signet rings. Whatever is impressed upon the wax we remember and know so long as the image remains in the wax; whatever is obliterated or cannot be impressed, we forget and do not know."[2] Perceptions and ideas are inscribed on a mental wax block, like "the imprints of signet rings." Other ancient authors use this same metaphor. Aristotle describes how experience presses an "image," or *eikon*, upon our memory "just as persons do who make an impression with a seal."[3] Despite the apparent metaphoricity of Aristotle's use of wax, this is a description of physical memory, and as a result, the metaphor of the wax tablet becomes invested with literality, or, as Douwe Draaisma states, "something is literally stamped into the body."[4]

Moving into the Enlightenment, in *Rules for the Direction of the Mind* (written approximately in 1628) René Descartes describes "sense-perception" as occurring "in the same way in which wax takes on an impression from a seal" and adds that this statement is more than "a mere analogy."[5] Descartes explains that "we must think of the external shape of the sentient body as being really changed by the object in exactly the same way as the shape of the surface of the wax is altered by the seal."[6] This formulation of sensation as waxen imprinting is not exclusive to touch: for Descartes, each of the other sensory organs, including the eyes, find themselves encased in malleable, skin-like membranes, which are then impressed by the objects perceived, "thus, in the eye, the first opaque membrane receives the shape impressed upon it by multi-coloured light."[7] Impressions become a means to describe sensations as they are registered within and throughout the machinations of the body.

In Descartes's writing, "impressions" are how matter and spirit touch. Cartesian impressions both split body from soul, and open space for a contact between a "corporeal" mode of operation and the "spiritual" capacity "through which we know things in the strict sense."[8] When discussing a purely cerebral "cognitive power," Descartes again invokes the wax image: "[T]he cognitive power is sometimes passive, sometimes active; sometimes resembling the seal, sometimes the wax. But this should be understood merely as an analogy, for nothing quite like this power is to be found in corporeal things."[9] If, according to Descartes, a body feels by being imprinted by what it senses, and the mind also thinks through a process analogous to imprinting, then Cartesian impressions on the body seem to be more literal than their mental equivalent.[10] Crucially, it is here, within the ambiguity of metaphor, that the spiritual can respond to the corporeal and flesh can be marked by mind.

Let us turn to another Cartesian invocation of the wax image: "[T]he 'common' sense functions like a seal, fashioning in the phantasy or imagination, as if in wax, the same figures or ideas which come, pure and without body, from the external senses. The phantasy is a genuine part of the body, and is large enough to allow different parts of it to take on many different figures and, generally, to retain them for some time."[11] At this particular juncture, Descartes does not clarify if the "as if in wax" is "more" than an analogy or merely one. Tellingly, the passage describes a process where mind and body seem to rub against each other, when spiritual or cerebral quantities—"figures or ideas which come, pure and without body"—are crafted "as if in wax" within an embodied space, "a genuine part of the body." The varying degrees of metaphoricity of the Cartesian wax seal image articulate, negotiate, but also obscure the relation between mind and body, thought and matter.

The image of the individual being imprinted recurs across the history of philosophy. Sigmund Freud takes up the metaphor of perception as a waxen tablet with a deep sense of the history of metaphors of mind, and their proximity to histories of technologies of writing. His "Mystic Writing-Pad," is an apparatus of "dark brown resin or wax with paper edging," which "some time ago there came upon the market."[12] To write on it is to make "depressions" and "presses" on wax.[13] The "Mystic Writing-Pad" that simultaneously erases writing and retains its trace, provides a metaphor of mind that encompasses the Freudian unconscious, while the "insistence" of Freud's "metaphorical investment" demands a comprehension of his analogy as a meditation on not the "perceptual apparatus of the mind" alone but also on the nature of writing and metaphor.[14] Draaisma compares the structure of the "Mystic Writing-Pad" to the structure of metaphors in general: "an instrument with two layers, a unification of word and image."[15] Freud's writing also stresses that metaphors of mind themselves spring from minds. Or, to quote Jacques Derrida, "the psychical is caught up in an apparatus, and what is written will be more readily represented as a part extracted from the apparatus and 'materialized.'"[16]

Scriptive metaphors of subjectivity persist within contemporary writing. The word "impressions" retains its Cartesian capacity to straddle mind and body: the theorist Sara Ahmed chooses to persistently refer to "impressions" because the term, encompassing perception, cognition, and emotion, can productively comprehend "experience" without making "artificial" distinctions between bodily sensation, emotion, and thought.[17] Eighteenth-century writings likewise exploit the wide reach of impressions' conceptual grasp. Brad Pasanek observes: "Fixed, struck, or stamped, impressions are variously made on and in the brain, the mind, the heart, the soul, the memory, the understanding, the imagination, and the passions. [. . .] Both words and images are stamped on hearts, minds, and souls. The mind is figured throughout the long eighteenth century as both that which stamps and that which is stamped."[18] While prominent seventeenth- and eighteenth-century philosophers like Descartes, John Locke, and David Hume differ in their epistemological models, their definitions of impressions, and their use of "impressions" as a "mere analogy" or as a corporeal process, they consistently deploy the idea of "impression" to describe the way the senses receive data from the external world. To remember, to experience, to feel, is to possess an experientially-impressed body and mind.

With the advent of the codex, parchment and then paper, "imprinting" and "impressions" became irrevocably connected to the technology of print as much as they were previously structured by the materiality of wax.[19] Print in the eighteenth century depended on a printing press literally *pressing* an inked surface upon the print medium (paper, or sometimes cloth) (figure 1). Amid the letterpress's process of composition, imposition, and presswork, "impression" becomes an important technical term for printers, encompassing a range of meanings: "impression" can stand for the process of printing a text ("taking an impression"), the quality of the result (a "good," "bad," "light," or "heavy" impression"), as well as a description of all copies of an edition printed at any one time.[20] Similarly, "imprint," as well as denoting stamping something onto something else, including type onto paper, also has a specific meaning in book production, referring to the printer's or publisher's information (the latter became more typical as the eighteenth century progressed), usually on the title page of a book.[21] The title page of the second, 1673 edition of *The Ladies Calling*, prominently displays "The second Impression" on its title page (figure 2),

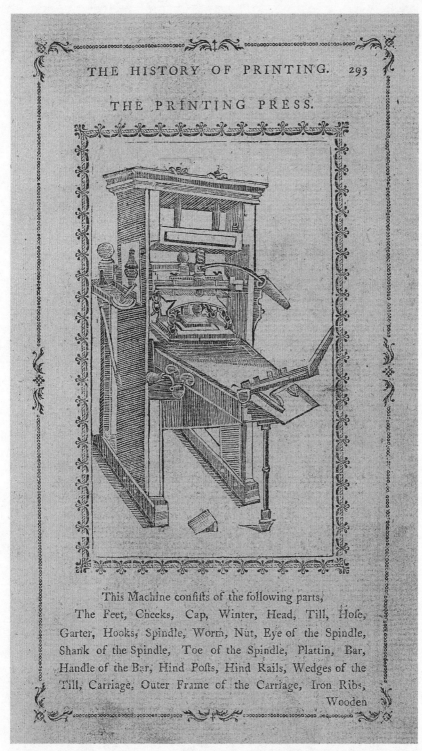

THE PRINTING PRESS.

This Machine confifts of the following parts,
The Feet, Cheeks, Cap, Winter, Head, Till, Hofe,
Garter, Hooks, Spindle, Worm, Nut, Eye of the Spindle,
Shank of the Spindle, Toe of the Spindle, Plattin, Bar,
Handle of the Bar, Hind Pofts, Hind Rails, Wedges of the
Till, Carriage, Outer Frame of the Carriage, Iron Ribs,
Wooden

FIGURE 1 A wooden printing press. Beinecke Rare Book and Manuscript Library, Yale University.

THE
Ladies Calling

IN TWO PARTS.

By the Author of the WHOLE DUTY OF MAN, &c.

The second Impreſſion.

Favor is deceitful, and Beauty is vain : but a Woman that feareth the Lord, she shall be praised. Pr.31.30.

At the THEATER in OXFORD.

M. DC. LXXIII.

FIGURE 2 Title page of the second edition of *The Ladies Calling*, 1673. Courtesy Chawton House Library.

with these words more emphatically imprinted on the page than anything else save for the title itself. This prominent paratextual "second Impression" binds Allestree's description of the "Impressions" that mark the romance reader to the technology that brought *The Ladies Calling* into existence.

Such is the eighteenth-century prominence of print that earlier media also reliant on "impressions" becomes retroactively associated with print technology. Coining, for instance, in Joseph Addison's *Dialogues Upon the Usefulness of Ancient Medals* (1721) becomes inscribed by print. Philander observes that coinage "was a kind of Printing, before the art was invented."[22] While I could potentially distinguish, as Pasanek does, "impressions" from "writing," "ink," "engraving," "coinage," and "spotting," it is also necessary to acknowledge how closely interconnected these tropes are and were, despite being grounded in different materials.

Speaking of different materials, the eighteenth-century book object is itself constructed out of multiple materials that have been diversely "impressed." The paper of British books like *The Ladies Calling* typically consists of linen rags that have been stamped into sheets. Paper watermarks are imprinted during the formation of the paper itself, "like a birthmark."[23] During the paper production process, copper wire is fixed to the mold, leaving a permanent imprint on the paper fibers scooped from the vat.[24] Turning to the binding, the copy of *The Ladies Calling* I examined at Chawton House Library was elaborately decorated with tooling, marks left by building up patterns with heated metal tools on the cover, leaving a design in the form of an imprint, and then further ornamented with gold leaf. Imprinting, impressing, and stamping make and mark the surfaces of eighteenth-century book objects.

Most famously, tropes of impressing, imprinting, and marking are sutured to the formulation of the Enlightenment subject as a blank page. Locke's enormously influential *An Essay Concerning Human Understanding* (1689) uses impressions and marks on the page to conceptualize how ideas are "printed" or "imprinted" on the mind.[25] Deidre Lynch, arguing for the role of typography in eighteenth-century constructions of "character," notes that at the center of the *Essay*'s description of human understanding is an "analogy" connecting the receiving of ideas and the process of individuation to typography.[26] While the page, marked by the printing press, is admittedly one of Locke's many metaphors of experience and character (the Lockean mind, for instance, is also an eye, or a site of storage), it strikingly speaks to the concerns evoked by Allestree's description. The mind as (im)printed page offers a formulation of experience and subjectivity as a mode of textual (re)production, forcefully conjoining ideas of "human understanding" with anxieties surrounding the consumption, production, and embodiment of literature.

GENDERING IMPRESSIONS AND THE IMPRESSED BODY

Impressions are gendered, as the Allestree epigraph crucially implies. The trope of being imprinted by experience could have bawdy connotations, with printing (and imprinting) used as a euphemism for penetration (and potentially impregnation).[27] References to imprinted minds can suggest sexually penetrated bodies. These connections between impressions and sexual penetration stem from a historically persistent understanding of sexual reproduction as involving female matter imprinted and molded by male templates. Aristotle's influential theory of generation involves the male seed providing the form of the child, while the female seed just provides the basic material out of which the child is formed. In other words, the female seed is shaped and molded by a male form. Accordingly, in the early modern period, impregnation is frequently described as an imprinting technique, with pregnant women compared to impressed wax, and later printed paper.[28]

Long-standing cultural associations that group femininity with matter and masculinity with shaping form can be tied to the gendering of the mind/body relation within the history of philosophy. Feminist theorist Elizabeth Grosz identifies a persistent representational alignment of "body" with "woman" and "man" with mind."[29] Certainly, eighteenth-century writers repeatedly situate the imagination between mind and body, invest it with the capacity to reduce or transform ideas into matter, and gender it as feminine. The power of the female imagination is perhaps most apparent in theories of the strength of the mother's imagination and its ability to imprint the flesh of the baby in utero: a striking example of the capacity for ideas, via the imagination, to literally mark the body.

Into the mid-eighteenth century, the theory of the mother's imagination's capacity to mark her unborn infant's skin, and mold its flesh in utero, held considerable purchase.[30] The mother's imagining mind could imprint matter. This power for a mind to mark a body was framed in explicitly textual terms. Kiran Toor writes, "What is perhaps most striking about the theory of maternal impressions is the indelible power granted to the imagination. Endowed with the ability to usurp the rules of generative resemblance, an image of an absent object— represented only in the mother's mind—can be inscribed as a trace onto the body of a foetus. No longer required to resemble its parents, the body of the child is *overwritten* by the imagination, even to deformity. [. . .] In this sense, the body of the child becomes a literal *text*."[31] The textuality of the marked child's body is overt in Jacques Du Bosc's analogy between maternal impressions and impressions from reading. In the popular conduct book *L'honneste femme* (1632), or *The Accomplished Woman*, which ran into multiple editions and at least eight English translations, Du Bosc describes the reading of "certain" romance narratives as leaving quasi-maternal impressions on their readers. "[N]othing is more common than to see Persons wholly changed after reading certain Books; they assume new Passions, they lead quite another Life. The Reason is manifest enough; for as Mothers, upon viewing some extraordinary Objects, often leave the Marks thereof upon their Infants, why should we not believe that the lascivious Stories in Romances may have the same effect upon our Imagination, and that they always leave behind them some Spots upon the Soul?"[32] The wrong kind of reading imprints the reader's imagination and dots suspect "Spots" upon the "Soul," just as the mother's infant is marked by images that have struck the maternal imagination. Du Bosc uses the maternally marked fetus to analogize the imprinted "Soul" of the romance reader, the baby's spotted flesh offering a corporeal counterpart to the romance reader's lasciviously spotted "Soul." Metaphor threatens to collapse into literality. Enraptured readers, powerful imaginations, and marked bodies are connected through more than analogy, and the description of "lascivious Stories in Romances" spotting their reader's "Soul" suggests—as with Allestree—the capacity for romances to prompt their readers into engaging in illicit sex. Romances, in other words, can indirectly result in their readers undergoing a sexual imprinting.

So Du Bosc's reference to sexually suspect "Spots," like Allestree's "ill Impressions," suggests how romance reading can mark the mind *and* body. Conversely, feminized, unmarked pages simultaneously suggest both a mind and a body "unblemished" by sexual experience or knowledge. Through the analogies between printed impressions and sexual penetration, the blank page can stand for ignorance, virginity, and appropriate femininity. This is exemplified in a "coxcomb's" remark in Mary Hays's *Emma Courtney* (1796): "[K]nowledge and learning, are insufferably masculine in a woman—born only for the soft solace of man! The mind of a young lady should be clear and unsullied, like a sheet of paper, or her own fairer face."[33] Hays suggests how images of "unsullied" whiteness, central to racialized discourse surrounding virginity, intersect with the eighteenth-century conceptualization of the subject as a blank page printed over by knowledge. The sheet of paper is compared to both the "mind of a young lady" and her "fairer face."

Another, earlier, pointed example is Laurence Sterne's *Tristram Shandy*'s (1759–67) description of the "concupiscible" Widow Wadman in volume 6. Instead of a detailing of her character or her body, she is represented by a blank page (figure 3), which "Sir" the reader is encouraged to draw on (*TS*, 6.38.566–567). The blank page is immediately followed by the exclamation, "Was ever any thing in Nature so sweet!—so exquisite!" (*TS*, 6.38.568). There are, of course, innumerable modes and methods of drawing on Widow Wadman's blank page, but it is striking the way it presents—albeit with Sternean irony—desirable femininity as a passive, blank, but inscribable text. In a novel that relentlessly connects pens with

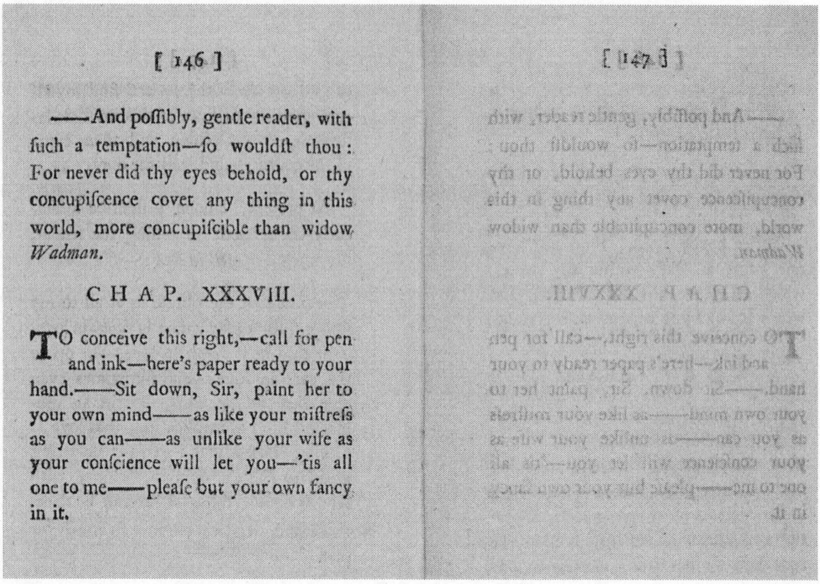
[146]

——And poſſibly, gentle reader, with ſuch a temptation—ſo wouldſt thou: For never did thy eyes behold, or thy concupiſcence covet any thing in this world, more concupiſcible than widow *Wadman*.

CHAP. XXXVIII.

TO conceive this right,—call for pen and ink—here's paper ready to your hand.——Sit down, Sir, paint her to your own mind——as like your miſtreſs as you can——as unlike your wife as your conſcience will let you—'tis all one to me——pleaſe but your own fancy in it.

[147]

FIGURE 3 The blank page in volume 6 of *Tristram Shandy*, 1762. Beinecke Rare Book and Manuscript Library, Yale University.

penises, the reader is invited, with an overt eroticism, to "call for pen and ink" and "paint her to your own mind" (*TS*, 6.38.566).

The Enlightenment trope of the subject as a page being written or imprinted by experience therefore maps onto a description of a white, feminine, virginal slate being stained, blotted, and altered by sexual experience. Allestree evokes these associations in his description of a romance reader whose impressions from her reading leads inexorably to her sexual "ruin" as a "natural consequent."[34] Allestree's words also suggest how anxieties around female, silent, solitary reading overlaid concerns surrounding masturbation's "suspicious solitude."[35] The popular antimasturbatory tract *Onania* (c. 1712), explicitly connects masturbation to the consumption of "*Ill-Books*" and silent reading of literature, while simultaneously "seriously" considering the "Impression" masturbation "must necessarily make on the Minds of those, that have given themselves over to it."[36] "*Ill-Books*," masturbation, and fornication are all multiply figured as marking, spotting, and tainting the mind. The trope of imprinting as penetrative sex conflates the reader's malleable imagination, marked by "*Ill-Books*," and the seduced woman's defiled body. To have an inscribable, malleable, penetrated subjectivity—to be, I will suggest, quixotic—is to be feminized, but feminized in a way that shifted from the mid- to late eighteenth century.

This is particularly the case given the burgeoning of sentimentalism in the mid- to late eighteenth century—the period this book focuses on—which brought with it an intense preoccupation with the human body as an eloquent object.[37] Sentimentalism stresses the body as offering a language of feeling through "its postures and gestures, its involuntary palpitations and collapses."[38] Sentimental bodies should be read as impressionable bodies: bodies that can become legibly, affectively impressed by feeling and aesthetic experience.

Through sentimentalism, the imprinted body is not merely matter stamped by experience, but is readable material, congruous with the printed book in its tactility and capacity to convey and transmit the passions. Mid- to late eighteenth-century impressionable bodies can be legibly marked by potentially sexually suspect stains of experience, but also, sometimes simultaneously, they are eloquently imprinted with the language of feeling. For instance, the eighteenth-century physician George Cheyne describes "Sensibility" as depending on the "Compactness and closer Union" of the nervous parts of the body.[39] This closeness allows each "Impression" received from the external environment to be speedily communicated to the "*Sensorium* in the Brain."[40] What ultimately results is a materialist formulation of feeling, and a definition of sensibility that depends on impressions. According to Cheyne: "*Feeling* is nothing but the Impulse, Motion, or Action of Bodies, gently or violently impressing the Extremities or Sides of the Nerves, of the Skin, or other Parts of the Body, which by their Structure and *Mechanism*, convey this Motion to the *Sentient* Principle in the Brain."[41] Such a definition of sensibility demonstrates the way impressions could constitute all the complexities of feeling: emotion and sensation. The "gently or violently impressing" of bodies and organs is synonymous with feeling itself. Formations of sensibility, as much as quixotic impressions, are structured around formulations of an imprinted body, congruous with a printed text. The self-conscious literature of sensibility, Alex Wetmore recently argues, correlates the feeling, eloquent body with the materiality of the book object, to the point where typographical impressions on the page become yoked to the communicative power of the legible, affectively imprinted sentimental body.[42]

What this book claims is this: toward the end of the century, when the idea of experiential "impressions" became much less used, and in an increasingly metaphorical sense, there was, paradoxically, a more emphatic and definitive positioning of the impressionable reading body as female. This transition can be tied to the well-documented politicization and interrogation of sensibility at the end of the century, as well as larger shifts around gender that Dror Wahrman identifies: from an earlier period that might have been "broadly prescriptive but allowing for individual deviations" of gendered roles and types, to the turn of the century, which was marked by a more inflexible branding of such deviations as "unnatural."[43] There was a turn from a characterization of quixotic impressionability as constituted by multiple performed, imprinted surfaces to a more anxious treatment of impressionability as intrinsically female and as politically fraught. Already prominent in gendered commentaries on the literary marketplace, as the century came to an end, feminized, impressionable bodies became even more frequent in literature, and a source of heightened concern.

MISREADERS IN THE MARKETPLACE

But first, to take a step back: the manifold significations of the gendered, impressionable reading body color the plentiful representations of reading women throughout the eighteenth century. Allestree's passionate, malleable reader, moved on an affective and bodily level, exemplifies a stereotype (to use another printing term) that pervades eighteenth-century print culture: the female reader who reads in the wrong way and chaotically and corporeally reproduces her reading.

The "misreader," or reader who misreads a text, is nearly synonymous with "Miss reader." The apparent ease with which she is moved, seduced, and changed by books, is described in reviews, plays, conduct literature, anti-novel tracts, and novels themselves. For example, Dorinda in Jane Barker's *The Lining of the Patch-Work Screen* (1726), is introduced as a woman rescued from her suicide attempt. She explains why she attempted to take her life: "It was such Romantick Whimsies that brought upon me the Ruin and Distress in which you behold me; I had read Plays, Novels, and Romances, till I began to think my self a Heroine of the first rate; and all Men that flatter'd, or ogled, me were Heroes."[44] Dorinda's voracious reading forms her conception of herself as a "Heroine of the first rate," and, at the same time, makes her more vulnerable to transgressive sex, in her case, with her footman.

Dorinda is typical of a century that, with increasing intensity, represented misreading as female. A similar story appears in *The World* (July 1754), describing Clarinda, whose education, focusing on dress, dance, and music, "immoderately softened the natural effeminacy of her mind," resulting in her spending all her spare time "in the ensnaring practice of reading NOVELS and ROMANCES; of which CLELIA was her favourite, and the hero of it continually in her head."[45] The man her father wants her to marry "was not the hero which CLELIA had impressed on CLARINDA's imagination," and, like Dorinda, she instead becomes interested in a servant, in her case, a French valet.[46] The narrator stresses the "softness" of femininity and romances: Clarinda seeks them out because they "represent the same softness" as her hyper-feminine education. It is Clarinda's "softness" that leads her to read "NOVELS and ROMANCES" and it is her softness that renders her sexually vulnerable. Soft women, it seems, read soft texts, which leave them even more "softened," that is, liable to sexual transgressions and imitative reading. Female romance readers read via their soft bodies.

Case studies of specific, historical female readers, as well as larger studies of female literary consumption, have demonstrated that there was little truth to the pervasive stereotype.[47] A growing body of scholarship suggests how depictions of impressionable female readers need to be understood contextually as a sign of larger anxieties. Given the belief that women were softer and possessed more sensibility than their male counterparts, the vulnerable reading woman, more impressionable and less reasonable, both signals the capacity of literature to affectively "imprint" readers of all genders and becomes a ready sign for larger cultural concerns.[48] These include the proliferation of printed texts, the ever-growing presence of women in the literary marketplace as authors and consumers—with writers such as Alexander Pope responding to what they saw as a "feminization" increasingly characteristic of literary activity—and a wide variety of concerns beyond the literary marketplace such as sexual difference, sensibility, labor, class, the health of the nation-state, the role of religion, and revolutionary politics.[49]

The trope of texts imprinting readers configured mid- to late eighteenth-century British articulations of the transformative power of print and the expansion of the literary marketplace. Pertinently, recent work by Richard De Ritter and Joe Bray has stressed the way female readers in the late eighteenth century were not solely portrayed as passive, but that representations of female reading were multifaceted and encompassed descriptions of them as active agents.[50] There were many ways of depicting the female reader in the late eighteenth century. I do not pretend here to provide a comprehensive overview of the diversity of representations of female readers in the period. Instead, looking at male as well as female reproductive readers, I will focus on the important figure of the impressionable quixotic reader, and how gendered conceptualizations of impressions shift and transition. Integral to representations of reproductive, embodied reading, the trope of the imprinted subject became complexly bound up in characterizations of the quixotic reader.

IMPRINTING QUIXOTES

Impressions, I will posit, provide a means to re-evaluate the moral panic around novel reading, the proliferation of quixotic narratives, and the gendering of the quixote in eighteenth-century Britain. The preoccupation with texts' capacity to imprint their readers' minds, bodies, and characters is integral to the eighteenth-century fascination with Miguel de Cervantes's novel *Don Quixote* (1605, 1615). In *Don Quixote*, an ordinary Spanish gentleman turns mad from his romance reading, believing himself to be a heroic knight. *Don Quixote*'s influence on British literature in the eighteenth century was, as J.A.G. Ardila puts it, "pre-eminent, to an extent that remains beyond compare."[51] There were numerous translations and theatrical adaptions, while characters and narratives indebted to *Don Quixote* appeared in novels, plays, poetry, letters, conduct books, and philosophical treatises. Don Quixote became part of what David A. Brewer terms a "textual commons"—part of a public canon of characters—that authors repeatedly drew upon, in literary, theatrical, and philosophical works.[52]

This collective corpus of quixotic narratives is not even limited to those that directly cite *Don Quixote*. The romance reader in Allestree's *The Ladies Calling*, for example, demands to be classified as quixotic. Like Don Quixote, she puts her book down only to attempt to live her reading. She tries to emulate the behavior of a heroine in a romance, using her books to "instruct" her, and, like Don Quixote, she is ultimately unsuccessful. While Don Quixote dies, lamenting his prior follies, Allestree's romance reader's sexual "ruin" is the result of her reading.[53]

To ask how to read the relation between Allestree's romance reader and Don Quixote invites the larger question about how to build a catalog of quixotic narratives. There are multiple methods. One can find texts with direct allusions to Cervantes's novel or focus on formal, narratological congruities to Cervantes's work. Aaron R. Hanlon observes the way catalogs of quixotic texts proliferate endlessly, to the extent that listing them becomes in itself a quixotic task.[54] He stresses the importance of considering quixotism systematically, rather than getting lost in the endless problem of categorizing citations.[55] April Alliston, Wendy Motooka, and Scott Paul Gordon also stress the way quixotism is a problem and a practice, rather than a direct importation of Don Quixote's character or Cervantes's narrative.[56] By working toward a systematic theory of quixotism, we can see how British quixotic narratives use Cervantes's novel as a prompt to represent concerns about the transformative power of literature and other media. Specifically, this book will argue that printing—and particularly a gendered framing of this technology—structured eighteenth-century conceptualizations of quixotism in particular and reading in general. In my interest in the quixotic narrative as a genre, I differ from Bray, who argues that to describe a reading practice as "quixotic misreading" is to dismiss it.[57] To read a reader (as it were) as quixotic is not to dismiss their reading practice as simply misguided, but to recognize its complexity and situate their representation within a literary, theoretical, and historical framework.

In the eighteenth century, Don Quixote's imitative reading proffers an epistemological problem inflected by contemporaneous formulations of impressions. Gordon and Motooka both describe how British writers draw on philosophical debates in their formulation of quixotism.[58] The quixote experiences the world from a highly specific perspective that immediately problematizes ideas of "common sense," cultural norms, and universal reason. For instance, Allestree's romance reader interprets her life through a lens marked by romances; after reading of heroines with multiple knights at her feet, she reads her own situation according to romance's conventions, reflecting "how much she looses time, that has not yet subdu'd one heart."[59] Her vision of the world and herself conforms to the laws of romance, but is at odds with Allestree's narration and his reader's presumed position.

It seems that to view the world through a quixotic perspective is to have been imprinted by impressions. For instance, Francis Bacon, in the opening to his *Historia Naturalis et Experimentalis* (1622), invokes impressions to describe the capacity for a person's (quixotic) subjectivity to interfere or mark their experience of the world. He states that his work as a natural philosopher would be easier "if the human intellect were flat and like a clean slate," but instead "men's minds are so marvellously beset that they altogether lack a clear and polished surface."[60] Instead of viewing the world through a "flat and clean" lens, pre-existing impressions blemish human perception: "[W]e plainly set the seal of our own image on the creatures and works of God rather than carefully examining and recognizing the seal that the Creator has set upon them."[61] Gordon observes how Bacon stresses that "the very objects that the mind receives—to observe, judge, analyze, assess—are already reshaped by cultural or personal forms."[62] Everyone's system or lens for perceiving the world is already imprinted by preconceived ideas. "We" are all quixotes. What is more, this quixotic vision is articulated—in ways redolent of Descartes—according to the valences of setting a waxen seal.

To be quixotic is to be problematically imprinted. Quixotes reason according to a set of rules that have been "impressed" or "stamped" upon them. Through the prism of Motooka and Gordon, quixotes, by doing so, problematize notions of universal reason, philosophical inquiry, and an empirically verified "reality."[63] In this book, I want to bring to Motooka's and Gordon's rich readings the observations—made by Sean Silver and Pasanek (among others)—that eighteenth-century epistemological philosophy was steeped in reference to material cultures and, relatedly, Wendy Wall's work on the gendering of print in the early modern period.[64] This book explores what happened after Wall's book ends, and what the mid- to late eighteenth-century gendering of print means for quixotic narratives.

Quixotic narratives, it needs to be said, are invested in impressions in another, more immediate way. They are, after all, about readers who try to embody and replicate their reading. Quixotic narratives self-consciously comment on print marketplace and literary-cultural (re)production. Cervantes's *Don Quixote* itself, with the second volume concerned with countering Alonso Fernández de Avellaneda's sequel, is saturated by a self-reflexive concern with print, authorship, and authority. Valuable work by Eve Tavor Bannet and Jodi L. Wyett situates eighteenth-century quixotism in relation to print culture and self-conscious meditations on transnational literary imitation, consumption, and female authorship.[65] Through examining the quixote's body as a site for gendered textual reproduction, *The Printed Reader* builds on Bannet's and Wyett's work, reading quixotic narratives as commentaries on textual transmission and a feminized literary marketplace through these texts' concern with the impressionable, book-like body of the quixote.

Quixotic narratives highlight how "it is reading, more than writing, that echoes the imprinting of the empiricist self."[66] Rebecca Tierney-Hynes identifies the problem of the absorbed romance reader as vital to the history of the eighteenth-century subject who comes to be constituted in and through language. Tierney-Hynes, Lynch, and Wahrman all argue for the contingent, unstable nature of the early modern self.[67] Relatedly, Lynch, with Silver, stresses the role of printed commodities and material objects within equivocal prototypes of modern subjectivity.[68] This book draws these projects together, in order to show not only how the material textures of eighteenth-century print objects are attached to tenuous constructions of a "self" but also how the varying metaphoricity of eighteenth-century formulations of "impressions" works to both destabilize and shore up shifting notions of gender and sex.

Bringing together work on the material text, the history of reading, philosophy, and eighteenth-century British quixotic narratives, this book stresses how representations of impressionable reading bodies were central to how the power of print was comprehended by mid- to late eighteenth-century British cultures. It connects developments in print technology to gendered conceptualizations of quixotism. The five quixotic narratives examined in this book each differently figure the interrelation between impressions, literary form, and anxieties around gendered textual proliferation. We begin with Charlotte Lennox's highly influential feminization of the quixote in *The Female Quixote* (1752) and end with Elizabeth Hamilton's popular political take on embodied reading in *Memoirs of Modern Philosophers* (1800). In Hamilton's work, the quixotic, impressionable body becomes entangled in the politicization of sensibility. Into the nineteenth century, developments in print technology meant that presses could produce on mass more consistent "impressions" of text on the page. This, I posit, has implications for the viability of "impressions" as an analogy in philosophy, given the way philosophers such as Hume drew on the irregularity of eighteenth-century print technology to describe the variations within which individuals registered experience. Certainly, at the turn of the century, "impressions" began to take on a more strictly figurative meaning in philosophical writings.

All that said, *The Printed Reader* does not track a neat, teleological progression from literal "impressions" to an allegorical use of the concept. Instead, what becomes visible is the historically complex entanglements of metaphor, the difficulty of disentangling the figurative from the literal, and the way literal impressions might be metaphorized, and metaphorical impressions literalized, within the same historical moment and often within the same text.

Chapter 1 reassesses Charlotte Lennox's important novel *The Female Quixote* (1752). Drawing on Thomas Hobbes and Hume, I argue that *The Female Quixote* describes the quixote's body as an imprinted page inflected with the ostentatious visuality of mid-eighteenth-century print. Eyes in this novel are imprinted, molded, and marked, even as they watch and read. The visuality of quixotic impressions in this novel has implications for Lennox's authorial positioning. She writes with a playful awareness of placing herself before the reader's eyes within a literary marketplace that frequently censored women writers and described feminized readers as being deviously marked and imprinted by their readings.

George Colman the Elder's short farce, *Polly Honeycombe, a Dramatick Novel of One Act* (1760), continues *The Female Quixote*'s concern with impressionable, quixotic female reading. In chapter 2, I argue that through placing quixotic novel reading onstage, *Polly Honeycombe* self-consciously compares the quixotic novel reader's embodiment of text to the actor's embodiment of script. The actor's body—described in Aaron Hill's writings on acting as an impressionable, imprinted surface—becomes the locale for a quixotic (re)production of text. In *Polly Honeycombe*, the presence of the actress's body underscores the layers of performed surfaces inherent in mid-eighteenth-century formulations of impressionable reading.

Laurence Sterne's *Tristram Shandy* (1759–67), the focus of chapter 3, interrogates the debates about gendered literary consumption and (re)production that *The Female Quixote* and *Polly Honeycombe* also self-consciously participate in. Concerned with the relation between literary and sexual reproduction, *Tristram Shandy* responds to the trope of the feminized, quixotic reader with quixotes who are equivocally male. The Shandy men attempt to render the male rather than the female body a site for literary and sexual generation. Playing on the sexual and affective resonances of "impressions," *Tristram Shandy* simultaneously satirizes eighteenth-century quixotic narratives about impressionable female readers and reiterates their tropes via impressionable masculine bodies. Ostentatiously marked by genital injuries or impairments, the surface of the tenuously male Shandean body becomes an impressionable erogenous zone.

In Richard Graves's anti-Methodist satire, *The Spiritual Quixote* (1773) (chapter 4), the equivocally male Shandean body becomes reworked into the ambiguously gendered, also impressionable Methodist body. *The Spiritual Quixote* suggestively compares religious enthusiasts (male and female)—who are presented as being unable to differentiate between impressions on the body that signify spiritual experiences and those that signify physical arousal—to the female, novel-reading quixote's collapse of book and body. The novel represents Methodism as a feminized religion and suggests that it thrives on malleable, quixotic bodies. With Methodism represented as penetrating and imprinting its converts, *The Spiritual Quixote* draws analogies between quixotic impressions, literary production, and religious enthusiasm, situating quixotism, and the fraught relationship between flesh and text, in British religious cultures.

Chapter 5 examines Elizabeth Hamilton's *Memoirs of Modern Philosophers* (1800), one of many politicized quixotic narratives at the turn of the century. Hamilton's novel represents radical philosophers as memorizing, fetishizing, and repeating phrases and words, resulting in a proliferation of feminized text. Similar to *The Spiritual Quixote*'s representation of quixotism as an enthusiastic entrapment in flesh, in *Memoirs*, quixotic "Modern Philosophy" is aligned with materialism and a spawning of print. *Memoirs*, like all the other texts discussed in the book, is preoccupied with quixotic reading bodies, the embodiment of writing, and textual reproduction. However, Hamilton, more than the other authors in this study, is concerned with distancing her own authorial and readerly practice from quixotic, reproductive consumption. In Hamilton's work we can see how late eighteenth-century articulations of quixotic impressions reflect solidifying gender norms. *Memoirs* depicts quixotic impressions more metaphorically than any of the other case studies, a sign that the trope of being imprinted by media was becoming more frequently comprehended on a strictly figurative level.

MARKING THE EYES IN *THE FEMALE QUIXOTE*

IN CHARLOTTE LENNOX'S *THE FEMALE QUIXOTE* (1752), Arabella, the titular quixote, describes how Orontes, "happening to see the Picture of the beautiful *Thalestris*, Daughter of the Queen of the *Amazons*," fell "passionately in Love with her" (*FQ*, 72). Arabella's anecdote reflects how the chivalric romances she reads invest images of female beauty with immense power. This tale of a man falling for a picture occurs in a novel that interrogates the imagination's capacity to collapse representations with "originals." Arabella, a wealthy young woman who has grown up secluded in her father's house, is quixotically in thrall to the pictures painted by the books she reads. She emulates the topoi of seventeenth-century French romances, behaving, and expecting to be treated, as if she is a princess in a romance. She is disappointed, for instance, that her father's choice of a suitor, Glanville, does not act like a hero in a romance and "should make so poor a Figure when he entertained her with Matters of Gallantry" (*FQ*, 30). While the figure of the female misreader is prevalent in texts throughout the century, representations of her proliferated following Lennox's influential novel. All Anglophone eighteenth-century quixotic narratives after Lennox can be read as being, to a greater or lesser extent, in conversation with her work.

With its overt interrogation of the gendered relationship between the novel, romance, and history, *The Female Quixote* occupies a centrality within contemporary critical debates around gender, genre, and the eighteenth-century novel.[1] Ending with the romance-reading Arabella renouncing *Clelia* for Richardsonian fiction, *The Female Quixote* can be—and has been—read as an allegorical literary history of the novel.[2] What I want to bring to this discussion is the way Arabella's imagining body is represented within the novel as a textual object. *The Female Quixote* centers her imprinted body in its exploration of gender and genre. Arabella looks quixotically outward, toward the page and toward the world she lives in, but also toward mirrors, examining and eyeing the desirability of her own body, viewing, reading, and rereading herself. *The Female Quixote* thus plays with the shifting distinctions between "seeing," "imagining," "reading," and "imprinting." Meanwhile, eyes are imprinted, molded, and deciphered, even as they themselves watch and read. To see why imprinted eyes are crucial to this novel's formulation of quixotism, it is necessary to attend to Enlightenment theories of the imagination.

MARKING THE EYES

The imagination occupies a centrality in Enlightenment philosophies of quixotism. Enlightenment philosophy conceptualizes the imagination, from the seventeenth century onward, as the faculty responsible for delusions, through its capacity to form chains of irrationally associated images and ideas.[3] With the capacity to imprint—as I discussed in the introduction—both mind and body, the imagination occupies a nebulous position between ideas and matter. Its vexed relation between body and spirit is echoed by its problematic capacity to conflate experience with fantasies and, on a more basic level, its power to conflate disparate ideas: the imagination straddles and potentially conflates such binaries as spirit/matter and memory/fantasy.

Crucially for the concerns of this chapter, the imagination's power to induce quixotism is repeatedly conceptualized by philosophers as a conflation of images. Enlightenment theories of the imagination return, again and again, to the eyes. Thomas Hobbes in *Leviathan* (1651), for instance, emphasizes the etymological link between the visual and the imagination: "[T]he Latines call *Imagination*, from the image made in seeing; and apply the same, though improperly, to all the other senses."[4] Hobbes writes:

> [W]hen a man compoundeth the image of his own person, with the image of the actions of an other man, as when a man imagins himselfe a *Hercules*, or an *Alexander,* (which happeneth often to them that are much taken with reading of Romants) it is a compound imagination, and properly but a Fiction of the mind. There be also other Imaginations that rise in men, (though waking) from the great impression made in sense: As from gazing upon the Sun, the impression leaves an image of the Sun before our eyes a long time after; and from being long and vehemently attent upon Geometricall Figures, a man shall in the dark, (though awake) have the Images of Lines, and Angles before his eyes: which kind of Fancy hath no particular name; as being a thing that doth not commonly fall into mens discourse.[5]

Hobbes's comment about "Fiction[s] of the mind" that "happeneth often to them that are much taken with reading of Romants" is testament to both the influence of *Don Quixote* within Enlightenment philosophy and the capacity for the impressionable reader to simultaneously "trouble and to constitute the ground" of empiricism.[6] This passage both invests the imagination with the power to form quixotic associations and moves from talking about the quixotic romance reader to describing the process of seeing. The Hobbesian quixotic imaginary is decidedly ocular, to the point where impressions are conceived as palinopsia, as persistent afterimages of sunlight. The consumption of romances, like staring at mathematical diagrams, leaves residual impressions or "*decaying*" images on the senses.[7]

These impressions, as Hobbes's reference to palinopsia signals, are emphatically physical. *Leviathan* formulates sensory experience as material pressings: Hobbes also describes smell, sight, and sound in terms of physical "pressure" and motions on and within the body, which "by the mediation of Nerves, and other strings, and membranes of the body" continue "inwards to the Brain, and Heart."[8] The eyes of both the mathematician and the romance reader are thus literally sculpted by what they see. Bodies internally reduplicate what the senses register. Adrian Johns explains in detail how this works for Cartesian formulations of sight: "[A]n image was thought to be 'imprinted' or 'painted' (both words were used) on the retina. [. . .] From thence, it was assumed, 'spirits' channeled in the optic nerves transmitted this image instantly to the brain. There it was again 'impressed' onto something called the *sensus communis*, and thus perceived by the mind."[9] To see is to be multiply imprinted or impressed.

Elsewhere, Enlightenment philosophy looks ocularcentric. John Locke describes how the mind, like an eye, has a problem seeing itself: "[I]t requires Art and Pains to set it at a distance and make it its own Object."[10] The Lockean mind, according to Richard Rorty, is an inner space that ideas pass "in review before a single Inner Eye."[11] Later in the eighteenth century, David Hume also treats the mind as that which sees but is also the object of the philosopher's gaze. He hopes his focus on impressions will recalibrate the way the mind is "seen," resulting in the philosophical equivalent of "a new microscope or species of optics."[12] Hume, more than even Hobbes, takes the eye as a starting point for interrogating the difficulty in disentangling seeing from remembering, and remembering from imagining: "When I shut my eyes and think of my chamber, the ideas I form are exact representations of the impressions I felt; nor is there any circumstance of the one, which is not to be found in the other. In running over my other perceptions, I find still the same resemblance and representation. Ideas and impressions appear always to correspond to each other. This circumstance seems to me remarkable, and engages my attention for a moment."[13] Hume, when posing the problem of distinguishing "impressions" (which, in his highly specific use of the term, refers exclusively to data from the senses) from the "ideas" formed by the mind, returns, again and again, to the eye. He writes, "That idea of red, which we form in the dark, and that impression which strikes our eyes in sun-shine, differ only in degree, not in nature."[14] He blurs the line, even as he draws it, between a material, corporeal eye that is marked or imprinted by the world it perceives and an inner eye that imagines images and colors in the dark. The difficulty of disentangling "ideas" from "impressions" prompts a collapse between mind and body, between imagined and experienced worlds.

This collapse is self-reflexively articulated through print. For instance, in the first sentence of the first book of his *Treatise of Human Nature*, Hume divides "[a]ll the perceptions of the human mind" into "IMPRESSIONS" and "IDEAS."[15] Christina Lupton notes how Hume's typographic emphasis draws attention to the materiality of the page, associating "IMPRESSIONS" with the technology of print. The small caps, imprinted forcefully into the paper of the page, mirror Hume's definition of impressions as offering a particularly "forceful" category of perception.[16] He certainly writes with a model of perception formulated around print, paper, and the book object, repeatedly referring to sensory impressions as analogous to his own writing and its mediation. For instance, he compares the externality of "several impressions" to the way the "paper, on which I write at present, is beyond my hand."[17] Hobbes and Hume, when interrogating the epistemological problems posed by the imagination, return, again and again, to the eye looking at paper.

Hume's descriptions of himself writing a manuscript both speaks to and elides the printed edition of his work his reader is consuming. Hume's suggestive references to print and imprinting could be said to participate in the skeptical turn Michael McKeon identifies in Cervantes's *Don Quixote*.[18] McKeon characterizes Cervantean quixotic epistemology as articulating a moment when "empiricism begins its slide into extreme skepticism."[19] Crucial to McKeon's argument is the technology of the printed book, and how it demands specific practices of reading and evaluation that do not apply to manuscripts: "Because the printed book is subject to close examination and exact replication in a way that storytelling and even manuscripts are not, publication tends to suppress standards of judgment that depend heavily on the context and circumstances of presentation."[20] The result is a quixotic practice inaugurated by print technology and steeped in epistemological skepticism.

A case in point is the thought experiment Hume proposes in his *Treatise*. He imagines two people reading the same "book," but one as a "romance, and another as a true history."[21] Hume's thought experiment deploys print's capacity to occlude the circumstances of a text's production and composition. He reasons that two readers might encounter the same "book" and "receive the same ideas, and in the same order," but the reader who reads the "book" as history would be more sympathetic and absorbed. The history reader "enters deeper into the concerns of the persons," while the romance reader, "who gives no credit to the testimony of the author, has a more faint and languid conception of all these particulars."[22] The two readers read the same words and are impressed with the "same ideas," but Hume stresses that the history reader's impressions of these ideas are "more strong, firm, and vivid" as opposed to the romance reader's "faint and languid" impressions.[23]

The assertion that history elicits stronger impressions and greater readerly absorption is complicated, not least by Hume's awareness of the popularity of romances and novels. In his essay "Of the Study of History" (1741), Hume takes the female reader of "Romances and Novels" as the starting point for his essay and begins with a mock-lament that women have an "Appetite for Falsehood."[24] He then relates a variation of his thought experiment in the *Treatise*. He recounts sending a woman who desired to read "Novels and Romances" Plutarch's *Lives*, "assuring her, at the same Time, that there was not a Word of Truth in them from Beginning to End. She perused them very attentively, 'till she came to the Lives of *Alexander* and *Cæsar*, whose Names she had heard of by Accident, and then returned me the Book, with many Reproaches for deceiving her."[25] Once again, albeit in a comic reversal, the printed book becomes a site of extreme skepticism, troubling judgment, occluding generic distinctions, and blurring empirical categories.

A shift can be identified between Hobbes's and Hume's formulation of quixotism: for the latter, the reading scene (of a book that might be a history or romance) supplants the mirror scene (or the viewing of a diagram). We could connect this to Rebecca Tierney-Hynes's stress on the way Hume's philosophy is linguistic: he describes "the boundarylessness of an identity permeated by the inaccuracies of language."[26] Tierney-Hynes also argues for a shift in the way reading was conceptualized during the eighteenth century, away from an older, seventeenth-century, more imagistic formulation of reading-as-seeing, to a newly textualized reading subject.[27] Accordingly, Humean impressions are invested in the technology of print and the scene of reading, as much as Hobbes might be in the scene of viewing.

In any case, Hume's figuration of perception as imprinting becomes a way to articulate a blurring of "truth and falsehood." This is nowhere more apparent than when he writes: "When the imagination, from any extraordinary ferment of the blood or spirits, acquires such a vivacity as disorders all its powers and faculties, there is no means of distinguishing betwixt truth and falsehood; but every loose fiction or idea, having the same influence as the impressions of the memory, or the conclusions of the judgement, is received on the same footing, and operates with equal force on the passions."[28] The imagination has the capacity to destabilize truth, and it becomes difficult for the Humean subject to distinguish between "ideas" from the imagination and "impressions" from the senses. Potentially all Humean subjects quixotically conflate the two.[29] Returning to Hume's two readers of the same book, it is significant that the only difference between the romance reader's and the history reader's experience is the *force* with which they receive the book's ideas, or whether they are subject to "faint" or "firm" impressions. The irregularities of eighteenth-century print technology meant that a pressing could produce a "light" or "heavy," "good" or "bad" "impression" on the page.[30] Hume repeatedly draws on the technology's residual inconsistencies to analogize "stronger" impressions with belief. He writes: "If we allow, that belief is nothing but a firmer and stronger conception of an object than what attends the mere fictions of the imagination, this operation may, perhaps, in some measure, be accounted for. The concurrence of these several views or glimpses imprints the idea more strongly on the imagination; gives it superior force and vigour; renders its influence on the passions and affections more sensible; and in a word, begets that reliance or security, which constitutes the nature of belief and opinion."[31] Hume tracks how "several views" or "glimpses" of an idea, and a resultant "superior," more forceful imprinting upon the imagination, can translate into a "belief" and "opinion" that has no stronger foundation than "the mere fictions of the imagination."

This imprinting, for Hume, is gendered. He deems "women and children" as "most guided by that faculty," the imagination, and they are therefore more liable to quixotically collapse impressions and ideas.[32] So for Hume, the reader most in thrall to literature, with the body most susceptible to flights of the imagination, is a young female reader, hungry, as we have seen, for "Falsehood." Yet the problem of quixotism, exemplified by female and infantile bodies, also presses at larger concerns. Just as Hume's lament about female consumers of romances, novels, and secret histories suggests history's close relationship with feminized genres, a feminine confusion between "ideas" and "impressions" is a potential issue for anyone who sees, imagines, and reads.

IMPRINTING LENNOX'S FEMALE READERS

The Female Quixote takes up this simultaneous gendering and universalizing of quixotism. In her novel, Lennox asks what happens when Hobbes's imagistic quixote is feminized, when the quixotic mirror scene is inhabited by a woman, who evaluates her own desirability simultaneously with experiencing a quixotically confused self-image. Throughout the novel, Lennox plays with the resonant distinctions and congruities between reading and looking, repeatedly analogizing Arabella's body with the printed page. The novel's narrative is impelled by what Arabella sees when she gazes at herself in the mirror:

> Her Ideas, from the Manner of her Life, and the Objects around her, had taken a romantic Turn; and, supposing Romances were real Pictures of Life, from them she drew all her Notions and Expectations. By them she was taught to believe, that Love was the ruling Principle of the World; that every other Passion was subordinate to this; and that it caused all the Happiness and Miseries of Life. Her Glass, which she often consulted, always shewed her a Form so extremely lovely, that, not finding herself engaged in such Adventures as were common to the Heroines in the Romances she read, she often complained of the Insensibility of Mankind, upon whom her Charms seemed to have so little Influence.
>
> (*FQ*, 7)

The narration persistently refers to sight when describing how Arabella's reading shapes her "Ideas" about "Life." She mistakenly identifies romances as "real Pictures of Life" and draws correspondences between the imaginative "Pictures" from her romance reading and her own reflection. Again, like Hobbes's romance reader, Arabella imaginatively compounds "Pictures" from her reading with the image of herself "shewed" by "Her Glass." Like Hobbes's romance reader, she gazes at her own reflection with eyes residually marked by her reading. That her "Form" resembles a romance heroine's by being "so extremely lovely" encourages her quixotic conflation.

The Female Quixote's transmutation of Cervantes's Don Quixote into a female reader is indebted to Adrien-Thomas Perdou de Subligny's *La fausse Clélie*, or *The Mock Clelia* (1670, translated into English in 1678), where the protagonist, Juliette d'Arviane, thinks she is the heroine of Madeleine de Scudéry's romance *Clélie, histoire romaine* (1654–60).[33] In Subligny's novel, as with Hobbes and Lennox, quixotism involves combining multiple mirrors, pictures, and pages. Early in the work, the Marquess of Riberville laments that he prompted a renewal of Juliette's quixotic behavior through comparing "the majesty of her Body, and the beauty of her Face, to a certain *Roman* Lady whom she resembles, and whose Picture hangs in the House."[34] To be quixotic in Subligny's, Lennox's, and Hobbes's writings involves amalgamating an image of oneself with a "Picture" of an ancient or mythic other.

Lennox's novel sets up important conventions for later quixotic narratives in the century, even as the mirror scene suggests how *The Female Quixote* looks back as well as forward. Unlike *Polly Honeycombe*'s and *Tristram Shandy*'s self-reflexive play with print and quixotically imprinted bodies (chapter 2 and chapter 3), *The Female Quixote*'s depiction of quixotism as a mirror scene is indebted to older formulations of the imagination as an illogical confluence of disparate images, even though, as we will see, it also describes quixotism in terms of print. *The Female Quixote* emphatically aligns the visuality of the page with the female body: Arabella turns from the page to a mirror and sees there something like what she has just read.

Through stressing the way impressions are watched and embodied in Lennox's novel, and where on the body they might be registered, I hope to build on interpretations like that of Norma Clarke, who writes that Arabella is a "blank page" who "knows nothing of the world except what she has read in books of romance."[35] Marta Kvande also references the Lockean model of subjectivity and describes Arabella's reading in emphatically material terms. For Kvande, Arabella's reading is a mode of "physiological conditioning."[36] Her sickness from her plunge into the river is read by Kvande as necessary for the "cure" of her quixotism that resolves the book. Kvande argues that Arabella's quixotism has physical origins; her illness from her swim "destroys the physiological effects of her romance reading, wiping the slate clean so that new images and new physiological patterns can be imprinted in her brain."[37] According to this formulation, for Arabella to be cured, the images books have made on her mind must be "wiped clean" so she is no longer a text that has been written by her romance reading, but is instead a slate that can be inscribed anew.[38] Such readings valuably stress the physicality of Arabella's reading and early eighteenth-century conceptualizations of impressions as physical etchings on the brain. Arabella's quixotism, as an (im)printing of her body, rendering her an unauthorized reproduction of the literature she consumes, is at the crux of *The Female Quixote*'s investigation of quixotism and print. However, these readings risk delineating Arabella as merely a passive receptacle of her literary consumption. Yes, Arabella is quixotically imprinted by her reading, but with the self-consciousness of an eighteenth-century novel object, she anticipates others reading, viewing, and admiring her.

Arabella "entered into her Seventeenth Year with the Regret of *seeing herself* the Object of Admiration to a few Rustics only, who happened to see her" (*FQ*, 8) (my italics). Being watched and read is, for Arabella, a necessary part of being a heroine: part of her emulation of her reading is demanding she be looked at and desired. She uses romances as prompts for the elaborate adornment of her body, such as when she dresses "after the same Model as the Princess *Julia*'s" (*FQ*, 269). Through anachronistically emulating Julia's fashion, Arabella not only quixotically seeks to embody textual description but also presents her body as a graceful object to be admired: "[N]othing could be more singularly becoming than her Dress; or set off with greater Advantage the striking Beauties of her Person" (*FQ*, 271). Arabella's costume both mimetically responds to her reading and demands that her body be noticed and interpreted in accordance with the conventions of a character in a romance. Continuing along these lines, Arabella's quixotism could be characterized as her attempting to transmute her body into a visual text that reiterates the romance tropes she has consumed and internalized.

For Arabella desires to *see* herself viewed by others and have the "Lustre of her Eyes" praised (*FQ*, 139). Helen Thompson accurately describes the way Arabella's reading results in a feminized quixotism, "quixotizing not the eyes that see a world of objects but the eyes that objectify themselves."[39] Her eyes become the subject of discussion after Sir George calls "the finest Black Eyes in the Universe," that is, Arabella's, "fair" (*FQ*, 188). Glanville, Sir George's rival for Arabella's affection, critiques the accuracy of Sir George's compliment: "Ah! Cousin, said he to *Arabella*, he must be little acquainted with the Influence of your Eyes, since he can so egregiously mistake their Colour" (*FQ*, 188). Arabella explains to Glanville that Sir George is using the "sublime Language" of romances, where "Fair is indifferently applied, as well to Black and Brown Eyes, as to Light and Blue ones" (*FQ*, 188). Thompson reads this as the romances that Arabella absorbs as a child determining "the truth of even the most irreducibly material thing, her own body," rendering her indifferent to the discrepancy between black and blue.[40] Taking this further, we can compare Arabella to the Hobbesian romance reader: her eyes have become palinopsiastically imprinted by the "Stile" (*FQ*, 173) of romance to such an extent that she sees her own dark eyes as "fair." Her interpretation and defense of Sir George's compliment puts her in a position where she figuratively gazes upon her own eyes, and evaluates their fairness. Her eyes, imprinted by romantic "Stile" and "Language," mark her vision with romantic tropes, including her vision of themselves.

CAST YOUR EYES UPON PAPER

The centrality of the gaze to Arabella's quixotic practice can be read alongside Lennox's references to readers' eyes elsewhere in her work. Throughout her oeuvre she plays on the way she, a female writer, invites the reader to look at her work and view it with admiration. Anna Viele asserts the centrality of the coquette in Lennox's oeuvre, arguing not only that Lennox's characterization of Arabella blends the coquette with the quixote but that a mode of coquetry was central to Lennox's professional negotiation of the mid-eighteenth-century literary marketplace as a woman writer.[41] In Viele's words, "Lennox's career is concerned with locating a means of coquetting (building an audience of people to please with her writing) without being criticized for it."[42] Through the figure of the coquette, Lennox emphasizes the visuality of her works, playfully describes her authorship as a feminine attempt to please, and suggests how the pages of her work might be viewed analogously to a desirable female body, or even beautiful female eyes.

Lennox plays the authorial coquette in the first "Trifler" essay of her periodical *The Lady's Museum* (1760–61). This essay opens by quoting the advice of a "polite old gentleman": *"Cast your eyes upon paper, madam; there you may lock innocently."*[43] The periodical's eidolon states that "[i]t is indeed very clear to me, that my friend in this borrowed admonition recommended reading to eyes which he probably thought were too intent on pleasing."[44] The italicized quotation is "borrowed" from Alexander Pope's "Letters to Several Ladies."[45] In Pope's letter, the line is repeated: "[C]ast your Eyes upon Paper, and read only such Letters as I write."[46] Manushag N. Powell observes how "[t]he impetus of the quotation is to direct women's eyes downward, away from live men and women and onto wise masculine writings."[47] The Trifler reworks the quotation "with a small deviation from the sense." By directing her gaze to blank paper she follows the command to lock eyes with paper; by becoming a writer she remains able to enjoy inviting eyes and "pleasing" an audience.[48] The eidolon in *The Lady's Museum* revisits the associations between gazes, pleasure, and paper that *The Female Quixote* constructs. The Trifler ultimately presents female authorship as a mode of coquetry, an eager inviting of readers' eyes. These associations are reiterated in a letter by a "reader" printed in *The Lady's Museum*, which states, "I can well suppose that the Trifler is eagerly perused by all the bright eyes of the Kingdom."[49] The phrase, occurring in a "reader's" letter, creates an imagined community of bright-eyed readers, while simultaneously articulating connections between authorship, readership, quixotism, and coquetry, since beautiful "bright eyes" are not only desirable objects of the writer/reader's gaze, but they also have a desiring relation toward the paper they peruse.[50] In short, the periodical's papery text exchanges coquettish glances with the reader's own "bright eyes." Lennox's periodical—one of the early periodicals to include illustrations—invites the reader's gaze on its paper, and then looks back.[51]

The first edition of *The Female Quixote*, through visual devices such as print ornaments, similarly invites its readers to cast their eyes upon its paper. Samuel Richardson, who advised Lennox about the plotting and length of her novel, printed the first volume of the first edition of *The Female Quixote*.[52] Janine Barchas argues that Richardson's use of printer's ornaments in *Clarissa* (1747–48) provides "hermeneutic pressure to existing pieces of type."[53] It is possible to formulate a similar argument about the interlineation of ornaments in *The Female Quixote*. Printers' ornaments decorate the seventeenth-century romance folios Arabella consumes, but they fell out of fashion in mid- to late eighteenth-century print.[54] Richardson, however, was reluctant to give up using ornaments.[55] The first pages of each of *The Female Quixote*'s nine books are ornamented with a headpiece and an initial (figure 4), quite appropriate for a novel featuring a heroine with an anachronistic relation to literary fashion.

Keith Maslen's painstaking tracking of Richardson's ornaments demonstrates that Richardson, as a printer, possessed a large stock of "cuts"—ornaments cut by hand using wood or metal—which he drew on when decorating the first volume of the first edition of *The Female Quixote*.[56] Richardson did not commission new ornaments for the first volume, and the extent that the ornaments were chosen with a specific signifying purpose remains a matter of speculation. Maslen postulates that the use and selection of the ornaments in eighteenth-century book printing was a matter for the compositor (who arranges the type), possibly following a general instruction by the master and potentially, on occasion, the author.[57] There is thus no fixed individuated "author" of the decorated eighteenth-century page: instead the look of the page hinges on collaborations and the availability of already existent cuts. The ornaments are a conventional part of book production, pressured onto the paper simultaneously with the text during the printing process. They ostentatiously present the page as a product of a printing press, but they are simultaneously productive of meaning: ornaments signify the page as a visual object while also guiding and interrupting readers' ocular negotiation of the page.

Take, for instance, the first page of the first edition of the novel, decorated with appropriate motifs (figure 4). The initial frames "T" within a border topped by an image of a book. This specific cut was used in sixteen different volumes that Richardson printed and reappears in the beginning of the subsequent book.[58] Even so, it is a particularly fitting choice at the commencement of a novel about (mis) reading. The dialogue between ornament and text extends beyond a self-referential joke. The vine-like tendrils in the initial, along with the grapes, vines, and birds in the headpiece (another frequently used piece in Richardson's stock of cuts), literally frame the characters—"characters" both in the sense of letters and fictive entities—as existing within a highly visual, stylized arcadia.[59]

This arcadia of printers' ornaments pictorially echoes the Marquis's castle and its unusual gardens, where Arabella grew up. "The most laborious Endeavours of Art had been used" to make the Marquis's property appear "like the beautiful Product of wild, uncultivated Nature" (*FQ*, 6). This description of the Marquis's property frames *The Female Quixote*'s narrative, and has been read by both

THE
Female QUIXOTE.

BOOK I.

CHAP. I.

*Contains a Turn at Court, neither new
nor furprifing—Some ufelefs Additions
to a fine Lady's Education—The bad
Effects of a whimfical Study, which
fome will fay is borrowed from Cervantes.*

HE Marquis of——for a long Series of Years, was the firft and moft
diftinguifhed Favourite at Court:
He held the moft honourable
Employments under the Crown,
difpofed of all Places of Profit as he pleafed,
prefided at the Council, and in a manner
governed the whole Kingdom.

Vol. I.   B   This

Regina Martin and Mary Patricia Martin as an allegory for Lennox's writing practice and for the novel as a whole: artful work that also emulates "Nature."[60] The novel's representation of the Marquis's grounds can also double as a description of Arabella herself.[61] Shortly after the delineation of the garden the narrator introduces her with a similar vocabulary: Arabella's "native Charms were improved with all the Heightenings of Art" (*FQ*, 7). The parallels between Arabella and the Marquis's property are further emphasized in the subsequent chapter, when her hair hangs "upon her Neck in Curls, which had so much the Appearance of being artless, that all but her Maid, whose Employment it was to give them that Form, imagined they were so" (*FQ*, 9). The tendrils among the ornamentation of the visually striking pages of *The Female Quixote*, like plants in the Marquis's garden and the locks of Arabella's hair, provide an artful (as opposed to "artless") environ for Arabella's quixotism. Like the Marquis's grounds, like Arabella's own body, like the Trifler's coquettish writing, the ornamented page self-consciously invites readerly gazes upon its artful simulation of "Nature."

Later editions of *The Female Quixote* also demand that their pages—and their heroine—be looked at. Both the 1783 edition printed for the *Novelist's Magazine* (Harrison and Co., vol. 12) and Cooke's edition of 1799 are illustrated.[62] In both editions the illustrations have an analogous function to the chapter titles of *The Female Quixote*; to quote Dorothee Birke's description of the latter, they "emphasize the difference between the kind of writing Arabella loves and the kind of writing Lennox herself has produced."[63] The illustrations are poised between elaborating on the romances that Arabella enjoys and describing her "foibles" with ironic distance. Of the four illustrations of the 1783 edition, two feature an imperious Arabella. These illustrations, like the narrator's descriptions of Arabella's elaborate dress, underscore how her self-presentation of her body as something to be seen, admired, and read is central to her quixotic practice. In one frame by William Angus (figure 5), Arabella commands her unwell suitor and cousin Glanville to live, while closing the bed curtain. Arabella, dressed in white, and almost at the center of the picture, commandingly dominates the darker surroundings, while the bedridden Glanville, his face swathed in sheets and clothes, is difficult to read. Miss Glanville, the character furthest in the background, contemplates the scene with quiet amusement. The illustration echoes the narrative's quixotic doubling, potentially presenting Arabella as a beautiful heroine, yet also offering multiple, more satirical viewpoints of her embodiment of romance tropes. The illustrations invite readers to cast their eyes on paper and, simultaneously, cast their eyes on Arabella's body. The illustration collapses coquettish page with coquettish quixotic body.

FIGURE 5 Illustration to the 1783 edition of *The Female Quixote*. Courtesy Chawton House Library.

ARABELLA'S BLUSHES

The placement of Arabella's tropic body within a novel results in the proliferation of romantic reflections and reiterations. Arabella is not just a quixotic copy of a copy—an emulation of a romance heroine—she is also, in a larger sense, as a fictional device, an imitation of Subligny and Cervantes. This is playfully acknowledged in the first chapter title: "*The bad Effects of a whimsical Study, which some will say is borrowed from* Cervantes" (*FQ*, 5). The main body of *The Female Quixote* is thus situated directly underneath a line of text that describes the novel in terms of transnational borrowing. Eve Tavor Bannet argues that quixotic narratives query the applicability of transnational literary imitations across the lines of class and gender.[64] Quixotic fictions necessarily comment on the appropriateness of global and temporal appropriation and adaptation, and on the pervasiveness of literary and cultural recycling.[65] Significantly, French romances are mediated to Arabella through "very bad Translations" (*FQ*, 7). Her quixotism is thus potentially an analogy for eighteenth-century and early modern authorial processes of translation, adaption, and appropriation.

Arabella and Lennox emulate imitations of imitations, while spurring future imitations. When Arabella attempts to emulate Clelia's swim across the Tiber, for instance, Lennox also, simultaneously, echoes Subligny's mock-Clelia's plunge into the river.[66] At the riverside, Arabella declaims to her young female companions:

> The Action we have it in our Power to perform will immortalize our Fame, and raise us to a Pitch of Glory equal to that of the renown'd *Clelia* herself.
>
> Like her, we may expect Statues erected to our Honour: Like her, be propos'd as Patterns to Heroines in ensuing Ages: And like her, perhaps, meet with Sceptres and Crowns for our Reward. [. . .] Once more, my fair Companions, If your Honour be dear to you, if an immortal Glory be worth your seeking, follow the Example I shall set you, and equal with me the *Roman Clelia*.
>
> (*FQ*, 363)

David Marshall observes how Arabella does not see herself as an end point in a concatenation of copies and translations.[67] She follows Clelia's example and simultaneously seeks to "set" an "Example" to the young women she addresses. She tries to encourage them to "follow" her "Example" by describing how their emulation could offer "Patterns" for both subsequent artworks and heroics (*FQ*, 363). Arabella thus situates herself as within an extensive imitative chain, following others, but also destined to be followed by others: a "Pattern" for "Heroines in ensuing Ages" (*FQ*, 363).

Certainly, quixotic romance consumption in *The Female Quixote* impels both a proliferation of images and a proliferation of book objects that can be both seen and read (manifest in the "huge" volumes that Arabella exhorts Glanville to read [*FQ*, 49]). On one level, Arabella's self-styling as a "Pattern" for ensuing heroics and artworks is part of her preoccupation with her body being viewed and admired. It is also a way for *The Female Quixote* to self-consciously anticipate its own legacy. As this book bears out, Lennox's novel was reworked and rewritten by authors such as George Colman the Elder, Laurence Sterne, Richard Graves, and Elizabeth Hamilton. More broadly, the elaborate, reduplicating chain of refracted images that *The Female Quixote* implicates itself within is part of both its treatment of literary history and its tracing of the romance's maternally inflected marks within and beyond the novel.

For *The Female Quixote*'s commentary on textual reproduction and adaptation implicitly invokes the theory of maternal impressions. Recalling Jacques Du Bosc's analogy between maternal impressions from the imagination and imaginative impressions from romance reading in *L'honneste femme* (1632) (see introduction), it is important to note that the romances that quixotically imprint Arabella belong to her dead mother (*FQ*, 7). Just as the misgenerated child, its flesh imprinted in utero, is a text written by the maternal imagination, Arabella's subjectivity is marked by her dead mother's imagination through her consumption of her mother's library. She reads her mother's romance collection "[f]rom her earliest Youth" (*FQ*, 7).

An absent mother is, admittedly, a trope widespread in eighteenth-century fiction. Ruth Perry observes, "There are many explanations for the striking motherlessness of literary heroines, ranging from reasons of literary expediency to deeper existential necessities."[68] In *The Female Quixote*, as with many other novels, maternal absence functions as a plot device, allowing the heroine to fall into more difficulty than if she had a reliable female guide. Here, however, maternal absence also results in a textualized maternal inheritance, with the mother only present through the books she has left behind her. So, Arabella reads and is guided by her dead mother's romances: she is, in a sense, "mothered" by them. Debra Malina, Margaret Anne Doody, and Anita Levy read Arabella's reading as a matrilineal inheritance that becomes a problem because it disrupts patriarchal authority, especially through her refusal to marry Glanville, the man chosen by her father.[69] Pointedly, the Marquis threatens in retaliation to burn his dead wife's books since they seem to encourage his daughter to disobey him (*FQ*, 55).

The Female Quixote also associates romance with the maternal through the character of Arabella's female mentor, the Countess, who fails to "cure" Arabella of her quixotism, despite her efforts. Critics are divided over the role of the Countess within the published novel. For Patricia Meyer Spacks, the Countess's inability to effect change is inextricable from her femininity: her gentle and ultimately ineffectual approach reflects "a woman's limited resources."[70] On the other hand, Patricia L. Hamilton argues that the maternal Countess initiates, and sets up, the cure that the paternal Doctor effects.[71] While the Countess arguably offers a more convincing possibility for Arabella's cure than Spacks suggests, Spacks is correct in noting that the Countess's association with the maternal is complexly bound to her failure to "cure" Arabella. Significantly, the Countess is unable to continue her re-education of Arabella because she needs to attend to her sick mother (*FQ*, 330). The Countess's departure to her own mother reinforces how she becomes another missing mother for Arabella, congruous to Arabella's biological mother, whose absence (and the books she left behind her) spurred Arabella's reproductive consumption of romance.[72]

A preoccupation with formative romance reading recurs in Lennox's later works, including *The Lady's Museum*, which contains a serialized translation of François Fénelon's *Treatise on the Education of Daughters* (1687), "translated by a Friend of the Author of the Museum."[73] Tellingly, the translation of Fénelon in *The Lady's Museum* stresses that particular care should be taken to educate girls from infancy because that is an age when they receive "the deepest impressions, and which consequently affects their whole life."[74] For Fénelon, the impressionability of infants is literal and material: "[T]he substance of their [infants'] brain is very soft, it hardens day by day; as for their mind it knows nothing: this softness of brain is the reason why every thing makes strong impressions."[75] The ignorance of children means their "brain hath as yet taken no impression," they have "no formed habits," and they have a "pliancy and inclination to imitate all they see."[76] Young brains become physically imprinted or impressed with the images and objects that they perceive: "sensible objects impress themselves [. . .] in very lively characters" and "images" are "engraven while the brain is so soft."[77] Arabella's romance reading could be said to similarly imprint her character. Like Fénelon's impressionable infant or the fetus marked by the imagination, Arabella's body becomes a site for the reproduction of images from (matrilineal) romances.[78]

Preceding his account of the importance of early childhood education, Fénelon (via *The Lady's Museum* translation) offers an account of what happens when female education is neglected. Girls are in danger of quixotism, of setting themselves up as

> *extraordinary women*, and read[ing] all the books that can feed their vanity; they are passionately fond of romances, of plays, of stories, of

chimerical adventures, wherewith much profane love is intermixed; they give a visionary turn to their understanding, by using it to the magnificent language of the heroes of romance; they even spoil themselves for the world, because all these fine airy sentiments, these generous passions, these adventures which the author of the romance has invented merely to please, have not the least relation to the real motives of action in the world.[79]

According to Fénelon's arguments, Arabella's problem is one of education: if more care is taken to mold impressionable infants' minds, young women would be less easily molded by their reading. Fénelon here also reiterates long-standing tropes around female reading that continue, undiminished throughout the century, positioning young women as vulnerable, impressionable, and quixotic: unthinking receptacles for textual reproduction. Henry Fielding, in a review of *The Female Quixote*, reads the plot as more probable than Cervantes's precisely because of the way it ties into established assumptions about feminine reading practices. A woman is more likely than a man to have her head turned by reading romances, Fielding asserts: "I make no Doubt but that most young Women of the same Vivacity, and of the same innocent good Disposition, in the same Situation, and with the same Studies, would be able to make a large Progress in the same Follies."[80] In *The Lady's Museum*, another translation from the French, "Of the Studies proper for Women," a translation of chapter 2 of Pierre-Joseph Boudier de Villemert's *L'ami des femmes* (1758), also advocating female education, explicitly critiques romance reading at a young age: "There is scarcely a young girl who has not read with eagerness a great number of idle romances, and puerile tales, sufficient to corrupt her imagination and cloud her understanding."[81]

So Lennox's periodical reiterates an already established vision of a world populated by poorly educated female readers reproducing their romance reading and offers itself as a solution to this problem, educating its female audience and encouraging them to reflect on their reading practices. Scholarship has stressed how *The Lady's Museum* is concerned with developing its audience's reading practices, whether it be written, as Judith Dorn argues, to widen "the scope of the reader's perception" or, as Powell describes, to "alert" its readers to "pleasures beyond narrative."[82] Yet *The Lady's Museum*'s relation to romance is not solely pedagogical. The anti-romance accounts in *The Lady's Museum* are qualified and complicated by the material published alongside them. For instance, there are essays by the coquettish Trifler, who jokingly laments "the too perceptible decline" of the kind of female "influence" over men Arabella quixotically believes herself to wield. Like Arabella, the eidolon imagines romance not as fantasy but as a period in history when "the smile of beauty was more powerful than the voice of ambition; when heroes conquered to deserve our favour."[83] *The Lady's Museum* also includes carefully documented accounts of historical women's sexual power and "profane love," such as "The History of the Dutchess of Beaufort," the mistress of Henry IV of France. Finally, anti-romance rhetoric is also published among romances themselves, including a translation from the Italian of Ludovico Ariosto's *Orlando Furioso*. It could be said that *The Lady's Museum*, like *The Female Quixote*—and, for that matter, Hume—uses the stereotype of the misreader as a starting point for raising larger questions about the unstable distinctions between romance and history and experiential impressions and imagined ideas. Both *The Female Quixote* and *The Lady's Museum* explore the gendering of particular reading practices and particular genres, and both cannily negotiate a place for female writers and consumers in a literary marketplace preoccupied with regulating, and often condemning, feminized literary consumption and production.

The Female Quixote and *The Lady's Museum* incorporate the figure of the romance reader into a larger meditation on philosophy, female education, and literature. Laurie Langbauer and Mary Patricia Martin argue that *The Female Quixote*'s alignment of romance with a maternal inheritance capable of erasure (books that can be burned) is part of its allegorical treatment of the romance within literary history.[84] *The Female Quixote* dramatizes romance tropes within the Richardsonian novel. While Arabella's quixotic actions overtly rework Scudéry, Cervantes, and Subligny, they also ironically nod to Richardson's *Clarissa*. For example, when Arabella "did not remember to have read of any Heroine that voluntarily left her Father's House, however persecuted she might be" (*FQ*, 35), the narration directly evokes *Clarissa*, and its "supposedly blameless heroine who provoked an ongoing ethical debate" when she ran away from her "Father's House" with Lovelace.[85] The distinctions between "novels" and "romances" were nothing if not fluid and complex, with eighteenth-century attempts at generic classification often positing romances and novels as interchangeable, something echoed by *The Female Quixote*'s narrator, who at one point claims to be "following the Custom of the Romance and Novel-Writers" (*FQ*, 180). That said, *The Female Quixote*, by presenting Arabella's emulation of romance as quixotic within a domestic novel and drawing comedy from the differences in the two modes, does offer a romance/novel dichotomy. An opposition of the two modes is reinforced by the Johnsonian clergyman's endorsement of Richardsonian fiction and his rejection of romances as "contemptible Volumes" (*FQ*, 373–374).

The bulk of work on *The Female Quixote* has focused on its complex articulation of the relationship between romance and the novel. *The Female Quixote* describes a world that is post-romance, and here I use the prefix "post" in the same way it is often used in "postcolonial," "postmodern," "postdigital," and "postfeminist": to signify a rupture and significant cultural shift, but also, simultaneously, to describe that what follows is crucially dependent on, and inseparable from, what has come before. To use Linda Hutcheon's description of postmodernism, what we have here is "neither a simple and radical break [. . .] nor a straightforward continuity," but instead something that is "both and neither."[86] *The Female Quixote* asserts the crucial interdependence of the novel and maternally marked romance, while simultaneously ostensibly disciplining its romance-reading heroine and placing her in a novelistic world where her behavior is anachronistic.

Lennox also seems to implicitly legitimize her—and Arabella's—work of cultural and generic recycling in her monumental study of Shakespeare scholarship, *Shakespear Illustrated* (1753), published the year following *The Female Quixote* and presented on the title page as "By the Author of the Female Quixote." Here, Lennox argues for Shakespeare's dependence on "bad" translations of existent stories. Commenting on his use of Matteo Bandello's "novel" as a source text for *Romeo and Juliet*, Lennox observes that it is "highly probable" that "he never saw, and did not understand the Original, but copied from a *French* Translation extant in his Time; or, what is equally probable, from an *English* Translation of that *French* one, both very bad."[87] Doody notes how "[i]t is part of Lennox's point that Shakespeare read romances and novels."[88] Just as *The Female Quixote* engages in a kind of literary recovery work, presenting the Richardsonian realist novel as drawing on the matrilineally marked history of romance, *Shakespear Illustrated* analogously traces Shakespearean drama's debt to feminized genres. Lennox complicates the mid-eighteenth-century gendering of novels and romances, arguing that Shakespeare, a male, canonical playwright, was an imitator of novels and romances that he also barely understood. While Arabella might imitate romances in bad translations, she is doing no more or less than what Shakespeare did, and also perhaps Richardson, as the aforementioned parallels *The Female Quixote* draws between the Richardsonian novel and romance suggest.

However, Arabella renounces her quixotism after a debate with a Johnsonian "good Divine," who advocates that she cease reading Scudéry's romances and begin reading Richardson's novels. At first glance, Arabella's renunciation of romance seems to spell subjugation to male authority; she acquiesces to the will of her father that she marry Glanville and to the will of the "good Divine" that romances are false. The "good Divine's" voice and presence, strongly redolent of Samuel Johnson, dominates the chapter, prompting the (since disproven) theory that the clergyman's speech was written by Johnson himself.[89] Lennox's successful mimicry of Johnson at the crux of the narrative means that the termination of Arabella's romantic quixotism is potentially mirrored by an erasure of a female authorial voice. The cessation of quixotism and romance becomes sutured to a dominant masculine voice in a "double renunciation" of female authority and authorship.[90] Evidence implies that Lennox originally planned for the Countess to play a larger role in guiding Arabella's gradual reformation over the course of a third volume, rather than a more sudden "cure" following a single chapter with a Johnsonian doctor.[91] Lennox probably took Richardson's and Johnson's—male authors'—advice in concluding the novel so abruptly. This is not, however, to encourage a reading of Lennox as a female author silenced by more powerful men. Recent work, such as Susan Carlile's excellent biography of Lennox, describes Lennox's friendships with Johnson and Richardson as intellectual partnerships between equals.[92] However, her fraught financial situation likely prompted her to follow Richardson's and Johnson's recommendations, and publish the work in two volumes, resulting in a published novel where the Countess's attempt to "cure" Arabella fails and the reformation of Arabella's quixotism hinges on her debate with the Johnsonian Doctor.

Wendy Motooka observes that the opposition between Arabella and the Doctor suggests more congruities than dissimilarities between them, with the "method" of Arabella's "madness" appearing "strikingly similar" to the Doctor's empiricist epistemology. I would add that the technology of print becomes crucial to the parallels the book draws between Arabella's and the Doctor's positions.[93] Arabella argues that her leap into a river is justified given the likelihood a potential ravisher could drive her into "the pathless Desart," immure her in a castle, or confine her on "some Island of an immense Lake" (*FQ*, 372–373). When the clergyman pronounces that there is "no such Castle, Desart, Cavern, or Lake," Arabella answers by referring to the Doctor's "own Principles" (*FQ*, 373). She observes how much the Doctor's experience of the world stems from his reading: "You allow that Experience may be gain'd by Books" (*FQ*, 373). The dispute directly echoes philosophical investigations into the trustworthiness of sense impressions for understanding the world, and implies, to quote Mack, "that all truth is textual truth."[94] Pertinent here is also McKeon's argument relating to print publication's ability to complicate "standards of judgment."[95] The discussion between Arabella and the Doctor, like Hume's *Treatise*, suggests an inherent difficulty of arriving at truth, and the possibility of universal quixotism.

According to the clergyman, romance reading is an issue because it generates extreme passions: it will set "Fire to the Passions of Revenge and Love; two Passions which, even without such powerful Auxiliaries, it is one of the severest Labours of Reason and Piety to suppress" (*FQ*, 380). However, the clergyman never enters into detail this argument about romance's ability to fuel erotic fires. When he states, "Love, Madam, is, you know, the Business, the sole Business of Ladies in Romances," Arabella's "Blushes now hinder'd him from proceeding as he had intended" (*FQ*, 381). Arabella's blushes mark a pivotal turn in the argument. The Doctor sees he has discomfited her, and rather than talking about love, he abruptly changes the direction of his argument and instead speaks about the violence depicted in romances (*FQ*, 381). The clergyman appears to conclude that it would be impolite, intrusive to proceed further. Arabella's blushes are treated as a bodily acknowledgment that she has been captivated by the "Love" depicted in romances, and her next words are to surrender to the clergyman's perspective.

Arabella's blush, and the Doctor's reaction, directly echoes a similar instance in Arabella's conversation with the Countess, after the Countess observes that contemporary society no longer bears any resemblance to the world depicted in romances: "[Arabella's] Blushes, her Silence, and down-cast Eyes gave the Countess to understand Part of her Thoughts; who for fear of alarming her too much for that Time, dropt the Subject, and turning the Conversation on others more general, gave *Arabella* an Opportunity of mingling in it with that Wit and Vivacity which was natural to her when Romances were out of the Question" (*FQ*, 326). Both the Countess and the Doctor respond to Arabella's blushes almost identically, interpreting them, and then changing the subject. Significantly, the Countess, a reader of romances, and the Doctor, who is an "absolute Stranger" (*FQ*, 373) to them, both interpret Arabella's tropic body along similar lines. This doubling underscores the way the Doctor and the Countess inhabit shared roles and, congruously, the way romances and novels are gendered and twinned throughout the narrative.

When Arabella blushes directly after the Doctor's reference to the role of love in romance, her red cheeks might potentially point to the way she is maternally imprinted by her romance reading. Her blushes are a visual imprint on her body, a mark which could signal that her reading has spotted the surface of her body with touches of pink and red. Her body, I have argued, is a text to be read and viewed, and the Doctor's sensitive analysis of Arabella's skin (and, for that matter, the Countess's similar interpretation) recalls Arabella's demand to Lucy, her maid, that her body be painstakingly observed. She orders Lucy to "relate exactly every Change of my Countenance; number all my Smiles, Half-smiles, Blushes, Turnings pale, Glances, Pauses, Full-stops, Interruptions; the Rise and Falling of my Voice; every Motion of my Eyes; and every Gesture which I have used" (*FQ*, 121–122). Arabella is determined that her body be scrutinized like a romance heroine's. "Full-stops," occurring here among references to orality, describes the end of her speeches, but I think it can also evoke more typographical pauses, the "single" dot that marks an end of a sentence, subtly locating Arabella's bodily expressions—her "Smiles, Half-smiles, Blushes, Turnings pale, Glances" (*FQ*, 122)—within the visuality of the punctuated, printed page.

So, the clergyman reads Arabella's body and, echoing the behavior Arabella enjoins Lucy, carefully notes her blushes. This is despite his dismissal of romance. His attentiveness to her blushes, coupled with his praise of Richardsonian novels, points to overlaps between the treatment of heroines' bodies in sentimental novels and romance. To be precise, Arabella's demand that there be attention paid to "every Motion of my Eyes; and every Gesture which I have used" (*FQ*, 122) presents her not only as the beautiful, watched heroine of romance, but also as a heroine of a Richardsonian eighteenth-century novel, whose bodily displays of affective impressions are signs that can be read, reproduced, and imitated. Pamela and Clarissa, just like romance heroines, have all their "Smiles, Half-smiles, Blushes, Turnings pale" recorded, read, reproduced, *and* held up as proof of their poignant virtue. Through its focus on Arabella's body as seen, as read, and as registered, *The Female Quixote*, then, foregrounds the continued reliance of the eighteenth-century sentimental novel on the structures of romance.

This is also apparent when Arabella tries and fails to swoon, "or something she took for a Swoon, for she was persuaded it could happen no otherwise; since all Ladies in the same Circumstances are terrify'd into a fainting Fit" (*FQ*, 300). The heroines of seventeenth-century romance often swoon, but so, famously, do heroines of mid-century novels. *The Female Quixote* here gently parodies Richardson's image of Pamela being watched as she faints. The swoon of both the romantic and the sentimental heroine articulates a model of physiology where affective impressions can immediately and reflexively inscribe a response on the body.[96] Thompson identifies Arabella's thwarted swoon as Lennox affirming a suspicion "of a now epistemologically corrupt mode of feminine reflexive response" already cuttingly undermined in both Eliza Haywood's *Anti-Pamela* (1741) and Henry Fielding's *Shamela* (1741). Arabella's affective models from her romance reading—and, *The Female Quixote* implies, the bodies of Richardsonian heroines—offer a Cartesian, mechanistic model of passion, where individuals are wholly subject to sensory and affective impressions.[97] This Cartesian physiological model animates romance, the sentimental novel, and, as I will discuss in chapter 2, mid-eighteenth-century theories of acting.

Yet while Arabella's thwarted swoon points to the limits of Cartesian physiology and affective reflexes, her blush that directly precedes her renunciation of romance does the opposite. Her blush seems to be a reflexive response that presents her body as an inscribable surface to be ostentatiously viewed and read even at the very moment that she renounces her quixotic behavior. The blush can simultaneously be interpreted as a Cartesian reflex that Clelia herself might embody and as a marker of her body's inauguration into both a more novelistic and a more sentimental mode of expression: Arabella's blush designates her body as a text analogous to Clarissa's or Pamela's hypertextual, epistolary bodies. So we have seen how Arabella's body has an unstable relation to sentimental and romantic embodiment of affect, and the embodiment of text in general. At times she successfully embodies the desirability of a romance heroine; elsewhere her body's reproduction of textual tropes is comically askew.

We have also seen how the visuality of the eighteenth-century printed page is conceptually central to *The Female Quixote*'s description of Arabella's quixotism. It is also pivotal to Lennox's complex self-positioning as a female author within a literary marketplace pervaded with anxiety about feminized literary production and consumption. Via a heroine who expects her imprinted body to be desired, admired, and read, *The Female Quixote* plays with the resonant congruities and dissimilarities between reading and viewing the printed page. This is key to *The Female Quixote*'s literary-historical tracking of romance tropes within the Richardson novel. Simultaneous with its attention to the trace of older romances within Richardsonian fiction, *The Female Quixote* examines how the motif of being quixotically (im)printed by the act of reading is bound to long-standing tropes of the imagination being captivated by images and, relatedly, the eyes being experientially marked by what they see. Arabella's display of her reading through her textualized body, and her ostentatious inviting of a readerly gaze, invites questions about the relationship between quixotism, embodiment, performance, and print. In George Colman the Elder's *Polly Honeycombe*, the subject of the next chapter, female reading is not only ostentatiously performed but is placed upon the mid-eighteenth-century stage.

PERFORMING PRINT IN *POLLY HONEYCOMBE,*
A DRAMATICK NOVEL OF ONE ACT

> Dr BROCKLESBY's medical Observations. 5s. bound.
> The King of Prussia's Campaigns. 3s. bound.
> The Deuce is in Him. A Farce. 1s.
> Polly Honeycomb. A Farce. 1s.
> The Musical Lady. A Farce. 1s.
>
> —"Books Printed for T. Becket and P. A. De Hondt," in Hugh Blair,
> *A Critical Dissertation on the Poems of Ossian*, 2nd ed. (London, 1765)

T HE ABOVE LINES, like so many other eighteenth-century publishers' book lists and catalogs, involve humorous and incongruous juxtapositions of titles; immediately listed after "Dr BROCKLESBY's medical Observations" and "The King of Prussia's Campaigns" are three theatrical farces. Among them is George Colman the Elder's *Polly Honeycombe, a Dramatick Novel of One Act* (1760), a play about quixotic novel reading that ostentatiously anticipates its inclusion in such lists through the interpolation of a fictive circulating library catalog in the preface to its printed edition. This chapter investigates the significance of this unperformable object within a printed play, and asks how we might read it. The circulating library catalog within *Polly Honeycombe*, and the play as a whole, suggests how mid-eighteenth-century depictions of quixotic readers respond to the generative relation between the theater and the novel, performance and print. Quixotic embodiment of text complexly yokes stage to page.

The farce's full title, *Polly Honeycombe, a Dramatick Novel of One Act. As it is now Acted at the Theatre-Royal in Drury Lane*, foregrounds the relationship between two forms. While "*Dramatick Novel*" might denote a novel that draws on dramatic conventions, "*One Act*" and "*As it is now Acted at the Theatre-Royal in Drury Lane*" describe a theatrical text. "As it is now Acted" or "As it is Acted" appears commonly on the title pages of printed plays in the mid-eighteenth century, advertising them as possessing a desirable likeness to their performed version.[1] "As it is now Acted" functionally binds print to performance, suggesting that the silent reading of the farce and its performance in Drury Lane occur simultaneously, or even that the act of reading produces an imagined performance of the text that is fundamentally connected to a similar performance onstage. Certainly, in *Polly Honeycombe*'s case, the cast and the circumstances of the Drury Lane performances mark the early printed editions of the play. For example, the dialogue of Mr. Honeycombe in the printed editions of *Polly Honeycombe* reflects the affectations and habits of Richard Yates, the original Honeycombe. Yates would repeat earlier lines when he forgot what to say next, and this habit leaves a trace in the repetitive nature of Honeycombe's dialogue, filled with "Hark ye, hussy" (*PH*, 87–88).[2]

If *"As it is now Acted"* suggests the close interrelationship between mid-eighteenth-century theater and print, *Polly Honeycombe*'s claim to be a *"Dramatick Novel"* works similarly. In the mid-eighteenth century, an intermingling of what, in our contemporary moment, we might compartmentalize as discrete literary forms was hardly unusual. *Polly Honeycombe* is not the only eighteenth-century text to titularly combine stage with page. For instance, Oliver Goldsmith's *She Stoops to Conquer* (1773) was submitted to Lord Chamberlain's office for a performance license with the title "The Novel; or, the Mistakes of the Night."[3] The circulating library catalog that prefaces *Polly Honeycombe* itself contains numerous mid-eighteenth-century titles that suggest a crossing between theatrical and novelistic forms, such as Sarah Fielding and Jane Collier's *The Cry: A New Dramatic Fable* (1754) (listed in the catalog as "Cry, A Dramatick Fable") and the anonymous collection of short stories *The Theatre of Love. A Collection of Novels* (1759). Other novels named in the catalog contain dramatic devices, such as Samuel Richardson's *The History of Sir Charles Grandison* (1753–54), which is prefaced by a list of "Principal Persons" as if the novel was a printed play, the "Persons" notoriously divided up into "Men," "Women," and "Italians."[4] The circulating library catalog's compilation of so many titles that are linked, in one way or another, to the eighteenth-century stage is suited to Colman's theme, but it also is an inevitable result of the interanimation between the eighteenth-century novel and the theater.

Interest in *Polly Honeycombe* has recently grown. David A. Brewer and Ros Ballaster have shown how the farce knowingly engages with the consumption of both printed and performed texts, elaborately acting out the complex interrelationship between eighteenth-century print culture and the stage.[5] Scholarly engagement with *Polly Honeycombe* can thus be read more broadly as part of burgeoning research on the historical relationship between performance and print and, specifically, the theater and the novel.[6] Emily Hodgson Anderson notes how eighteenth-century "writers and audiences saw more connections than divergences between theater and the novel."[7] Ballaster agrees that there is a close relationship between eighteenth-century novels and the theater, but rather than arguing for the similarity between stage and page in the mind of their audiences, she argues that the two forms set themselves up as rivals.[8] *Polly Honeycombe* suggests how both Ballaster and Anderson are correct: the two forms are set up as competing, but also as interconnected modes of quixotic reproduction.

This chapter, then, involves situating quixotism, and quixotic impressions, among an interrogation of the novel/theater relationship. My argument is that *Polly Honeycombe* demonstrates quixotic impressions as reaching beyond the printed page, into the theater in ways that underscore the embodied nature of quixotism and its fraught relationship with text and flesh. The heroine Polly—like Arabella of *The Female Quixote* (chapter 1)—is imprinted by her reading of feminized texts. The play's prologue implicitly evokes Charlotte Lennox's novel in its description of romance being superseded by the novel: "*Cassandra's Folios now no longer read, / See, Two Neat Pocket Volumes in their stead!*" (*PH*, 68). In *The Female Quixote*, Arabella is described as infatuated with "so many huge Folio's" (*FQ*, 49). Most seventeenth-century French romances in English, including *Cassandre*, were printed as folios, a format where sheets are folded once, with a minimum leaf height of thirty centimeters.[9] Novels, on the other hand, were more compact in size and could fit in women's pockets. These, in the mid-eighteenth century, were bags tied around the waist, beneath the dress, which could be accessed through slits in the seams.[10] By describing novels in the prologue as "*Pocket Volumes*," *Polly Honeycombe* stresses from its opening how the smaller size of novels allows them to exist in a close proximity to the reader's body. More immediately, by virtue of being a performed text, *Polly Honeycombe* can use the body of the actor to emphasize the physicality of reading and quixotism. Yet this relationship between page and performance is double-edged: just as the actor's body offers a corporeal articulation of quixotism, *Polly Honeycombe*'s self-conscious deployment of print presents the actor's body as a textual object.

PRINT AND THEATER IN *POLLY HONEYCOMBE*

Print spurs performance, and performance prompts print. The anonymous author of *An Essay on the New Species of Writing founded by Mr. Fielding* (1751) writes, "As in the Playhouse, so in the Press. A Piece is no sooner perform'd at *Drury-Lane* or *Covent-Garden*, than the News Papers are fill'd with Advertisements of—This Day are publish'd, Remarks on, or a candid Examen of the late new Tragedy or Comedy."[11] *Polly Honeycombe* was no different; the printed play was available within a week of the farce's premiere.[12] On the pages of eighteenth-century periodicals, advertisements and reviews of performances of *Polly Honeycombe* appear alongside notices of its printed edition. This close temporal alignment between performance and print is echoed by the close physical proximity between the Drury Lane theater and the circulating libraries in London.[13] The consumption of one medium feeds into the consumption of the other.

The intimate, competitive co-existence of eighteenth-century plays and print culture motivates plays' repeated and explicit references to the circulation and consumption of printed matter. Polly Honeycombe's infatuation with novels is far from unusual on the eighteenth-century stage. Earlier in the century, Biddy in Richard Steele's play *The Tender Husband* (1705) is infatuated with chivalric romances to such an extent that a character describes her as a "perfect *Quixot* in petticoats."[14] Another spirited Polly on the stage, Polly Peachum, of John Gay's famous *The Beggar's Opera* (1728), is, like Polly Honeycombe, prompted to disobey her parents because of the ideas she has imbibed from her reading. When the good-for-nothing Macheath vows eternal constancy, Polly Peachum replies, "I have no Reason to doubt you, for I find in the Romance you lent me, none of the great Heroes were ever false in Love."[15] However, Polly Peachum's mother blames her disobedience on "[t]hose cursed Play-books she reads," grouping plays with romances.[16] This reference to the play's printed form is not only a self-reflexive gesture reserved for the reader of the play; it is a reference that renders the play's printed form visible to the audience in the theater.

As for *Polly Honeycombe*, it is both a straightforward satire on novel reading and something more. The plot focuses on Polly's attempts to imitate novel heroines. She is the daughter of two parents determined to marry her to money, and the suitor they approve is Mr. Ledger, who speaks in the jargon of finance and, in Polly's words, is "more tiresome than the multiplication-table" (*PH*, 86). Polly, Clarissa-like, defies her parents' choice of husband and fixes her affections on the social climber Scribble, who ventriloquizes the language of romance (as Sir George similarly does in *The Female Quixote*). Both Ledger's and Scribble's names associate their characters with different forms of inscription and further bind *Polly Honeycombe* to the page, even when it is staged. Polly's quixotism is encouraged by her nurse, who is Scribble's aunt and has a vested interest in the bourgeois Polly marrying Scribble.

This was the plot of one of the most popular farces of the eighteenth century.[17] *Polly Honeycombe* was performed fifteen times in the first season of its appearance.[18] Each time, it was performed after a longer play: *Polly Honeycombe* is an afterpiece, written to be only part of a night's performance and staged after a more substantial piece of work. For instance, on the night of its premiere, *Polly Honeycombe* was performed after Aaron Hill's version of Voltaire's *Mérope* (1749).[19] Though it was often paired with similarly humorous, self-reflexive plays such as *The Beggar's Opera*, it was just as likely to be preceded by a tragedy.[20]

Polly Honeycombe also had a successful publishing history, running through seven printed editions during the first three theatrical seasons it was staged, and it later appeared in collections of Colman's *Dramatick Works* (1777).[21] The farce also features on several circulating library lists.[22] This was not unusual in the mid-eighteenth century, when plays typically ran into several editions and could rival the popularity of novels in circulating libraries, but as the first work of an unknown playwright, *Polly Honeycombe* was a notable success.[23] It is necessary, here, to dwell on *Polly Honeycombe*'s performance and print history because—as I hope is already clear—this is a farce dominated by self-reflexive references to its own dissemination.

Contemporary responses to the play, such as a review published in both the *London Magazine* (December 1760) and the *Edinburgh Magazine* (January 1761), commended it for its "successful attempt to display the pernicious effects produced by the modern novels and romances, so readily supplied by the circulating libraries, on female minds."[24] Certainly, *Polly Honeycombe* satirizes female novel reading, but it also resolutely resists being read as a straightforward lesson on how not to read. The preface to the printed play, by quoting a wish from Colman's fictive "Mother" that "your Farce may do some good on the Giddy Girls of this Age!" (*PH*, 63), suggests that there might be problems with this very injunction. In the preface, Colman does not present her as the most perceptive reader, writing dismissively of her "talents for Criticism" (*PH*, 61).

Colman's "Mother" also criticizes how *Polly Honeycombe* deviates from dramatic conventions of closure. She writes that "the *Catastrophe*" contradicts "all known rules" because "the whole Piece, instead of concluding bluntly with a sentence in Prose, should have been tagged with a Couplet or Two" (*PH*, 60–61). For a comedy, *Polly Honeycombe* does end unconventionally. As well as the lack of concluding couplet, the farce ends without a marriage between Polly and Scribble, or even Polly and the paternally sanctioned lover, Ledger. Nor is she reconciled with her parents or "cured" of her novel-reading ways. In an ending Ballaster argues resembles novels in its abruptness, the play finishes with Polly as triumphant, surrounded by chaos.[25] The problem of her quixotism is unresolved. She remains as determined as ever to disobey her parents and be a novel heroine. Through its sudden ending, the farce's anti-novel message, such as it is, is undercut.

The play's preface, by commenting on this deviation from dramatic conventions, trumpets the irresolution as a deliberate authorial choice, rather than an inadvertent error. The interpolation of his "good Mother's" criticism in the preface—criticism that Colman himself in the preface treats with amused contempt—allows him to forestall, effeminize, and trivialize potential criticisms of his play. A critic cannot level similar objections to *Polly Honeycombe* without being implicitly compared to the character of Colman's "Mother." This was noted by Tobias Smollett in the *Critical Review* (December 1760), where he observes that the preface anticipates criticism by acknowledging that those aspects of the play that might be seen to be errors, "which might otherways incur censure," are committed voluntarily.[26] Even so, the deviations from eighteenth-century dramatic conventions were read as flaws, with the *Theatrical Review* (December 1771) calling the ending "inconclusive and unsatisfactory."[27] Eighteenth-century responses to *Polly Honeycombe* tend to commend the farce's ostensibly anti-novel stance and critique the "novelistic" complexities that subvert its apparent anti-novel position.

We can see this in the critical reaction to the moral (and novelistic) ambiguities posed by the portrayal of Polly's parents. Clara Reeve notes disapprovingly in *The Progress of Romance* (1785) that *Polly Honeycombe*'s anti-novel message is contradicted by its treatment of Polly's parents. In a didactic work, the parents should be figures of authority, but in this farce, Reeve observes, they are subject to mockery.[28] A letter in the *London Chronicle* (January 1761) is more virulent in its scorn for the characters of Mr. and Mrs. Honeycombe, describing them as "insufferable": "The author does not seem so much as to intimate that they had accustomed themselves to read Novels; and yet he represents one as a foolish old Dotard, and the other drunk with Ratifia from the Apothecary's."[29] The writer recognizes that a portrayal of parents as clowns in an anti-novel play would only be explicable had these parents "accustomed themselves to read Novels."[30] In *Polly Honeycombe*, Mr. and Mrs. Honeycombe could even be said to resemble novel-reading quixotes. Though an old married couple, they behave like young lovers from a sentimental novel, and the play derives much of its comedy from this incongruity. Polly describes them as squeezing "their hard hands to each other, and their old eyes twinkle" (*PH*, 75). By engaging in bouts of contextually inappropriate "*kissing and fondling*" (*PH*, 79) and, more urgently, by being farcical, rather than authoritative, the parents, without being sentimental novel readers themselves, are ambiguously aligned with both quixotism and the novel. As *Polly Honeycombe*'s contemporary audience recognized, Mr. and Mrs. Honeycombe immediately complicate any reading of the farce as unambiguously anti-novel.

CHARACTER AND QUIXOTISM

Eighteenth-century writers identified the novel and the drama as having strong continuities, but also crucial differences.[31] John Dryden's influential essay *Of Dramatick Poesie* (1668) asserts that drama provides a "lively" image of human nature that narration alone is unable to produce.[32] Colman himself compares theater to "the colder Form of the novel" in his *Critical Reflections on the Old English Dramatick Writers* (1761).[33] Like Lennox's scholarship on Shakespeare (chapter 1), Colman's *Critical Reflections* is interested in earlier playwrights' adaptations of "romantick Novels."[34] However, more so than Lennox, Colman is fascinated by the capacity of the theater as a medium to transform these source texts: he writes about how the form of the drama means that a dramatic adaptation of a novel can provide "true Character" and describe "the Workings of the human Heart," even when this is lacking in the original novel.[35] Similarly, Sarah Fielding and Jane Collier describe how the use of dramatic features in their novelistic "Dramatic Fable" *The Cry* gives "life and action to our history."[36] According to Fielding and Collier, "dramatic representation" heightens readers' sympathetic interest in the characters of the story: "It must be allowed that characters should be animated to gain our attention, and some degree of sympathy is necessary [. . .] the nearer things are brought to dramatic representation, the more are you acquainted with the personages, and interested in the event of the story."[37] In this formulation, a proximity to "Dramatick" representation implies a lively animation that immediately elicits sympathetic interest.

However, Fielding's earlier essay *Remarks on Clarissa, Addressed to the Author* (1749) opines that "*Clarissa* is not intended as a Dramatic, but as a real Picture of human Life, where Story can move but slowly, where the Characters must open by degrees, and the Reader's own Judgment form them from different Parts, as they display themselves according to the Incidents that arise."[38] Fielding draws attention to the structural difference between novels and theater. She distinguishes the "Dramatic" from the "real Picture" that Richardson's *Clarissa* (1747–48) offers. While print can aspire to the immediacy drama provides, Fielding suggests that the slower pace of (Richardsonian) novels, with their repeated retelling of events, unfolding over an extended period of time, produces a sense of multifaceted, "real" characters. The different temporalities of novels and plays result in different experiences of character. When being read, the text can be consumed for an extended period, drawing out events and characterization, allowing for a more sustained relationship with characters than watching them as part of an evening's performance. Moreover, characters in a novel can develop and "open" over months or years, allowing the reader to understand them "by degrees." Plays like *Polly Honeycombe* that preserve the unity of time are unable to do this. The farce, shorter than even a full-length play by virtue of being an afterpiece, would appear to be the last place to look for the novelistic encounter with character that *Clarissa* achieves.

The physical, sensory conditions of mid-eighteenth-century theater also need to be considered. In playhouses the audience was as well-lit as the stage and audience members often interacted with each other loudly in ways that had little relation to the play being performed.[39] A weekly periodical that Colman produced with Bonnell Thornton, *The Connoisseur*, humorously notes the tendency of the theater audience to compete with "the business of the play" for attention and, among other requests, asks of the prostitutes in the audience "and those who come to market, to drive their bargains with as little noise as possible" (November 1754).[40]

The presence of an actor could also interfere with the audience experiencing a sympathetic, novelistic relationship to the character being performed. Catherine Gallagher, drawing on David Hume's writings, argues that eighteenth-century philosophy suggests it is easier to sympathize with a character who has never existed, and who does not have a body, than with an embodied person.[41] The body of the person who is the subject of sympathy becomes a "proprietary barrier" that resists the investment of sympathy she identifies as crucial to the experience of a "realist" novel.[42] The bodies of actors in the theater thus present a "proprietary barrier" to the audience.[43] Sympathizing with Polly, by this argument, is precluded through the body of Jane Pope. Pope began playing Polly as a teenager at Drury Lane, but she kept the role well into her thirties. The structure of eighteenth-century theater encouraged actors to monopolize a part until they retired from a company, which led to close associations between actors and particular roles.[44] Pope had a strong proprietary relationship with Polly, and her body could be said to prevent Polly from being a "nobody" available for an audience member to sympathetically invest in. Arguing along these lines, it is Pope's embodiment of Polly (and print), rather than Polly's own inner life, that becomes staged.

Consequently, Lisa Freeman argues that the theater offered an eighteenth-century concept of character not as a novelistic "emanation of a stable interiority, but as the unstable product of staged contests between interpretable surfaces."[45] I agree with this claim for the intrinsic exteriority of mid-eighteenth-century theater. However, Freeman also potentially overstates the difference between characterization in the theater and the novel. Deidre Lynch and Dror Wahrman have stressed the way character in mid-eighteenth-century writing was constituted as externalized surfaces.[46] Given such a formulation of character, *Polly Honeycombe* shows us the extent theatrical characters *can* resemble those in mid-eighteenth-century novels. This is not because the theatrical characters onstage are particularly complex or interiorized, but precisely because they are generic types and self-consciously represented as circulating commodities, made up of legible surfaces or different "Parts," to quote, again, from Fielding's *Remarks*.

Quixotism itself invokes the distinction between individualized and generic character "types," or what we could term a "Theophrastian" character, after the classical collection *Characters* by Theophrastus (a collection imitated throughout the eighteenth century).[47] *Characters* outlines various moral types, such as the "buf-foon" and the "flatterer." In April Alliston's astute exploration of quixotism, char-acter, and the novel, she argues that quixotic narratives dramatize the central con-cern of character in eighteenth-century novels: the relationship between the "type" and the "particular." Quixotes literally *act out* the formal tension between Theophrastian characters and the particularity of overcharged, or more individu-alized, characters.[48] Alliston agrees that character is constituted by external, imprinted surfaces. However, she proffers that an *"anxiety of interiority"* is the result of the interplay between the overcharged surface of the particularized character the quixote is and the Theophrastian "type" the quixote aspires to be.[49] Such an anxiety is identifiable in *Polly Honeycombe*, but it extends beyond competing forms of characterization and is manifest in the collision between competing media (novel and theater).

Alliston's model needs to be qualified further—indeed, inverted—before it can be applied to quixotic representations on the eighteenth-century stage. Unlike *The Female Quixote*, where Arabella, the individualized quixotic character, is com-pared to the generic Romantic "type" she emulates, in *Polly Honeycombe*, Polly imitates (among others) the individualized characters from Richardson's novels and can herself be classed as a particular "type": the voracious, female novel reader. *Polly Honeycombe's* contemporary audience commended the farce for its represen-tation of this "type." In two consecutive letters published in the *Public Ledger* (December 1760), by a "young lady" who signs herself "E.W.," the farce is com-mended for accurately representing the novel-reading women who populate the town.[50] E.W. writes that Polly's "character is new on the Theatre, though there are 976000 originals in town."[51] For E.W., then, Polly exemplifies a particular cate-gory of person, the deluded female novel reader, of which there are numerous "orig-inals." It is Polly's ability to exemplify the traits of these 976,000 that makes her, as a fictional character, praiseworthy. E.W. also calls Polly the "very image" of her "Cousin *Fanny*": "Poor *Fanny* has so stuffed her head with novels, that every good disposition of her mind, which formerly were many, are absolutely buried and lost; and the poor girl, who is now grown a little *old-maidish*, might have been married and happy, but for the crude lessons she imbibed from these impure fountains."[52] The letter deploys the standard conventions of anti-novel rhetoric. Novels are "impure fountains" that are drunk or "imbibed," suggestively permeating and pol-luting their readers' bodies. Strikingly, it is "Fanny," the apparent, living "origi-nal," who is a Theophrastian character. For E.W., *Polly Honeycombe's* success hinges on Polly's resemblance to this generic (but living) "type."

Though Polly can be identified with this novel-reading "type," she is not solely defined by it. Rather, the novel-reading "type" is a role she performs. Brewer argues that the farce is both conventional and unorthodox because of the eager, self-aware performance that animates Polly's character. She laughs in the middle of the play and in the epilogue, thoroughly enjoying playing her quixotic role (*PH*, 102, 109).[53] This, on top of the way the farce does not end with Polly "*old-maidish*" or regretful of her novel-reading ways, points to how Polly is not deluded like "[p]oor *Fanny*" or, more generally, the eighteenth-century stereotype of the novel-infatuated woman that Fanny epitomizes. Instead, Brewer suggests, Polly's behavior appears as a playful acting out of novelistic form, aware that it does not adequately fit her situation.[54] Polly thus is both a "type" and a self-conscious performance of this type. Or, to be precise, the novel-reading "type" is one of many surfaces that structure Polly's character, creating both an anxiety of interiority and an exuberantly performed exteriority.

ACTING AS SHE READS

Polly Honeycombe stresses the theatricality of Polly's quixotism. "Well said, Sir George!" are the first words Polly exclaims, and the first words of the play proper (*PH*, 70). She speaks them with a book in her hand, interrupting her reading to directly address a fictional character as though he is a person of flesh and blood, capable of hearing her appreciative words. Polly then resumes reading her (fictive) novel (she later refers to it as *The History of Sir George Truman and Emilia* [*PH*, 76]). Her pose mirrors that of an actor at a rehearsal holding a script, and her eager sympathy with characters from the novel she reads prompts her to theatrically mimic their movements. *The History of Sir George Truman and Emilia* itself parodies sentimental literature's emphasis on somatic affect through its hyperbolic descriptions of characters' emoting bodies. See, for instance, the description of Emilia's blushes: "Thou hast seen, perhaps, [. . .] the artificial vermilion on the cheeks of Cleora, or the vermilion of nature on those of Sylvia; thou hast seen— in a word, the lovely face of Emilia was overspread with blushes" (*PH*, 70). The metaphor compares Emilia's blushes to makeup, or "artificial vermilion." Paul Goring argues that central to the experience of sentimental literature was the reader being affected by the descriptions of emoting bodies: the "signifiers *produce* the internally felt signifieds."[55] *The History of Sir George Truman and Emilia* takes this to its satirical extreme, with the narrator implying that the reader should be moved by the signifier—the blush—regardless of whether it is actually internally felt by the character or not. Cosmetic blushes offer the sign of affect without any implication of "inner" feeling. In the introduction to this book, I discussed how the imprinted body frequently blurs into the imprinted mind in eighteenth-century philosophy: both mark and are marked by each other. The artificial blush can be "read" as if it is a symptom of a feeling mind or a feeling body, but ultimately it is a free-floating signifier, detached from "authenticity." Polly's novel, by comparing Emilia's blushes to both the "paint" of cosmetics and nature, syntactically fuses performed and "natural" marks of emotion on the body.

Polly's response to her reading also valorizes the performance of legible signs of passion *as* passion. When Sir George and Emilia declare their love for each other, Polly is so impressed by their textualized bodies that their signs of feeling become inscribed on her flesh. After Polly reads that Sir George brings Emilia's hand to his chest, "where the pulses of his heart beat quick, throbbing with tumultuous passion," she touches her own chest, *"acting it as she reads"* (*PH*, 70). The implication is that her own heart is beating similarly, that her body is quixotically replicating Sir George's affective impressions. Her placement of her hand on her heart is not an exact reproduction of either Sir George's or Emilia's movement. Instead, Polly's theatrical reading renders her gesturing body the locus of the love scene: she inscribes on her own body both Emilia's bashfulness and George's "tumultuous passion" (*PH*, 70). Her hand is pressed, like Emilia's, but she is feeling the throbs of her own heart. The placement of this scene at the opening of the farce implies that Polly's theatrical reading—her embodied reproduction of the marks of emotion on Sir George's and Emilia's novelized bodies—spurs her behavior in the rest of the play. The structure of the farce traces her rebellion against her parents and her attempts to write her own narrative back to her pleasure in performed reading.

I will discuss shortly the impressed body as it is conceptualized in eighteenth-century acting theory. For now, I will situate the marks of passion on Polly's (acting) body in relation to the pages of *Polly Honeycombe*'s printed edition. The print publication of *Polly Honeycombe* contrasts the detailed descriptions of fictive, emoting bodies in *The History of Sir George Truman and Emilia* with concise stage directions describing Polly's actions. Julie Stone Peters describes a shift in printed stage directions, from the seventeenth century into the eighteenth century, with a new emphasis on directions that aimed to "bring the performance to the reader—that attempt to make it vividly present in the instant."[56] Stage directions, ostensibly written to guide the actress playing Polly, also serve to direct the performance occurring in the reader's imagination. Their curtness is ostentatiously unlike phrases from Polly's novel. Yet directions such as *"reading and acting"* also refer the actress, and the reader, back to the novel Polly is dramatically embodying (*PH*, 70). *The History of Sir George Truman and Emilia* becomes both a prop and an elaborate set of stage directions. The actress and Polly simultaneously respond to the novel's descriptions of emoting bodies. Blushes, glances, and other marks of "tumultuous passion" (*PH*, 70), facetiously imagined in *The History of Sir George Truman and Emilia*, become a basis for performative re-inscription on the bodies of Polly and the actress.

The self-consciousness of the reading scene underscores the theatricality of Polly's quixotic reading. She articulates her appreciation of the novel by interrupting her reading of it: she breaks off from the description of Emilia's blushes to exclaim, "This is a most beautiful passage, I protest!" (*PH*, 70). So Polly moves between being an enraptured reader and a commentator. By pausing her reading in order to narrativize her own emotional transport, she subverts her declarations of rapture at the very moment of their articulation, implying that her absorption in the story is as momentary as it might be intense. On the pages of the printed play, quotation marks and dashes separate the words of the novel from Polly's commentary, marking an overt shift from the exaggerated sentimentalism of *The History of Sir George Truman and Emilia* to Polly's delighted appreciation of it.

The sense that Polly's reading involves a theatrical display of sensibility is reinforced by stage directions such as "*affectedly*" (*PH*, 70). In any case, she moves from being a characteristic "type"—the infatuated, quixotic female reader (when she reads)—to an astute, self-conscious commentator on her own sensibility. Like an actor on the eighteenth-century stage, Polly can fall out of character. The play also hints that Polly uses the established associations between sensibility and class to prove (to herself at least) her refined taste and sensibility and assert that she is above her bourgeois parents. She demonstratively empathizes with the character of the baronet, Sir George, and states, "Lord, lord, my stupid Papa has no taste. He has no notion of humour, and character, and the sensibility of delicate feeling" (*PH*, 70). Polly seeks to perform, through her reading, the role of the young woman of sensibility and "delicate feeling" (*PH*, 70).

By asserting the performed nature of Polly's sentimental reading, I do not mean to implicitly oppose her reading practice to a model of "authentic," internalized feeling. Instead, it is important to note how the play suggests that possessing feeling involves an adroit externalization of it. Useful here is Goring's argument that the "performing body" is significant "within not only works of fiction but also the activity of reading" and that during the eighteenth century, reading practices were public and performed.[57] Goring argues that sentimental literature invites its readers to "inhabit roles" and "rehearse a language of gesture."[58] Literary appreciation becomes "measured and assayed in terms of *visible sensibility*."[59] So we could say that behind Polly's concern with acting out her sympathy is sentimentalism's inherent theatricality that demands that the impressions texts make on their readers be embodied and enacted. Demonstrating one's sensibility and appreciation of sentimental literature involves having a body that legibly performs feeling. Polly's quixotic reading can therefore be comprehended in the context of a period that conceptualized sentimental reading as theatrical. To have sensibility is to possess a physiology that lends itself to legible impressions to such an extent that one's flesh becomes both a spectacle and a text. In *Polly Honeycombe*, the impressed body of Polly (and the actress) is closely aligned with the book she holds. Both the surface of the actress's/Polly's body and the pages of her book are inscribed with the signifiers of emotion.

THE PLASTIC IMAGINATION

Let us examine these surfaces in closer detail. Both Polly's and the actress's performances of emotion involve an impressed body becoming a text, a text that the audience can decipher and interpret. Eighteenth-century critics focused intently on actors' gestures and expressions, that is to say, on actors' externalized performances of emotion.[60] Post-Cartesian theories of acting—particularly Aaron Hill's influential writings—conceive a language of bodily expression involving the actor's mind marking the actor's body, via the imagination. They stress the actor's emoting body as a site for the articulation and reproduction of affect, envisaging the actor's face as a screen upon which, to use Lynch's words, "the operations of a natural semantic system might be viewed with special distinctness."[61] The actors' externalization affect is "read" by the audience, and audience members can respond sympathetically and even mimetically.[62]

We could even say that acting bodies are envisaged as bodies of print in mid-eighteenth-century acting theory. Hill—whose translation of Voltaire's *Mérope* preceded *Polly Honeycombe*'s premiere—conceptualizes acting as involving legible signs of passion being imprinted on the actor's body and asserts that skillful actors require a malleable body and a strong imagination. Hill describes the actor's idea of a particular passion as exerting a physical pressure, which then impresses the actor's spirits and muscles.[63] Central to this transformation is what Hill calls the actor's "*Plastic Imagination*," an attribute that is "the happiest Qualification which a *Player* shou'd desire to be Master of."[64] It is an imagination that can mechanically imprint the actor's body with the passions envisaged in the actor's mind, so that the actor can "assume such impressions, at will."[65]

Hill's concept of "plasticity" overlaps with impressionability, encompassing a mutability of form, the power of education, and the capacity for ideas to mold matter. Catherine Malabou notes, in the eighteenth century, "plasticity," "*plasticité*," and "*Plastizität*" enter the language.[66] References to "plastic" imaginations in the early eighteenth century often anticipate formulations of the creative, powerful imagination usually identified with Romanticism.[67] However, Hill's use of "plastic" here is more mechanistic; it evokes print technology and formulates a capacity to mechanically embody text and passion. For example, in his poem "The Art of Acting" (1746), he writes of the actor's plastic imagination:

> Print the *ideal pathos*, on the *brain*:
> Feel the thought's image on the *eyeball* roll;
> Behind that *window*, sits th' attentive SOUL:[68]

An idea of the passion is printed on the actor's brain, like paper being impressed by a printing press. Similarly, in his *Essay on the Art of Acting* (1753), Hill states that when the imagination conceives "a *strong idea* of the passion," the idea "cannot *strongly* be conceived, without impressing its own form upon the muscles of the *face*."[69] After the "*Imagination* assumes the *Idea*," its "*Marks*, and characteristical Impressions, appear, first, in the *Face*; because nearest to the *Seat* of the Imagination," and then the rest of the body follows, prompted by the animal spirits.[70] The result is a particular passion being "muscularly stamp'd" on the body.[71] The actor's body, like the quixotic reading mind, becomes analogous to a printed page, overlain with signifiers.

Hill's theories remained influential years after they were published.[72] Colman and Thornton's *The Connoisseur* appears indebted to Hill when it describes acting as a feat of imaginative reproduction, analogous to writing or drawing: "[I]f it is necessary for the writer to work up his imagination to such a pitch as to fancy himself in the circumstances of the character he draws; what less must the actor do, who must look as the person represented would look, speak as he would speak, and be in every point the very man?"[73] Similarly, Robert Lloyd's poem *The Actor* (1760), addressed to Colman's collaborator, Thornton, and which Colman references in *Critical Reflections*, draws on Hill both for its description of affective contagion, "POET and Actor thus with blended Skill, / Mould all our Passions to their instant Will," and for its description of the actor's imprinted body:

> THE pliant Muscles of the various Face,
> The Mein that gave each Sentence Strength and Grace,
> The tuneful Voice, the Eye that spoke the Mind,[74]

Ultimately, Hill, Lloyd, and *Polly Honeycombe* describe a process of reproduction, where passions depicted on paper become themselves imprinted on actors' and readers' bodies. Hill's *Essay on the Art of Acting* is a key example that takes as a starting point the close interrelation between printed pages and "stamp'd" bodies: it contains quotations from plays by Thomas Otway, John Dryden, Shakespeare, and Hill himself as exemplars of particular passions (such as joy or grief) for the budding actor to use as the basis for their performance. For instance, in the case of "anger," Hill quotes Shakespeare's Henry V's rallying speech to his troops (act 3, scene 1), a speech that rouses them to a fierce, battle-ready state by describing the bodily signs of anger.[75] The soldiers are encouraged to "imitate" the "action of the tyger" and to "[s]et the teeth close, and stretch the nostril wide."[76] Hill (via Shakespeare) implies that the printed descriptions of external signs of passions and the feelings themselves are interchangeable. Similarly, in *Polly Honeycombe*, Polly, the sentimental reader of Sir George's and Emilia's raptures, is so moved by descriptions of external marks of emoting bodies that she physically imitates them. In both *Polly Honeycombe* and Hill's treatise, passion cycles between imprinted bodies and imprinted pages. Printed descriptions of affectively impressed bodies produce, through their readers, more affectively impressed bodies, bodies that can themselves then be described and printed.

THE "EXTRACT"

A congruous cycle of print and imprinted bodies is articulated and induced by the "Extract" of a fictive circulating library catalog, included in the preface to *Polly Honeycombe*'s print edition. The "Extract" is itself enclosed in an extract from a letter by Colman's "mother," who introduces the circulating library catalog as a found object, a "bulky pamphlet" in the possession of some young female novel readers (*PH*, 62). The "Extract" from this circulating catalog concludes the play's preface. It is a long list of published, eighteenth-century fiction titles, displayed in alphabetical order over two columns, an unperformable object in the printed play (see figures 6 and 7).[77] The "Extract" is ostentatious about its dependence on print and paper: it is difficult to look at the "Extract" and *not* see how its meaning depends on the layout of the printed page and the act of silent reading. Unable to be acted, arduous to read aloud, it is a plotless, narrativeless list, long and repetitive enough to make reading it, as we would read prose or the script of the play, laborious. It demands that the arrangements of the titles of the page and the patterning in the columns be noted, that our eyes pick out the longer titles and the italics as we scan the page. Its meaning comes from print devices: the patterning of the listed titles, the repetition, the columns, and the few well-chosen italics. It highlights the conventions of the eighteenth-century novel title, also noted in the play proper by the Nurse's comments on "[t]he *Ventures* of Jack this, and the history of Betsy t'other, and sir Humphrys, and women with hard christian names" (*PH*, 72).

via, or Love-Letters between a Nobleman and his Sister.

Amorous Friars, or the Intrigues of a Convent.

Anti-Gallican, or the History and Adventures of Harry Cobham.

Anti-Pamela, or feigned Innocence detected.

Apparition, or Female Cavalier, a Story founded on Facts.

Auction.

Beauty put to its Shifts, or the Young Virgin's Rambles, being several Years Adventures of Miss * * * * in England and Portugal.

Bracelet, or the Fortunate Discovery; being the History of Miss Polly * * *.

Brothers.

Bubbled Knights, or successful Contrivances; plainly evincing, in two familiar Instances lately transacted in this Metropolis, *the Folly and Unreasonableness of Parents laying a Restraint upon their Childrens Inclinations in the Affairs of Love and Marriage.*

Card.

Chiron, or the mental Optician.

Chit-chat, or a Series of interesting Adventures.

Chrysal, or the Adventures of a Guinea, with curious Anecdotes.

Clarissa, or the History of a young Lady; comprehending the most important Concerns of private Life, and particularly shewing the Distresses that may attend the Misconduct both of Parents and Children in relation to Marriage.

Cleora, or the Fair Inconstant; an authentick History of the Life and Adventures of a Lady, lately very eminent in high Life.

Clidanor and Cecilia, a Novel, designed as a Specimen of a Collection, *adapted to form the Mind to a just Way of thinking, and a proper Manner of behaving in Life.*

Clio, or a secret History of the Amours of Mrs. S n—m.

Cry, A Dramatick Fable.

Dalinda, or the Double Marriage.

Devil upon Crutches in England, or Night Scenes in London.

Emily, or the History of a Natural Daughter.

Fair Adulteress.

Fair Moralist.

Fair Citizen, or the Adventures of Charlotte Bellmour.

Fanny, or the Amours of a West-country young Lady.

Female Foundling; shewing the happy Success of constant Love, in the Life of Mademoiselle D —— R ——.

Female Rambler, or Adventures of Madam Janeton De * * *.

Female Banishment, or the Woman Hater.

Female Falshood.

Fortunate Villager, or Memoirs of Sir Andrew Thompson.

Fortune-Teller, or the Footman Innobled.

Friends, a *sentimental* History.

Gentleman and Lady of Pleasure's Amusement, in Eighty-eight Questions, with their Answers, on Love and Gallantry. To which are added, the

FIGURE 6 Second page of the "Extract" in *Polly Honeycombe*, 1760. Forrest Collection, Kislak Center for Special Collections, Rare Books and Manuscripts, University of Pennsylvania.

The "Extract" provides the readers of *Polly Honeycombe* with something withheld from the theater audience. It is an object Polly herself might have owned and used, like the other textual props onstage, such as her "excellent ink-horn" in her pincushion and "a case of pens, and some paper" in her fan (*PH*, 91), secreted among her intimate belongings in imitation of a Richardsonian heroine, or even the *"Pocket Volumes"* referred to in the prologue (*PH*, 68). In essence, the "Extract," as a potential prop of print and paper, concealed from the audience in the theater, further presents Polly as possessing a textual subjectivity.

The "Extract" itself is a show of promiscuous literary consumption. It contains a dizzying number of titles, ranging from "respectable" works, such as Richardson's *Pamela* (1740) and *Clarissa* (1747–48) and Voltaire's philosophical fiction *Zadig* (1747), to the translation of Claude Prosper Crébillon's *Sopha* (1742), which Patrick Spedding argues "became a symbol of immorality and decadence" in eighteenth-century England.[78] There are also a number of prostitute narratives in the "Extract," from those arguing for social reform, such as *The Histories of Some of the Penitents in the Magdalen House* (1759), to the scandalous, such as *Memoirs of Fanny Hill* (1750), John Cleland's much less popular abridgement of his infamous *Memoirs of a Woman of Pleasure* (1748–49).[79]

The strong presence of prostitute narratives in the "Extract" both reflects mid-eighteenth-century preoccupations with the figure of the prostitute and suggests specific congruities between circulating library texts and the circulation of female bodies, as well as the close spatial and cultural interrelations between the London theater and the sex trade. Such associations are strengthened by the formal similarities of the "Extract" to a popular catalog of London prostitutes: *Harris's List of Covent-Garden Ladies*. In April, eight months before *Polly Honeycombe*'s first performance and publication, the 1760 edition of *Harris's List of Covent-Garden Ladies* was published, the first installment in a series of roughly annual publications produced throughout the second half of the eighteenth century.[80] Even in the years before it was printed, Jack Harris's list had a semi-mythical status as a circulating manuscript catalog of women, and Harris's "sisterhood" of prostitutes is mentioned in Colman and Thornton's *The Connoisseur* (January 1755; October 1755).[81] While the 1760 printed edition is now lost, it most likely resembled the 1761 edition: an alphabetized catalog of London prostitutes, providing brief descriptions of them with their locations.[82] The connections between the "Extract" and *Harris's List* extend beyond them both being alphabetized catalogs. Kitty Fisher, for instance, features in both catalogs: her name occurs in the title of a circulating library object in the "Extract" (*The Juvenile Adventures of Miss Kitty F[isher]* [1759]), and she appears as an item in the 1760 and 1761 editions of *Harris's List*.[83] To read another prostitute narrative listed in the "Extract," *Memoirs of the Celebrated Miss Fanny M[urray]* (1758–59), is to read about Murray being "enrolled" in Harris's "parchment list."[84] Circulating women, like circulating books, it seems, are items to be cataloged.

The "Extract" therefore builds on already established cultural connections between the consumption of erotic, circulating-library material, female sexuality, and the list form. The "Extract"—in part through these connections to prostitute narratives and *Harris's List*—draws on established anti-novel narratives that designate the circulating library as a site for sexually fraught textual consumption. *Polly Honeycombe* further references these tropes when Polly asks her nurse to pick up some books from the library on the way to collect Scribble's love letters, associating love letters with circulating library texts (*PH*, 76). This, together with the suggestive connections in the "Extract" between circulating women and circulating books, resonates with Emma Clery's argument that anti-circulating-library discourse frequently rhetorically conflated books that were borrowed and the bodies of female readers. Library books, passing through the hands of temporary owners, becoming grubbier and steadily more defaced, suggested a parallel fate for the female readers who consumed and internalized the stories.[85] Anti-circulating-library discourse, in other words, relied on the same tropes of female circulation and loss of value Bonnie Blackwell identifies in it-narratives, where the "endurance" of a circulating object narrator "throws into high relief the transitory nature of female value" with the object-narrator "both witness to and metonym for the waning market value of a woman once initiated into sexuality."[86]

The profuse it-narratives in the "Extract," like the prostitution narratives, are largely tales of circulation, where the main character passes through multiple hands. Beyond the pornographic *Sopha*, there is *Sedan, in which many new and entertaining Characters are introduced* (1757). Directly above the title of Richardson's *Clarissa* is Charles Johnstone's *Chrysal; or the Adventures of a Guinea, with curious Anecdotes* (1760). *Adventures of a Cat* (1760) and *Adventures of a Black Coat* (1760) appear alongside *Adventures of Frank Hammond* (1754), a more conventionally human "character." The circulating library "Extract" agrees with Lynch's argument that people in mid-eighteenth-century England related to character in a way governed by economic transactions.[87] It also affirms the close interconnections between material "things" and the mid-eighteenth-century novel: novel characters and novels are structured by their manifestation as commercial, material, circulating paper commodities.[88] This point could be taken even further given that the paper of early editions of *Polly Honeycombe*—including the pages of the "Extract"—would have been made from linen rags, textile waste collected by rag-pickers, then beaten and stamped into sheets.[89] Thus, in the most fundamental

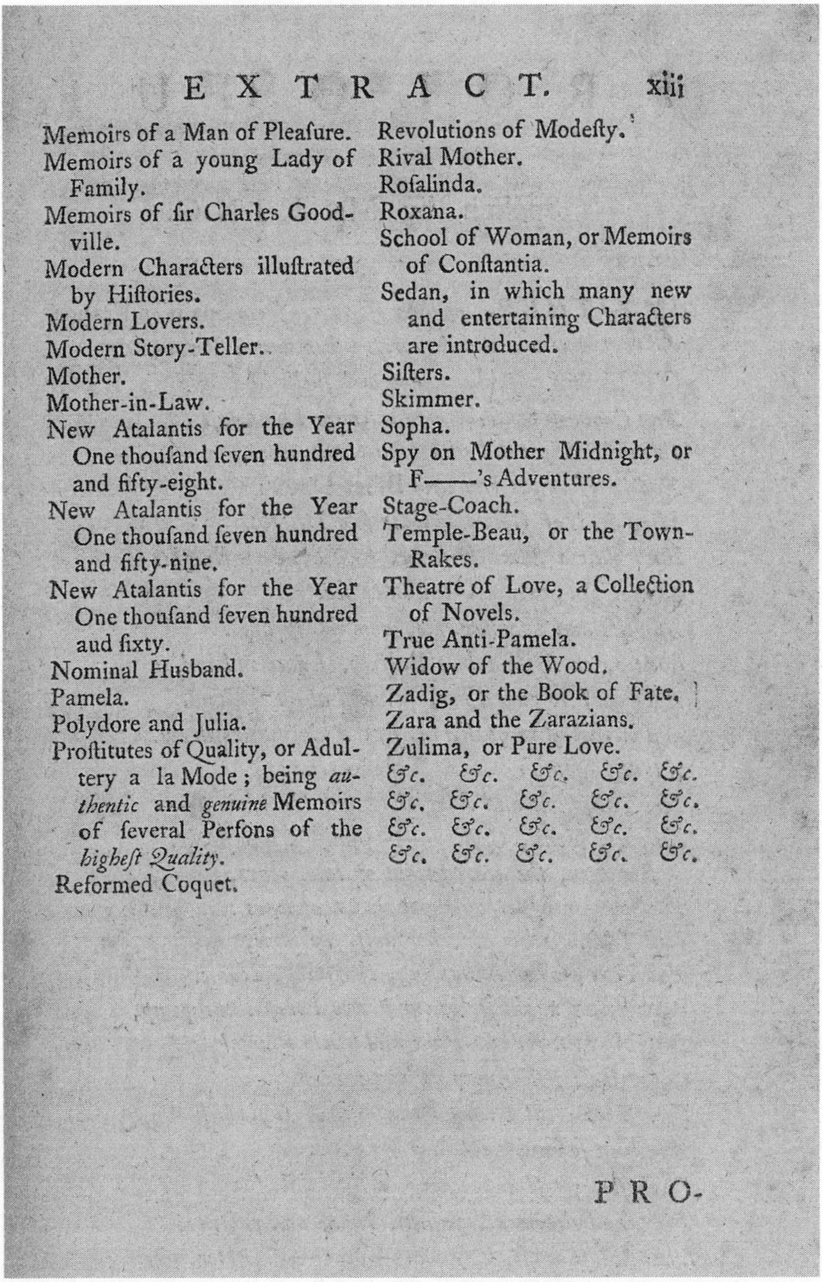

Memoirs of a Man of Pleafure.

Memoirs of a young Lady of Family.

Memoirs of fir Charles Good-ville.

Modern Characters illuftrated by Hiftories.

Modern Lovers.

Modern Story-Teller.

Mother.

Mother-in-Law.

New Atalantis for the Year One thoufand feven hundred and fifty-eight.

New Atalantis for the Year One thoufand feven hundred and fifty-nine.

New Atalantis for the Year One thoufand feven hundred aud fixty.

Nominal Husband.

Pamela.

Polydore and Julia.

Proftitutes of Quality, or Adultery a la Mode ; being *authentic* and *genuine* Memoirs of feveral Perfons of the *higheft Quality.*

Reformed Coquet.

Revolutions of Modefty.

Rival Mother.

Rofalinda.

Roxana.

School of Woman, or Memoirs of Conftantia.

Sedan, in which many new and entertaining Characters are introduced.

Sifters.

Skimmer.

Sopha.

Spy on Mother Midnight, or F——'s Adventures.

Stage-Coach.

Temple-Beau, or the Town-Rakes.

Theatre of Love, a Collection of Novels.

True Anti-Pamela.

Widow of the Wood.

Zadig, or the Book of Fate.

Zara and the Zarazians.

Zulima, or Pure Love.

&c. &c. &c. &c. &c.
&c. &c. &c. &c. &c.
&c. &c. &c. &c. &c.
&c. &c. &c. &c. &c.

FIGURE 7 Final page of the "Extract" in *Polly Honeycombe*, 1760. Forrest Collection, Kislak Center for Special Collections, Rare Books and Manuscripts, University of Pennsylvania.

way, a variety of imprinted consumer goods constitute the bodies of eighteenth-century print objects. Throughout the "Extract," *Polly Honeycombe* self-consciously probes mid-eighteenth-century close cultural associations between the commercial circulation of printed objects, consumer goods, and female bodies.

Part of the ostentatious dependence of the "Extract" on paper and print for meaning comes from carefully chosen italics. Evidence points to the italicizations in the "Extract" being Colman's authorial interventions, rather than faithful transcriptions of the titles themselves.[90] The deployment of a sprinkling of italicized words in the "Extract" is reminiscent of Hume's typographical emphasis in his definition of impressions, when his use of small caps seems to enact the imprints of forceful sensory experiences upon the Humean subject (see chapter 1). The "Extract" analogously uses a sprinkling of italicized words to suggest novels' impressions on a malleable reader's subjectivity. For example, italics are used in the full title of *Clidanor and Cecilia*, describing the text as being *"adapted to form the Mind to a just Way of thinking, and a proper Manner of behaving in Life"* (*PH*, 64).[91] Colman's typography enacts the capacity of this novel—and the other titles in the "Extract"—to imprint, mold, or *"form the Mind"* of the reader.

I have described how the "Extract" resists conventional modes of reading. However, through Colman's astute use of italics and short and long titles, a narrative can be gleaned from the "Extract," a narrative that appears to involve quixotic reading and filial disobedience. For instance, the careful deployment of short titles in the "Extract" suggestively positions novels as quasi-maternal competition, vying with their young readers' parents for influence. For example, the "Extract" refers to William Guthrie's *The mother; or, The happy distress. A novel* (1759) as simply "Mother" (figure 7). Directly beneath "Mother" is "Mother-in-Law" (figure 7).[92] In case the reader of the catalog had not yet noticed the joke, there is another "mother" in the adjacent column, "Rival Mother" (figure 7).[93] These titles seem to foreshadow the discord between children and parents in *Polly Honeycombe*'s plot, while also speaking to larger debates about the capacity of novels to disrupt paternal authority and reproduce themselves through impressions on their quixotic readers, or, in other words, their power to "mother" their readers.

The sparing placement of longer titles in the list works similarly. We have the famous full title of *Clarissa*, which concludes, "and particularly shewing the Distresses that may attend the Misconduct both of Parents and Children in relation to Marriage" (figure 6). This is complemented by the italicization and the use of the full title of the *Bubbled Knights* on the same page: *"the Folly and Unreasonableness of Parents laying a Restraint upon their Childrens Inclinations in the Affairs of Love and Marriage.*" These words, along with the aforementioned italics in the full title of *Clidanor and Cecilia*, and "*sentimental*" in "Friends, a *sentimental* History," are the only italicized words on the page (figure 6). Novels, the "Extract" seems to hint, "*form the Mind*" of their young readers by impressing them with ideas of opposing their parents in "*the Affairs of Love and Marriage*" and encourage them to associate such disobedience with the fashionably "*sentimental*." Yet the "Extract" also aligns the quixotic novel reader with the ideal reader of *Clarissa*, identifying the same paradox Sarah Raff discusses: "Both orthodox and quixotic models of reading envision fiction's radical influence upon its receiver."[94] The eighteenth-century novel's moral imperative is to "*form the Mind*" of the reader (figure 6). Or to put this another way, both the quixotic reader and the ideal reader of didactic fiction potentially have a mind that, in Locke's words, is "unwary, and as yet, unprejudiced," like a sheet of paper that receives "any Characters."[95]

In short, the "Extract" uses print to describe the impressions novels leave on the mind of their readers. It can be read as both a narrative about and a portrait of an insatiable novel reader, through its imagining of the Lockean *tabula rasa* as overlain with contemporary novel titles. The cumulative nature of Lockean individual consciousness, which conceptualizes the subject as essentially a collector of sensations, is mirrored by the list form of the "Extract."[96] Each book title potentially signifies an experience impressed upon the reader's mind, metaphorizing the reading subject as a collection of circulating objects. Julie Park argues for overlaps between eighteenth-century collections of objects and eighteenth-century formulations of "selfhood": "So central did the acquisition and display of objects become to forming the self—and invariably a feminine self—that objects threatened to displace the subject as a locus for selfhood in eighteenth-century England."[97] Sean Silver's recent exploratory work, itself titled *The Mind Is a Collection*, tracks eighteenth-century metaphors that render the mind as a collection of objects, sometimes as a museum, sometimes as a cabinet, sometimes as a library.[98] *Polly Honeycombe*'s circulating library list, however, is not quite a list of acquirable objects, but rather an advertisement of the transient experience of rapidly reading a novel that circulating libraries offer. The circulating library reader owns nothing after the reading of a borrowed novel beyond the marks the experience of reading leaves in the mind. Similar to a theatrical performance, then, sensory experiences or impressions are the commodities the library catalog advertises. The "Extract" uses print to articulate economies of experiential and affective impressions, ultimately blurring the Lockean subject into a list of commodified experiences.

QUIXOTISM AS EXTRACTION

Its very title, "Extract," contributes to the catalog's representation of the quixotic reading subject as created by imaginative impressions from their reading. *Polly Honeycombe* suggests how we could develop an allegory of quixotism as extraction: to do so allows us to consider the quixotic reader as both stemming from an original text and independent of it. Thinking along these lines offers another close interconnection between Polly's quixotic subjectivity and the portion of text—the novelistic extract—she reads in the opening scene of the farce.[99] The word "extract" itself describes production: the primary definition of "extract" in Samuel Johnson's dictionary being "[t]o draw out of something," which Johnson then elucidates through examples that describe this drawing out as involving one substance being chemically extracted from another.[100] Johnson also correlates the word "extract" with the female body. As an illustration to the third definition of "extract" ("[t]o take from something of which the thing was a part"), he quotes Adam's characterization of Eve from John Milton's *Paradise Lost* (1667):

> Bone of my bone, flesh of my flesh, myself
> Before me: woman is her name, of man
> *Extracted*.[101]

In both Johnson's dictionary and *Paradise Lost*, Eve, the archetypal woman, is an extract. Extraction has connotations here not only of generation, but also with female flesh. There are established associations between femininity and the fragmentary: Elizabeth W. Harries notes how "fragments are felt to be feminine" in eighteenth-century writing, and argues for an identification of femininity with the incomplete and the irregular in eighteenth-century literary culture.[102] Harries shows how feminized forms can be simultaneously identified both with the fragmentary and with frivolous excess.[103] Relatedly, the concept of "extraction" simultaneously evokes feminized generation and feminized lack.

Such coalescence of gender and genre plays out in *Polly Honeycombe*, with its title encouraging its audience and readers to associate Polly, the female character, with *Polly Honeycombe*'s genre. As a result, the text's fragmentary nature, an "afterpiece" with (as we have seen) an unconventionally open, novelistic ending, becomes implicitly gendered as feminine. Taking this further, the eighteenth-century feminization of quixotism could itself be connected to the way quixotism offers both an uneven embodiment of texts and an unauthorized reproduction of print.

This much seems clear: the copious proliferation of novels in the quixotic "Extract" implies both a gendered fragmentation and a feminized excess. The "Extract" presents a massive generation of texts, its length only underscored through its aforementioned unreadability and unperformability. That it is itself only an extract, a selection from a larger circulating library catalog, suggests the entire catalog is so enormous it defies transcription. This delineation of copious generation continues into the series of twenty "&c." that close the "Extract" (figure 7).[104] The mass of "&c.," clustering at the end of the list, draws the reader's attention to "&c." as a typographic object. The only other place "&c." appears in the play is also in the preface, again following a list of commodities, when Colman's mother describes "black caps, black fans, black gloves, &c. from the milliner's" as being scattered on the table, alongside textual objects, "three or four books, half-bound, and a bulky pamphlet" (*PH*, 62). The "&c." here signals a careless profusion of feminine products that are too trivial to list. The multiplicity of "&c." at the end of the "Extract" similarly suggests that here are novels which are too inconsequential and too numerous to include.

Or perhaps they are too obscene to include. "&c." also had a specific sexual suggestiveness in the eighteenth century. Patrick Spedding and James Lambert argue that "&c." had an elliptic function like the dash, "alert[ing] the reader to the fact that an obscenity has either been used or has been narrowly avoided."[105] Certainly, "&c." was used as a substitute for a variety of obscenities, and among them genitalia.[106] The series of twenty "&c." at the end of *Polly Honeycombe*'s "Extract" is structurally an opening, with *Polly Honeycombe*'s main text beginning immediately after the circulating library catalog. Appearing after the list of "&c.," *Polly Honeycombe* becomes another title in the circulating library "Extract," or, as the bawdy implications of the "&c." might suggest, *Polly Honeycombe* is birthed by the circulating library catalog. In any case, *Polly Honeycombe* self-reflexively positions itself as a product of the same textual proliferation and circulation it parodies. This is especially the case as the bulk of the titles in the "Extract" belong to the 1750s, which, as well as lending the printed play topicality, directly connects *Polly Honeycombe* to the other print objects that were advertised, borrowed, and read alongside it.[107] On multiple levels, the "Extract" anticipates *Polly Honeycombe*'s mediation, not only as a circulating library text, which was listed in similar catalogs, but also as a work that was itself frequently extracted in periodicals. As was often the case with popular mid-eighteenth-century plays, periodicals republished scenes from *Polly Honeycombe*, as well as its prologue and epilogue, the printed columns of the periodicals often echoing the columns of the "Extract" itself.[108] So, *Polly Honeycombe* was frequently extracted, begins with an extract, and suggestively connects its heroine's subjectivity to both an extract from the novel she reads aloud and an extract from a circulating library catalog. Quixotism itself becomes aligned with a process of extraction and circulation.

In its depiction of mass literary production and consumption, the "Extract" draws on circulating libraries' association with the manufacture as well as the distribution of novels. Anti-circulating-library rhetoric associated their creation of novels with their creation of quixotic readers.[109] For example, "T. Row," in a letter in the *Gentleman's Magazine* (1767), writes:

> [M]any a young person being entirely corrupted by the giddy and fantastical notions of love and gallantry, imbibed from thence [romance reading]. There is scarce a month passes, but some worthless book of this kind, in order to catch curiosity by its novelty, appears in the form of two volumes 12mo. price five or six shillings, and they are chiefly the offspring, as I take it, of the managers of the circulating libraries, or their venal authors. Some few of them, indeed, have come from better pens, but the whole together are an horrible mass of hurtful insignificance, and, I suppose, may amount now to above an hundred volumes; I speak at the lowest. The author of *Polly Honeycomb* made a commendable attempt to stop the progress of this growing evil, and parents might learn, if they pleased, to debar their children the use of such pernicious books, from thence.[110]

This letter in the *Gentleman's Magazine* overwhelmingly portrays "worthless book[s]" as distastefully commercial items, part of a "horrible" and "hurtful" feminized marketplace. The grossly material entities of "two volumes" are manufactured with no other motive but that of making money. Row uses the language of diseased reproduction, describing circulating libraries as producing on "mass" an "offspring" of "hurtful" texts and, through these, corrupted readers. *Polly Honeycombe*'s partial participation in this discourse is evident in both Polly's avid consumption of texts onstage and the depiction in the "Extract" of an endless "mass" imprinting quixotic readers. Yet *Polly Honeycombe* also mocks these tropes, with the audience encouraged to cheer for Polly as she astutely outwits her parents and escapes a loveless marriage. The farce's novelistic, inconclusive ending allows *Polly Honeycombe* to be read as both an anti-novel farce and a pro-novel comedy.

So, on one hand, Polly is represented as being formed via the circulating library "Extract," but she also goes beyond it. I have argued that Polly's exuberant performance of quixotism means she is not simply a passive receptacle for novels: novels not only shape Polly; they become a tool she uses to outmaneuver her parents. The circulating library catalog is undeniably tied to Polly's subjectivity, but not wholly constitutive of it. Though Polly reads plenty of novels, and enjoys read-ing them, she also reads other material, such as her prayer book (*PH*, 73).[111] Per-haps this is why, unlike, say, Biddy Tipkin of Steele's *Tender Husband*, Polly can use her reading as a guide to formulate her own successful narrative. She tells her nurse that she has "such a head full of intrigues and contrivances" (*PH*, 73) as a result of her novel reading, aligning herself with Lovelace, the manipulative seducer of Richardson's *Clarissa*, who proclaims himself to have "the *most plotting heart in the world*," rather than with the novel's tragic heroine.[112]

Polly's ability to weaponize her novel reading is explicit in David Garrick's epilogue to *Polly Honeycombe*, where the actress playing Polly proclaims how "*NOV-ELS will teach us all the Art of War*," and engender a battle between husbands and wives, parents and daughters, with novel readers victorious: "*Daughters should gov-ern, Parents should obey*" (*PH*, 110). Polly also distinguishes the novelistic love she feels for Scribble from the more naïve love between her parents, stating, "*We Girls of Reading,* [. . .] *Pity our parents, when such passion blinds 'em*" (*PH*, 109). The fear of female novel-reading expressed in conduct books, that novels will teach young women to disobey their parents and husbands, becomes a reason to read them. Polly learns from novels how to build "ladders of ropes," or "of escaping out of window, by tying the sheets together," or "of throwing one's-self into the street upon a feather-bed," or "of being catch'd in a gentleman's arms" (*PH*, 88–89). *Polly Honeycombe* turns anti-novel discourse on its head. Here, novels instruct girls in reducing their parents to fools with an adroitness difficult not to admire. Polly might be a circulating-library reading quixote, but she is also a savvy heroine of an eighteenth-century play, who uses novel reading to triumph over her parents.

Thomas Keymer, commenting on mid-century novelists, writes that their literary self-consciousness is a direct and "practical self-consciousness about the mechanisms and institutions of print culture: specifically, about the relationship between authorial production and its materialization as a printed object."[113] *Polly Honeycombe*'s incorporation of typographical objects like the circulating library catalog evidences a similar reflective engagement with the material form of the printed book and its dissemination. Yet its self-consciousness about its manifesta-tion in print intersects with its self-consciousness about its theatrical form. The farce repeatedly suggests how novels are to Polly what a script is to an actor.

Polly Honeycombe brings print alongside performance to describe the quix-otic reader as multiply imprinted, or made up of multiple layers of externalized, imprinted surfaces. The preface's "Extract" could be numbered among such sur-faces, presenting the quixotic reader as a Lockean *tabula rasa* imprinted by novel-reading experiences, while the opening scene of Polly reading stages a complex interaction between several affectively impressed bodies, on the stage and on the page. Throughout, *Polly Honeycombe* describes quixotic reading as spurring embodied textual proliferation. This leads us into chapter 3. In *Tristram Shandy*, the trope of the female, quixotic novel reader, which *Polly Honeycombe* parodies, is masculinized. Quixotic and impressionable male bodies occupy the center of the page.

> [I]f I can so manage it, as to convey but the same impressions to every other brain, which the occurrences themselves excite in my own——I will answer for it the book shall make its way in the world, much better than its master has done before it——Oh *Tristram! Tristram!* can this but be once brought about——the credit, which will attend thee as an author, shall counterbalance the many evils which have befallen thee as a man.
> —*TS*, 4.32.400–401

TRISTRAM, THE FICTIVE AUTHOR AND narrator of Laurence Sterne's *The Life and Opinions of Tristram Shandy* (1759–67), describes successful writing as involving the transmission and transposition of "impressions" from his own "brain" to his readers' (*TS*, 4.32.400–401). What is more, Tristram appears to equate this goal of imprinting his own sensations on the reader's brain with a recuperation of his manhood; if successful, he imagines he can "counterbalance the many evils" that have wounded his masculinity, such as the injuries to his name, nose, and genitals. Raymond Stephanson notes how Tristram here equates the successful creative act with recuperated masculinity.[1] The passage does this and more: it places experiential and affective "impressions" at the center of Tristram's thwarted autobiographical project, and it uses them to suggest how Tristram's writing of his autobiography is an attempt at an exclusively male act of reproduction. Tristram writes to reproduce his own "impressions" upon the "brain" of his readers. Doomed to be the last member of a line plagued by impotence— "nothing was well hung in our family" (*TS*, 5.17.449)—Tristram describes his autobiographical writing as a form of reproduction where, despite the "evils which have befallen [him] as a man" (*TS*, 4.32.401), he can leave, via the conveyance of "impressions," a second self, which "makes its way in the world, much better than its master has done before it" (*TS*, 4.32.401).

Tristram's attempt to reproduce through his writing is only one of the many ways that he and the male members of his Shandy family attempt to compensate for a wounded masculinity by trying to metaphorically father through language. Of course, these attempts at reproduction fail: there is no way that Tristram can conceivably "convey the same impressions to every other brain, which the occurrences themselves excite in [his] own" (*TS*, 4.32.400–401). While in *Polly Honeycombe* the female quixotic body becomes analogized to the printed page, and becomes a sexualized site that spawns text, here the focus shifts to a male body and its fraught relationship with the reproduction of text. The Shandean body is castrated, impotent, but also pleasurably textual.

This passage is one of many that blend bodies and books by punning on the multiple resonances of imprinting and impressions: "impressions" here encompasses marks on the "brain" that stem from sensory experience, a sexualized penetration and marking that Tristram equates with his virility, and the typographical impressions on the page that the reader holds. Throughout *Tristram Shandy*, experiences are described as imprinting the senses and marking the Shandy men. Tristram, for instance, tells us he owes "one half" of his philanthropy to the "impression" that was "imprinted by my uncle *Toby*" when Toby spared the life of a fly (*TS*, 2.12.131). Deidre Lynch argues that early eighteenth-century texts describe a "fascination with the puns that could link the person 'in' a text to the printed letters (alphabetic symbols, or 'characters' in another sense) that elaborated that text's surface."[2] *Tristram Shandy* points to how this preoccupation continues into the second half of the eighteenth century. Tristram owes his "character" to experiential "impressions."

"Impressions" can also be read alongside other, more bawdy connotations of "impressions." Occurring alongside references to chaotic male-only reproduction, the word evokes sodomy, in the early modern sense of the term. Unauthorized, illegal imprinting, such as the production of counterfeit coins, was conflated with "deviant" non-reproductive sexual practices through the idea of "sodomy."[3] *Tristram Shandy*, as this chapter will discuss, offers through its remasculinization of quixotic impressions a description of tenuously masculine bodies that sodomize and are sodomized.

Elsewhere in the text, "impressions" takes on an explicitly typographical, lexemic sense. For instance, when discussing how the word "whiskers" has become irrevocably associated with bawdy connotations in Navarre, Tristram darkly remarks: "There are some trains of certain ideas which leave prints of themselves about our eyes and eye-brows; and there is a consciousness of it, somewhere about the heart, which serves but to make these etchings the stronger—we see, spell, and put them together without a dictionary" (*TS*, 5.1.413). The "we" implicates the reader, Tristram, and the people of Navarre in following a particular train of thought that begins with "whiskers" and ends with something unmentionable and sexual. The chain of associations leaves decipherable marks on the body. Here, as in *Polly Honeycombe* and *The Female Quixote*, impressions traverse the boundaries between the literal and metaphorical, cerebral and embodied. For the citizens of Navarre, and, this passage suggests, the reader who consumes their narrative, mental impressions become legible marks, visible on the body. People become like pages, with the imaginative associations they make spelled across their faces. Jarred Wiehe has recently argued how *Tristram Shandy* reshapes the "geography of erogenous zones" away from the genital.[4] Building on this, we could say the Navarre passage begins by connecting "whiskers" on the upper lip to something unmentionable and concludes with "eyes and eye-brows" becoming a site on the body where eroticized "etchings" are made. The entire surface of the face in this passage threatens to become a penetrable site for lexical marks: the face is where unspoken thoughts become imprinted on the body.

I want to stress this formulation of the Shandean body as a site enveloped by an impressionable, erogenous surface, where genitals become displaced by whiskers and noses. In this text, even the imagination becomes tantamount to androgynously gendered genitalia. *Tristram Shandy* is rife with descriptions of imaginations swelling (*TS*, 1.15.46), being tickled (*TS*, 3.24.28), and becoming dangerously heated (*TS*, 3.39.279, 6.23.541, 8.12.671). While imaginations were yoked to female reproductive bodies via metaphors of mental wombs, and the possibility of maternal imaginative impressions on the fetus, they were also relatedly and repeatedly connected to the male genitalia. The leading eighteenth-century physicians Albrecht von Haller, Robert Whytt, and Herman Boerhaave ascribed erections to the imagination, a link that facilitated constructions of the imagination as a sexual site.[5] Stephanson observes that in *Tristram Shandy* the imagination acts like an erection, "desirously 'straddling' and 'sliding into' the many 'slits' which all the armaments of judgement are powerless to prevent."[6] Yet sexed images are never straightforward in this text, and nor are imaginations solely penetrative. They also pregnantly swell (*TS*, 1.15.46) and can be mounted by Satan (*TS*, 3.36.267).

Before getting further into *Tristram Shandy*'s exploration of gender, reproduction, and bawdy impressions, it is necessary to position it as a quixotic narrative. *Tristram Shandy*'s complex relation to quixotic tropes is a productive scholarly subject. Susan Staves, for instance, argues that Sterne "shows us not just one eccentric quixote isolated from sane humanity by his eccentricities, but rather a vision of all men as equally eccentric quixotes isolated from each other."[7] Wendy Motooka builds on Staves, noting how *Tristram Shandy* not only presents men as quixotic, but complexly remasculinizes the feminized eighteenth-century quixote, writing that the work "revels in the feminized, limited and arbitrary sallies of the early eighteenth-century quixote [. . .]. Sterne's novel is 'odd' because it delights in the prospect of a world full of 'rational' men who think like female quixotes."[8] We could add that Sterne's men not only think like female quixotes, but have bodies that quixotically spawn text. *Tristram Shandy* is both a quixotic narrative and an anti-quixotic narrative. It subverts the eighteenth-century feminization of quixotism and connects narratives about impressionable female bodies to larger cultural anxieties surrounding male artistic creation.

Whether this remasculinization of quixotism endorses or mocks misogyny is a fraught question. The extent to which *Tristram Shandy* is or is not sexist has been the subject of much debate.[9] Juliet McMaster and Paula Loscocco have both argued that the book is about misogyny rather being in itself a misogynist text.[10] More recently, Elizabeth W. Harries has tentatively stated, "I think the novel is sexist, and I think it is not," arguing that it is a novel that both "shores up *and questions* cultural myths about gender."[11] Certainly, *Tristram Shandy is* animated by its male characters' misogyny and reiterates conventional wisdom about feminine literature and female bodies. Yet it also uses impressions to unsettle gendered tropes in eighteenth-century literary culture, providing descriptions of erotic pleasure that exist beyond the penis and repeatedly representing male-gendered bodies as being as (sexually) penetrable as the female body is typically identified as being.

This chapter will begin its examination of *Tristram Shandy*'s complex treatment of gendered, quixotic impressions with the fictive readers "Sir" and "Madam." I will discuss how the book both reiterates and problematizes eighteenth-century stereotypes around sexed quixotic reading practices and feminized literary consumption and production. "Sir" is one of many impressionable, penetrable "males" in a book dominated by them. The wounded "maleness" of the Shandy men, and their thwarted attempts to reproduce without female input or influence, destabilizes sexual difference. Moreover, the dominant image for quixotism in *Tristram Shandy*—the hobby-horse—further serves to represent a permeable, quixotic, impressionable masculinity. By attending to the figure of the impressionable quixotic reader in this chapter, I will show how *Tristram Shandy* simultaneously reiterates and attacks eighteenth-century gendered metaphors surrounding reading, quixotism, and reproduction. It takes these tropes to their (il)logical conclusion, resulting in a text that both is exuberantly anti-woman and, with the self-consciousness that pervades the text, *examines* this misogyny.

READING THE READERS: SIR/MADAM

Tristram's concern with his capacity to penetrate his reader is seen in his one-sided conversations with a variety of fictive readers, most notably "Sir" and "Madam." When considering how reading is represented as an (unsuccessful) sexual act in

Tristram Shandy, criticism has emphasized Tristram's relationship with Madam.[12] Helen Ostovich, for example, writes that the "liveliest, most disputacious reader-relationship in the novel is the one between Tristram and his female reader, Madam," intensified through the "sexual overtones" that typify their exchanges.[13] However, while Madam the reader is the butt of bawdy jokes, Tristram's relationships with his male readers are also sexualized, and potentially to a greater degree.[14] There is a tendency for writings about Tristram's interactions with "Madam" and "Sir" to treat them as addresses to distinct types of readers, distinguished via their sex or reading practices.[15] It *is* the case that Tristram's interactions with the fictive readers represent them as separate characters, and they are used by Sterne to critique different styles of reading. However, divvying up readers of *Tristram Shandy* into "Sir" and "Madam" overlooks the way that, whatever reader Tristram is addressing, the presence of another sex is always felt.

What I mean to say is this: while reading *Tristram Shandy*, it is difficult for the reader, whatever sex, *not* to identify both with "Madam" and with "Sir." For a start, Tristram sexualizes and feminizes his readers in a work that is preoccupied with the dilemmas of being a man and, during the eighteenth century, appealed more to men than to women.[16] The text's numerous male readers therefore participate in Tristram's relationship with his female reader, "Madam." For example, in the most famous of the exchanges between Tristram and "Madam," Tristram accuses Madam of inattentiveness. She has failed to notice when Tristram tells her "as plain, at least, as words, by direct inference, could tell you such a thing" that "*my mother was not a papist*" (*TS*, 1.20.64). This passage is written so that almost every reader will miss what is an exceedingly subtle reference about why Tristram's mother is not Catholic. It is nearly impossible, on first reading, to connect Tristram's comment that "if it was not necessary I should be born before I was christened, I would this moment give the reader an account of it" (*TS*, 1.19.64) with Mrs. Shandy's religion, especially as the discussion of how Catholicism allows baptism before birth by "injection" occurs in the succeeding chapter. Reading *Tristram Shandy* for the first time, then, the reader, irrespective of gender, is implicated in Madam's mistake.

Consequently, Madam is ordered to reread the chapter. Tristram explains why: "'Tis to rebuke a vicious taste which has crept into thousands beside herself,—of reading straight forwards, more in quest of the adventures, than of the deep erudition and knowledge [. . .] this self-same vile pruriency for fresh adventures in all things, has got so strongly into our habit and humours,—and so wholly intent are we upon satisfying the impatience of our concupiscence that way,—that nothing but the gross and more carnal parts of a composition will go down" (*TS*, 1.20.65–66). Inevitably, the act of reading "straight forwards" is described in sexual terms. To read for the plot, or to use Tristram's more sexually suspect word, "adventures," involves a "vile pruriency" (*TS*, 1.20.66).[17] Barbara M. Benedict argues that Tristram's treatment of the fictive female reader "Madam" involves associating women with a "debased" literary culture.[18] According to Benedict, Tristram's exchanges with Madam attack gendered literary forms like "*French Romances*" (*TS*, 1.18.57).[19] Tristram does draw on the stereotype of the voracious female reader, devouring tales of romance or "adventures" with an increasingly perverse palate. However, unlike anti-novel or anti-romance tracts, Tristram implicates all readers, as well as himself, in the trend of "reading straight forwards" (*TS*, 1.20.65). The "she" slips into the "we." Tristram accuses his reader not only of impatience and the thoughtlessness of quick reading, but of possessing a physiology habituated to a corporeal kind of reading, where "nothing but the gross" and "carnal parts" are absorbed (*TS*, 1.20.66). *All* his readers are capable of a bodily, prurient reading, bringing his male readers close to the anti-novel stereotype of the female reader.

Alternately, the reader, irrespective of sex, is also prompted to identify with the male reader and is privy to Tristram leaning forward and explaining why he has "imposed this penance on the lady" (*TS*, 1.20.65): "I wish the male-reader has not pass'd by many a one, as quaint and curious as this one, in which the female-reader has been detected. I wish it may have its effects;—and that all good people, both male and female, from her example, may be taught to think as well as read" (*TS*, 1.20.66). Given that no "male-reader" could have worked out why Mrs. Shandy was not a Catholic on first reading, the passage reads as a playful accusation of the "male-reader" and thus an injunction for "all good people, both male and female," to learn from her example (*TS*, 1.20.66). Sterne, through the use of the fictive readers "Sir" and "Madam," prompts his readers not only to think consciously about their own habits of reading but also to identify with "both male and female" fictive readers. There is an easy fluidity between gendered reading practices. The male reader is proved capable of feminine misreading, and the female reader is privy to homosocial generalizations about female misreaders.

This fluidity is apparent in Tristram's preface, which is addressed explicitly to men, to bearded "subtle statesmen and discreet doctors" (*TS*, 3.20.228), yet also involves Tristram imagining himself and his reader as a pair of heterosexual lovers. Tristram describes himself as the "caressing prefacer stifling his reader, as a lover sometimes does a coy mistress into silence" (*TS*, 3.20.232–233). Indeed, the majority of Tristram's descriptions of reading as sex between himself and his reader occur after he has explicitly gendered his readers as male. Ostovich quotes Tristram's remark that "when a man is telling a story in the strange way I do mine, he is obliged continually to be going backwards and forwards to keep all tight together in the reader's fancy" (*TS*, 7.33.557–558) as evidence for his eroticized relation-ship with the female reader.[20] Yet Tristram's words about going "backwards and forwards" directly follow a reference not to Madam but to Sir. The bawdy jokes in *Tristram Shandy* are nothing if not ambiguous; as Michael Hardin states, they are "*plural*" in their meanings and allusions.[21] From one angle, representing a male author and reader as a heterosexual dyad as Tristram does in the preface mascu-linizes him and serves as a heterosexual veil for Tristram's homoerotic relation-ship with his male reader. From another, Tristram's metaphor involves position-ing male reading bodies as his "coy" mistresses.

The preface presents Tristram's ideal reader as male-bodied, but tenuously so. His male readers become one of many impressionable male bodies that this book depicts. The problem with "Madam" might be that her corporeal "straight forwards" reading processes only "the gross" and "carnal parts" (*TS*, 1.20.66) of the composition, and Tristram wants a reader who can be impressed by *all* the parts of his writing. Tristram's preface describes his desire that his bearded readers be gifted with wit and judgment and that these, and other such qualities, "be poured down warm as each of us could bear it [. . .] into the several receptacles, cells, cel-lules, domiciles, dormitories, refectories, and spare places of our brains" (*TS*, 3.20.228). Sterne's source for this passage is François Rabelais's *Gargantua and Pan-tagruel* (c. 1532), rendered by John Ozell's revision of Thomas Urquhart's transla-tion (1750) as: "[B]e pleased but to contemplate a little the form, fashion, and carriage of a man exceeding earnestly set upon some learned meditation, and deeply plunged therein, and you shall see how all the arteries of his brains are stretched forth, and bent like the string of a cross-bow; the more promptly, dexterously, and copiously to suppediate, furnish, and supply him with store of spirits, sufficient to replenish, and fill up the ventricles, seats, tunnels, mansions, receptacles, and cel-luls of the common sense."[22] Both Rabelais and Sterne are concerned with the materiality of the reading body. Rabelais describes a body responding to study-ing, where studying leads to a chain of physiological processes within the body of the reader (including the generation of semen).

However, Sterne takes this one step further, with Tristram describing him-self as pouring fluid *into* the reader's body. In case the reader missed the potential bawdy implications of male bodies being filled with fluid by Tristram, he contin-ues, orgasmically: "[H]ow should I tickle it off! [. . .] writing away for such readers!—and you,—just heaven!—with what raptures would you sit and read,—but oh!—'tis too much,——I am sick,——I faint away deliciously at the thoughts of it!——'tis more than nature can bear!——lay hold of me,—I am giddy,—I am stone blind,——I'm dying,——I am gone" (*TS*, 3.20.229). When his readers are permeable enough, Tristram envisages a rapturous pleasure, expressed in short exclamations about how he is losing control. Though the tense slips into the present, the scene of consummation is framed as a fantasy sequence. Tellingly, this rapturous union involves Tristram wielding more power with his pen than the references to his physical and literary impotence imply he is capable of. It is what would happen *only* if Tristram was blessed with an ideal reader—"could this effusion of light have been as easily procured, as the exordium wished it" (*TS*, 3.20.233)—only if he could penetrate his reader's (ostensibly male) body.

MALE INTELLECT, FEMALE MATTER?

Impressions, then, are central to both the complex, shifting gender configurations of the reader within *Tristram Shandy* and the text's description of textual and sexual reproduction. Sterne both participates in and critiques characterizations of women as quintessentially and "naturally" soft and impressionable. For instance, Tristram draws upon the contemporary characterization of female bodies as being sexually impressionable in his discussion of Dolly and the sealing wax. He directly echoes John Locke's *An Essay Concerning Human Understanding* in his discussion about how the sensory organs need to be neither too dull nor too soft when retaining ideas.[23] Tristram suggests what might epitomize an impressionable sensory organ: "When *Dolly* has indited her epistle to *Robin*, and has thrust her arm into the bottom of her pocket hanging by her right side;—take that opportunity to recollect that the organs and faculties of perception, can, by nothing in this world, be so aptly typified and explained as by that one thing which *Dolly*'s hand is in search of.—Your organs are not so dull that I should inform you---'tis an inch, Sir, of red seal-wax" (*TS*, 2.1.99). On one level, the suggestive conflation between Dolly's vagina and the "red seal-wax" provides a bawdy reworking of Locke and Descartes; in Locke's work, the "Organs" that act "like Wax" and are imprinted by sensory impressions are not red.[24] This passage, like so much of *Tristram Shandy*, draws on the capacity for impressions to metaphorically stand for sexual acts. Printing a page, imprinting wax, or inditing an "epistle" can describe the feminized subject being marked by sexual (and in this case masturbatory) acts or experiences.

A gendering of impressionability as feminine is also central to the theory of reproduction to which Tristram and Walter Shandy subscribe. Whether the origins of a person lay in the father's sperm or the mother's egg was debated at the time of Sterne's writing.[25] Both Walter and Tristram decide on a model that makes the mother "*not the principal agent*" in producing life (*TS*, 5.31.468) and emphasizes the ostensible imprintability of the female body. Their model involves the man providing what is basically a miniature version of the person-to-be, while the woman simply provides the raw material for the baby's growth. Still, *Tristram Shandy*'s description of a "little gentleman" within a sperm, who has "skin, hair, fat, flesh, veins, arteries, ligaments, nerves, cartileges, bones, marrow, brains, glands, genitals, humours" and is, bathetically, "as much and as truly our fellow-creature" as the "Lord Chancellor of England," satirizes the "minutest philosophers" who placed the sperm at the center of theories of generation (*TS*, 1.2.3). Tristram treats sperm with mock-reverence, and acknowledges that the homunculus "may appear" to be "ludicrous" (*TS*, 1.2.2). Through its treatment of reproduction, *Tristram Shandy* both eagerly reduces women to malleable flesh and aligns men with shaping form, but it also, simultaneously, upsets this gendered dichotomy.

Certainly, Walter and Tristram both enjoy characterizing women as ductile matter. Loscocco observes that Walter (as well as Tristram) follows a medieval tradition that attributes men to reason and women to flesh, or lust.[26] Or, as Carol Kay writes, women in *Tristram Shandy* are aligned with "biology," men with "wordy play."[27] A telling example of this is the comparison Tristram makes between the metaphorical birth of Walter's hypothesis and Mrs. Shandy's birthing of Tristram. Tristram digresses from the story of his own birth, to describe the development of Walter's hypothesis (*TS*, 2.18.168–19.181). Tristram writes, "It is the nature of an hypothesis, when once a man has conceived it, that it assimilates every thing to itself as proper nourishment; [. . .] my father was gone with this about a month" (*TS*, 2.19.177). The "hypothesis" becomes a metaphorical fetus within Walter's brain. Sterne draws on the established literary trope that genders the pregnant mind as male, in opposition to the biologically pregnant female body.[28]

That Tristram chooses to spend time describing Walter's cerebral gestation rather than his own biological birth is symptomatic of his narration as a whole; it excludes women, reducing them to shadowy presences, to desiring bodies and blank pages.[29] We are told, "[A]ll the SHANDY FAMILY were of an original character throughout;——I mean the males,—the females had no character at all,—except, indeed, my great aunt DINAH," who had an illegitimate child (*TS*, 1.21.73). Echoing Alexander Pope's "Epistle II" (1735), which pronounces, "'Most women have no Characters at all,'" Tristram cheerily informs the reader that all Shandy women have "no character."[30] The only woman who is allowed to have character, Dinah, is defined by her sexuality, or as Ruth Perry puts it, the women "barely exist in the narrative except in their concern for the phallus."[31] Both Tristram and *Tristram Shandy* could be said to be formed by an inept patriarchy that attempts to both relegate women to the margins and appropriate the power of the fertile mother.[32]

Yet this real marginalization of women in the text only serves to place tenuously gendered men in the foreground. For instance, Walter's "hypothesis" comes at the conclusion of his attempt to locate the soul in the body, an attempt that is treated in unequivocally satirical terms. Walter's search for the soul is inextricably connected to his theories of birth; since he concludes the soul is in the cerebellum, a natural birth will break or disperse "the network" around the soul (*TS*, 2.19.178). Ultimately, the hypothesis that is "born" from Walter's ridiculed search is impractical to say the least: it is an embrace of the then deathly caesarean section.[33] Mrs. Shandy turns "as pale as ashes" (*TS*, 2.19.179) when Walter mentions it to her. Walter, seeing she would never agree to it, has to reluctantly content "himself with admiring—what he thought was to no purpose to propose" (*TS*, 2.19.179). The narration of Walter's hypothesis/fetus, like Tristram's attempt to birth his readers, describes a male-only attempt at conception as impotent, impractical (and in this case deadly, if put into practice). Walter's attempts to seize on the productive power of the mother are represented as barren, though a dark humor persists in Walter's momentary reduction of Mrs. Shandy to a malleable, gestating body he can cut and control with his own "newborn" idea.

MARKS OF ILLEGITIMACY

Despite Walter's theories, he cannot control what happens at Tristram's own, mishap-filled birth, or, for that matter, Tristram's conception. The power of the maternal imagination seems to compromise paternity in the sexual mishap that opens *Tristram Shandy*. Mrs. Shandy disrupts sex with her husband by asking, "*Pray, my dear,* [. . .] *have you not forgot to wind up the clock?*" (*TS*, 1.1.2). Tristram later explains that Mrs. Shandy's question results from her imagination combining "ideas which have no connection in nature" (*TS*, 1.4.7). Since Walter winds up the clock the same night that he settles "family concernments," it becomes the case that Tristram's "poor mother could never hear the said clock wound up,— but the thoughts of some other things unavoidably popp'd into her head,—*& vice versâ*" (*TS*, 1.4.7). This is one of many references in the text to Locke's theory of the association of ideas.[34] We are told that Mrs. Shandy's interruption, stemming from her imaginative conflation of ideas, disrupts the transference of "animal spirits [. . .] transfused from father to son" (*TS*, 1.1.1). According to Tristram, the sad results fall on him: "the effects of which I fear I shall carry with me to my grave" (*TS*, 1.4.6–7). In other words, Tristram describes his inheritance from his father as being disordered by his mother's imagination. Rather than seamlessly inheriting his father's "animal spirits," Tristram describes himself as being irrevocably shaped by his mother's wayward combination of ideas.

Crucial to Tristram's description of himself as being marked by a female imagination is the theory that I discussed in the introduction: that ideas and images in the mother's imagination, whether during conception or afterward, could shape the fetus and lead to monstrosities. The theory of the maternal imagination was exploited in a famous hoax by Mary Toft, who, in 1726, managed to convince respected men such as Nathanael St. André and Samuel Molyneux (physicians to the king) that she had given birth to several rabbits because she had thought about them intensely while she was pregnant.[35] Though belief in the power of maternal impressions became less popular as the century progressed, both the Toft hoax and the theory of the capacity of the mother's imagination to shape infants in the womb were persistently referenced by writers throughout the century.[36] Bonnie Blackwell argues that Mrs. Shandy "has a clear historical pedigree" that comes directly from Toft.[37] Mrs. Shandy's maiden name (we learn from the marriage contract) is Mollineux (*TS*, 1.15.43), and she requests to be attended by "the famous Dr. *Manningham*" (*TS*, 1.18.50), suggesting Richard Manningham, who played a crucial part in the Toft affair.[38] Such references encourage readers to note how both Toft's fake rabbit birth and Tristram's misgeneration involve the mother's imagination ostensibly affecting the child.[39] Just as Toft's fixation with rabbits leads to the impression of rabbit forms on her fetuses, Elizabeth Shandy's inextricable correlation between clocks and intercourse disrupts Tristram's inheritance from his father and is responsible, at least Tristram seems to believe, for all of his misfortunes (*TS*, 1.4.6–7). Moreover, just as the mother's imagination can prevent a child from resembling its father, the theory also meant that the child could look like men who were not the father; an illegitimate child could resemble its mother's husband if the husband's image was imprinted on the mother's imagination. As *Aristoteles Master-piece* (1684) states (a popular text on reproduction and sexual practices, and alluded to in *Tristram Shandy* [*TS*, 2.7.117]), "[N]othing is more powerful than the Imagination of the Mother; [. . .] wherefore it is apparent that likeness can confirm no Child to be a lawful Fathers own."[40] Thus, from multiple angles Mrs. Shandy's imagination can compromise Walter's claim to be Tristram's father.

That said, there is also a sense that Sterne ridicules the men for believing in the power of the maternal imagination, a satirical focus that also characterizes the numerous texts that lampooned the Toft affair. In these pieces, the doctors associated with the Toft hoax were portrayed, Lisa Cody argues, as both "lustful villains" and "emasculated, feminine dupes, whose credulity lined them up with women."[41] The titles of satires, such as "The Doctors in Labour" and "St. André's

Miscarriage," question divisions between men and mothers. In short, whether we read Mrs. Shandy's imagination as having the power to destabilize Walter's paternity, or Walter as foolish for believing this is a possibility, the maternal imagination has implications for Walter's masculinity, structured as it is around paternity.

To press this further: while Wiehe is correct in noting how *Tristram Shandy* articulates queer erotic pleasures beyond the penis, jokes about procreational mishaps seem to attach themselves to Walter's character.[42] A large part of Walter's character is his fraught relation to patrilineality. J. Paul Hunter notes how Tristram's "too-frequent" affirmations of Walter as "my father" signal the text's wider concern with paternity.[43] There are several "clues" in the text, suggesting that Walter did not conceive Tristram, such as Walter's sciatica and Tristram's calculations about the narrow time during which he could have been conceived by Walter.[44] The bend sinister of the Shandy arms, "this vile mark of Illegitimacy" (*TS*, 4.25.373), is yet another motif of thwarted patrilineality.

Tristram and Walter, male quixotes in *Tristram Shandy*, endeavor to respond to this disruption in paternal authority by authoring masculine texts in a competitive project of quixotic writing, following a Shandean logic that repeatedly conflates writing with life. The same process that subjects Tristram to impressions from his mother's imagination implies that, in a parallel process, Tristram can potentially be imprinted as his father's child through Walter's textual production. Walter's "*Tristra-pædia*," a complete book of education for Tristram and a response to the death of Walter's first son, Bobby, can be read as an attempt both to compensate for the mortality of bodies and to control life through writing.

So Walter writes his *Tristra-pædia* in an attempt to reassert himself as Tristram's father and control his development, or, in Tristram's words, to create "an INSTITUTE for the government of my childhood and adolescence" (*TS*, 5.16.445). Walter does succeed in marking Tristram's brain; Tristram writes that "whenever my brains come to be dissected, you will perceive, without spectacles, that he [Walter] has left a large uneven thread" (*TS*, 6.33.558). However, the writing of *Tristra-pædia* also compromises Walter's ability to act as an adequate father as Tristram is growing up: Walter spends years struggling with his writing, and Tristram "was all that time totally neglected and abandoned to [his] mother" (*TS*, 5.16.448). Walter's *Tristra-pædia* and Tristram's attempt to reproduce himself through writing his own life are potentially pleasurable, but also overtly unsuccessful, attempts at male-only reproduction. *Tristram Shandy* responds self-consciously to anxieties about feminized literary production with a tale of thwarted patrilineality and men suspicious about maternity.

HOBBY-HORSES

A fraught masculinity is also present in *Tristram Shandy*'s description of the relationship between a Shandy man and his quixotic, "hobby-horsical" obsessions. In eighteenth-century Britain, the hobby-horse can describe a fixed interest ranging from an eccentric preoccupation to a monomaniacal obsession. The word "hobby-horse" designates a child's toy, a stick with a horse head, but was also used metaphorically to describe a hobby, or a diversion.[45] In *Tristram Shandy*, it also suggests obsession. The image used to symbolize Shandean quixotism is an adult astride a child's toy, simultaneously suggesting both a playfulness inappropriate to adult decorum and Don Quixote himself, on his poor-bred steed. This quixotic image is repeated with Yorick and his horse, which is identified as surpassing even Don Quixote's mount in its unsuitability. Tristram claims Yorick's horse answers Cervantes's description of Don Quixote's steed: "a hair-breadth in every thing,—except that I do not remember 'tis any where said, that *Rosinante* was broken winded" (*TS*, 1.10.18).

Quixotism and hobby-horse riding are not interchangeable, but they are closely related. The hobby-horse is described as a "ruling passion" in *Tristram Shandy*, echoing Alexander Pope's *Essay on Man* (1733–34), which describes a porous, humoral body becoming dominated by a ruling passion like a disease: "As the mind opens" it becomes susceptible to "Imagination" plying "her dang'rous art."[46] According to George Cheyne, hobby-horses, or innocent amusements, can "keep the Mind easy, and prevent its wearing out the Body, as the Sword does the Scabbard."[47] For Cheyne, the hobby-horse supplements or manages the difficult relation between mind and body, between matter and spirit. Carol Houlihan Flynn observes that Cheyne's faith in the power of the hobby-horse is part of the widespread, eighteenth-century interest in the ways the mind and body intersect.[48]

Like "impressions" and indeed so many other eighteenth-century metaphors, then, the trope of the hobby-horse acts as a point of contact between the mind and the body, the metaphorical and the literal. Cheyne's hobby-horse could transition from the more cerebral figuration to physical literality. He prescribed to Samuel Richardson a "chamber horse" to benefit his body and mind. This home exercise machine was designed to provide "all the good and beneficial Effects of a hard Trotting Horse except the fresh Air."[49] Richardson's biographers, T. C. Duncan Eaves and Ben D. Kimpel, enjoy imagining Richardson riding the horse: "Some chamber horses had springs, but the one Cheyne describes [. . .] must have acted like a joggling board, supported by both ends and limber in the middle, with hoops to brace the arms and a footstool to support the feet, on which Richardson was to ride while reading or dictating. Richardson used this machine, and it is pleasant to imagine him dropping Pamela's advice to her little family from this gently bouncing perch, perhaps balanced by Mrs. Richardson."[50] For Eaves and Kimpel, Richardson riding his chamber horse is an image of quixotic writing. The riding of the chamber horse lends his authorship buoyant eccentricity. More strikingly, Richardson's simultaneous writing and riding unifies Cheyne's formulation of a hobby-horse as a mental diversion, and its material embodiment as a "Chamber Horse." The hobby-horse becomes a hinge between mind and matter, flesh and literature, metaphor and literality.

The hobby-horse occupies a similar positioning in *Tristram Shandy*; it touches both mind and body. For example, Tristram describes how a quixote like Toby comes to be permeated by an obsession: "A man and his HOBBY-HORSE, tho' I cannot say that they act and re-act exactly after the same manner in which the soul and body do upon each other: Yet doubtless there is a communication between them of some kind, and my opinion rather is, that there is something in it more of the manner of electrified bodies,--and that by means of the heated parts of the rider, which come immediately into contact with the back of the HOBBY-HORSE.—By long journies and much friction, it so happens that the body of the rider is at length fill'd as full of HOBBY-HORSICAL matter as it can hold" (*TS*, 1.24.86). Focus drifts toward "the heated parts of the rider" that "come immediately into contact" with the horse. The hobby-horse's placement between the legs associates the hobby-horse bawdily with the body. The hobby-horse might be, as William Mottolese asserts, a prosthesis, deployed by Shandy men in attempt to repair impotence and castration, or, as Ross King suggests, a failed attempt to supplement (through language) the evacuation of masculinity, but it must also, as Wiehe argues, reflect *Tristram Shandy*'s preoccupation with pleasure beyond the penis.[51] The hobby-horse seems to offer a dildo-esque source of sexual pleasure.

The way a hobby-horse can be both a dildo and a quixotic obsession is apparent in Tristram's description of the relationship between hobby-horse rider and hobby-horse: there is the implication that some kind of intercourse takes place; "the body of the rider is at length fill'd as full of HOBBY-HORSICAL matter as it can hold" (*TS*, 1.24.86). There is perhaps, through the description of the rider's body becoming "fill'd" with "hobby-horsical" substance, the suggestion of pregnancy.[52] In any case, the hobby-horse rider becomes penetrated by ideas via "the heated parts of the rider, which come immediately into contact with the back of the HOBBY-HORSE" (*TS*, 1.24.86). Toby's penetration by ideas of fortification is emphatically described as sexual, involving friction on the genitals and rear, "the heated parts of the rider" (*TS*, 1.24.86).[53] The hobby-horse rider, the male quixote, and the Shandy man, are penetrated.

The permeability and figurative pregnancy of the Shandy male suggests a male body at risk of falling out of masculinity. Thomas Laqueur has influentially and controversially argued that the eighteenth century marked a shift from an ancient one-sex model to the two-sex model, where anatomical differences, what we term "sex," became the biological basis for gender.[54] Miriam L. Wallace, noting the permeability of the Shandean male, argues that *Tristram Shandy* reflects shifting gender paradigms; the Shandy men are placed within the two-sex system, but their bodies are changeable, permeable, and threaten to betray their gender.[55] In other words, the bodies of the Shandy men are male-gendered, but anxiously and problematically so.

The permeable Shandy male also reflects shifts in eighteenth-century ideas of masculinity. The Shandy men are sentimental men: susceptible to feeling, sensitive to what is going on around them, and readily affected by narratives. Carol Kay argues that the Shandean marginalization of women stems from the sentimental man's fear of "womanishness": "The modern domesticated male, who fears that his civilized polish and sensitive feeling is a kind of womanishness, finds a new way of asserting his masculine superiority over the women he comes close to. So in *Tristram Shandy* [. . .] sentimental man excludes sentimental woman."[56] However, this attempt at a "remasculization" (to use Kay's term) of the sentimental man backfires, with the anxious exclusion of women only highlighting the potential effeminacy of the Shandean body.[57] Toby's very name is eighteenth-century slang for the posterior.[58] As for Walter, his misogyny is inextricable from his horror at his own sexuality: "a passion, my dear, continued my father, addressing himself to my mother, which couples and equals wise men with fools" (*TS*, 9.33.806).[59] Walter believes sex "bends down the faculties, and turns all the wisdom, contemplations, and operations of the soul backwards," transforming men into "satyrs and four-footed beasts" (*TS*, 9.33.806). According to Walter, sex between himself and his wife—to whom he is speaking—by coupling him with a fool brings him close to a foolishness he genders as feminine. He tries to keep himself uncontaminated by both sex and the feminine, yet his efforts work against him. Walter's repeated use of the word "ass" to refer to "the desires and appetites of the lower parts of us" (*TS*, 8.31.716) becomes a means to further describe his body as sexually penetrable. "Ass" is a word that associates itself not only with the animal but with the rear, and the opportunity to pun on the word is exploited in the confusion between Walter and his brother Toby directly after Walter inquires, "[H]ow goes it with your ASSE?" (*TS*, 8.32.717). Toby thinks he is referring to "the *part* where he had had the blister" (*TS*, 8.32.717). A page earlier, Tristram urges his reader not to mount his "father's ass." "[M]y father's ass——oh! mount him—mount him—mount him—(that's three times, is it not?)—mount him not" (*TS*,

8.31.716). Tristram's repeated injunctions to the reader not to "mount" his father, and the slippage between ass/asse and ass/arse, represent Walter as somehow liable to sexual penetration. In short, Walter's positioning as "father" and his ostentatious disdain for the feminine only serve to demarcate his body as penetrable and impressionable. *Tristram Shandy* overwhelmingly presents male-only attempts at production as erotic and erratic. Walter's and Tristram's literary attempts to compensate for the "many evils which have befallen thee as a man" are complicated by the problems of language and representation.

QUIXOTIC WRITING

Tristram Shandy might depict the Shandean male body as erotically penetrable rather than penetrating, yet Tristram and Walter do remain complexly preoccupied with phallic lack. Tristram associates his facility at writing with conventionally masculine heterosexual prowess, and his literary production reinforces rather than compensates for his problems. Tristram's pen and penis seem to fail simultaneously:

> ——Do, my dear Jenny, tell the world for me, how I behaved under one [disaster], the most oppressive of its kind which could befall me as a man, proud, as he ought to be, of his manhood——
>   'Tis enough, said'st thou, coming close up to me, as I stood with my garters in my hand, reflecting upon what had *not* pass'd——'Tis enough, Tristram, and I am satisfied, said'st thou, whispering these words in my ear, **** ** **** *** ******;—**** ** ****——any other man would have sunk down to the center——
>
>   (*TS*, 7.29.624)

When Tristram writes of his sexual mishap, he loses control of his story; he passes the narration of his life on to Jenny, asking her to "tell the world" what happened. The dashes and the ellipses ensure that whatever "had *not* pass'd" is itself muted. Jenny's words themselves are "whispered" by her and then censored before they are inscribed on the page, replaced by asterisks. This is only one of several instances of words being censored or omitted in the book and replaced by asterisks.[60] In some cases, these asterisks can be decoded. For example, earlier in the book, the coded word "******* ***" is easily decipherable in context as "chamber pot" (*TS*, 5.17.449). Yet Tristram's conversation with Jenny is mediated to the reader in such a way that we cannot be sure precisely what it is that Jenny says, and the asterisks function as an erasure of her words. Alex Wetmore notes how Sterne's asterisks, or "stars" or "lights," are also inverted "dark" stars that become sources of obscurity.[61] Tristram's representation of Jenny's whispers as dark stars causes them to plummet into meaninglessness, mirroring the sinking movement "down to the center" (*TS*, 7.29.624) that in this passage affects Tristram's penis, his pen, and meaning itself. The failure of Tristram's "manhood" occurs at a moment when Tristram himself seems to be unable to communicate Jenny's words to the reader. Language and heterosexual masculinity simultaneously fracture.

Even the striking typographical elements *Tristram Shandy* is famous for—the black and white pages, notational scoring, the numerous dashes—as well as drawing attention to the book as an embodied object, can be also read as attempts to surmount (and satirize attempts to surmount) the limits of printed language. William Holtz writes how the typographical devices in *Tristram Shandy* "would seem to be as parts of one of the grand comic themes of *Tristram Shandy*: the general inadequacy of man's abilities to his conceptions, the disparity between his aspirations and his accomplishments—whether he aims to make love, to write a book, or simply communicate a thought."[62] We can take Holtz's perhaps inadvertent gendering of "inadequacy" further here and read the typographical features of *Tristram Shandy* as feeding into the book's general preoccupation with problematic paternity. They potentially demonstrate a failure on Tristram's part to translate his own experience into language. Impotence itself can be characterized as quixotic. To be a quixote is to strive for and farcically fall short of a desired model: it is a failure to live the textual tropes.[63] None of the Shandy males are up to the task that they set themselves, whether it be, as in Walter's case, "fathering" via a book of education or, in Tristram's case, reduplicating himself through his writing. The characters in *Tristram Shandy* suffer a castration that can be figurative, as in the case of Tristram's unfortunate naming, or painfully literal, as in the case of Tristram's accidental circumcision from the sash window, Walter Shandy's sciatica, and the wound in Toby's groin.[64] The suggestion is that their attempts at masculinity, and perhaps even masculinity itself, are quixotic.[65]

At the same time, the ostentatious visuality of *Tristram Shandy* points to possibilities beyond the failure of heteronormative masculinity. The typography suggests the potential eloquence of the "material thingness of texts," which, analogous to the legible sentimental body, becomes more visible when words splinter.[66] See, for instance, Tristram's description of Walter's distress: "A fix'd, inflexible sorrow took possession of every line of his face.—He sigh'd once,—heaved his breast often,—but utter'd not a word" (*TS*, 3.29.255). As well as this passage reflecting sentimentalism's "investment in the body as a signifier," the punctuation spills into a description of Walter's face.[67] The lines on Walter's face—which themselves have a signifying function—become reproduced on the page through Sterne's dashes.

The surface of Walter's face is therefore not only legible and impressed by feeling; it becomes directly transposed onto the papery objecthood of *Tristram Shandy*'s innovatively punctuated page.

An even more obvious example of the book asserting its existence as a material object, with implications for its articulation of tenuous, imprinted masculinities, is the missing chapter 24 of volume 4. The book moves from chapter 23 to chapter 25, and, in the first edition, from page 146 to 156. Tristram observes: "—No doubt, Sir—there is a whole chapter wanting here—and a chasm of ten pages made in the book by it—but the book-binder is neither a fool, or a knave, or a puppy— nor is the book a jot more imperfect, (at least upon that score)—but, on the contrary, the book is more perfect and complete by wanting the chapter, than having it" (*TS*, 4.25.372). Tristram ironically speaks in the language of descriptive bibliography and mocks the reader for presuming to discover the binder's mistake. While bookbinding errors are not unusual in eighteenth-century books, the anomalous pagination is a deliberate typographical effect: Tristram announces that he "was obliged to tear out" the missing chapter from his manuscript because it was "so much above the stile and manner of any thing else" he has been able "to paint in this book" (*TS*, 4.25.374). The torn manuscript becomes a paginated "chasm" in a printed book, simultaneously gesturing toward the book production process and collapsing a manuscript object into mass-produced print.

The missing chapter is both a sublime, unprintable object and a signifier of Tristram's inability to write the rest of the book at a similar level. On one hand, given his emphatic suturing of his authorial prowess to his "manhood" throughout the text, the ostentatious *lack* of chapter 24 has implications for Tristram's masculinity. Yet the "chasm," like other Shandean wounds, is a potentially pleasurable opening, rendering the book "more perfect and complete" through its absence (*TS*, 4.25.372). The first edition, by skipping nine pages (147–155), ostentatiously disrupts the page numbering of the volume, with a recto-verso swap. From the missing chapter—two-thirds of the way into the volume—until the volume's end, the established conventions of page numbering are inverted, with odd-numbered pages on the verso and even-numbered pages on the recto of each leaf.[68] It is useful to revisit here the early modern formulation of "sodomy" as encompassing unauthorized imprinting as well as "deviant" sexual practices. Sterne's typographic device takes the back of the page for the front. The pagination remains unsettlingly odd today, to the point where most contemporary editions of *Tristram Shandy* resist this inversion of conventional book production practices by skipping an even number of pages. For instance, the Florida edition of *Tristram Shandy* skips from page 361 to page 372 to avoid what the editors describe as the "awkward" situation of odd-numbered versos and even-numbered folios through the rest of the edition.[69] *Tristram Shandy*'s reversal of the recto/verso, back/front binary renders its leaves, like its male characters, deviantly imprinted.

RIDING THE READER

It makes sense, at this juncture, to return to where this chapter opened: discussing how Tristram's authorship functions as a failed form of reproduction. I have suggested how Tristram's endeavor to translate his experiential impressions accurately and seamlessly onto the page can be read as quixotic. Tristram trumpets his own control over the reader, but only in a way that emphasizes how little power he actually has to control the reader's response to his written life and opinions, and subsequently how little control he has over this second, written "life" of his.

Tristram presents himself as riding his readers. Ostovich notes how "Tristram plays persistently on the notion of Madam Reader as hobby-horse," and I would add that this metaphor is extended to all his readers.[70] Tristram repeatedly uses motifs of horse riding for his writing—"What a rate have I gone on at, curvetting and frisking it away, two up and two down for four volumes together, [. . .] I'll take a good rattling gallop; but I'll not hurt the poorest jack-ass upon the road" (*TS*, 4.20.356)—and the reader is indeed taken for a ride, a ride for nine volumes of what declares itself to be a "COCK and a BULL" story at its end (*TS*, 9.33.809). Elsewhere, Tristram threatens to give the reader fifty pages of an account of the siege of Calais: "[I]n Rapin's own words," then does not, "gentle reader!——I scorn it——'tis enough to have thee in my power——but to make use of the advantage which the fortune of the pen has now gained over thee, would be too much [. . .] ere I would force a helpless creature upon this hard service" (*TS*, 7.6.584). Tristram has the power to force his reader to read fifty pages of Rapin, if he so desires, reducing his reader to a "helpless creature" who can be steered in any direction he pleases. But not far beneath Tristram's declarations of his own power over the reader is an anxiety about his lack of it. Readers can put the book down at any time; they can resist Tristram's efforts to steer them, and remain unmoved, despite his best efforts.[71] Tristram demonstrates his uncomfortable awareness of this. At some points in the book, Tristram behaves toward his reader/horse with almost obsequious gratitude: "I would go fifty miles on foot, for I have not a horse worth riding on, to kiss the hand of that man whose generous heart will give up the reins of his imagination into his author's hands" (*TS*, 3.12.214). Elsewhere, Tristram writes about "*that ear* which the reader chuses to *lend* me" (*TS*, 7.20.605). There is bitterness to this italicization: it hints that it is the reader's choice to grant Tristram attention—divided though it may be—and to take it away.

Inherent in Tristram's anxieties is the sense that the idiosyncrasies or deficiencies of each reader render him powerless to predict or control his reader's response. For instance, his comment, "As the reader (for I hate your *ifs*) has a thorough knowledge of human nature, I need not say more to satisfy him," emphasizes that the reader's reaction to Tristram's narration depends on the reader's own "knowledge" and experience (*TS*, 1.12.30). In another of many examples, Tristram writes: "If the reader has not a clear conception of the rood and the half of ground which lay at the bottom of my uncle *Toby*'s kitchen garden, and which was the scene of so many of his delicious hours,—the fault is not in me,—but in his imagination;—for I am sure I gave him so minute a description, I was almost ashamed of it" (*TS*, 6.21.534). Tristram can give such a "minute" description of Toby's kitchen garden that he is "almost ashamed of it," but he cannot judge the clarity of his reader's "conception" of the garden because he cannot know for sure what is going on in the reader's mind. He can only blame the reader's imagination for being at "fault" if the reader fails to have a clear impression of what Tristram is describing (*TS*, 6.21.534).

Tristram's control of his readers is overtly limited by their particular idiosyncrasies, individual physiologies, temperaments, and imaginations. When Tristram guesses the reader's reaction to Walter's theory of the importance of Christian names, he writes: "I fear the reader, when I come to mention it to him, if he is the least of a cholerick temper, will immediately throw the book by; if mercurial, he will laugh most heartily at it;—and if he is of a grave and saturnine cast, he will, at first sight, absolutely condemn as fanciful and extravagant" (*TS*, 1.19.57). The reader will "throw the book by," "laugh," or condemn the theory "as fanciful and extravagant," depending on the reader's particular humoral "type" (*TS*, 1.19.57). Of course, Tristram has no way of predicting his readers' reactions, and though he provides a list, it is only how he tentatively "fear[s]" the reader will behave, rather than what he knows the reaction to be. Indeed, the shortness of the list—Tristram gives the reader only three options—serves to highlight the infinite number of reactions readers could have, to this or to any passage in *Tristram Shandy*.

Tristram's attempts to control his reader's response are thwarted: for *Tristram Shandy* depicts a world where almost every character is governed by a specific ruling passion or quixotic obsession. Staves writes that Sterne "maneuvers the reader into joining the cast of quixotes. First he cajoles him into admitting that every man has his hobby horse. [. . .] Sterne forces the reader to betray and acknowledge the extent to which he himself is locked into fixed patterns of response, hobby-horsical patterns which lead him to destroy or ignore the reality the novel presents to him."[72] Ultimately, the reader's situation as another comic quixote thwarts Tristram's attempts at reproduction; Tristram can only guess from what quixotic perspective the reader is registering his writing.

Masculine reproduction miscarries yet again through Tristram's written "I" being placed ostentatiously at the edge of existence. Through the bulk of his narrative, Tristram retells events he does not himself remember, having been still an infant or not yet born. When he writes closer to the present tense he tends toward a narrative of travel or escape (from death). Tristram cannot make the "I" of the book that he is writing coincide with the "I" who is writing the book, and Sterne exploits this problem for all its creative potential. Tristram notoriously writes, "I have brought myself into such a situation, as no traveller ever stood before me; for I am this moment walking across the market-place of Auxerre with my father and my uncle Toby, in our way back to dinner——and I am this moment also entering Lyons with my post-chaise broke into a thousand pieces—and I am moreover this moment in a handsome pavillion built by Pringello, upon the banks of the Garonne, which Mons. Sligniac has lent me, and where I now sit rhapsodizing all these affairs" (*TS*, 7.28.622). There is a potential parody of Richardson, on his medicinal hobby-horse, "writing to the moment." Through writing about himself writing, Tristram the writer-narrator splits into a multitude of Tristrams. He falls, inevitably, behind his written selves. Even the "I" who "now sit[s] rhapsodizing all these affairs" can never perfectly coincide with the Tristram who could be said to hold the pen: one is represented as being written, the other is committing the act of writing. Tristram is dispersed and fractured. In *Tristram Shandy*, between the real and the representation, between the active, written mind and the writing body is a gap Tristram quixotically attempts to surmount, but to no avail. A big part of the joke is that, of course, all these Tristrams are written. There is no "real" Tristram, and Tristram's own existence, as a character in the text, is tied to his failed attempts to translate himself onto the printed page. Sterne's presence as the ultimate author of *Tristram Shandy* is also palpable in this passage's description of quixotic writing. He notoriously sought comparisons between himself and his fictional characters; he deliberately cast himself as Tristram during his lifetime and signed letters as "Tristram Shandy."[73] Sterne himself becomes part of another layer of quixotic authorship in the text, another example of the gap between the "I" printed on the page and the centered, authorial "I."

Tristram's quixotic attempt at male-only reproduction does produce pleasure, comedy, and lots of Tristrams, but the results are also chaotic and beyond Tristram's control. It is impossible for his written selves to catch up with his writing self. He is living faster than he can write: "[I]nstead of advancing, as a common writer, in my work with what I have been doing at it—on the contrary, I am just thrown so many volumes back [. . .] at this rate I should just live 364 times faster than I should write—It must follow, an' please your worships, that the more I write, the more I shall have to write—" (*TS*, 4.13.341–342). Tristram's quixotic failure at perfectly reproducing himself leads to infinite textual creation. His attempt at male-only reproduction results in a vision of prodigious textual production that outstrips in its excess even *Polly Honeycombe*'s circulating library "Extract" (chapter 2), Bridgetina Botherim's speech (chapter 5), or other, similar instances of feminized textual copia.

Given what we have so far explored, it is possible to say that *Tristram Shandy* persistently marginalizes women, while simultaneously representing such marginalization as resulting from men who are so anxious about their masculinity that they are only men in part. Sterne responds to eighteenth-century debates about fiction by inverting, critiquing, and rehearsing gendered tropes about reading and impressions. Much, but not all, of this serves to fundamentally question assumptions about gender, and the very binaries on which fallacious logic about women, and female quixotes, is based. *Tristram Shandy* articulates an anxiety about the female imagination and, with a sprightly, even infectious joy, reiterates sexist tropes of the feminine as flesh, as matter, or as malleable bodies. Yet the text also self-consciously satirizes male anxieties about the feminine and describes a Shandean body as encased in a legible, erogenous surface. Through its representation of permeable male bodies and "hobby-horsical" intercourse, *Tristram Shandy* describes masculine imaginative practices of production as potentially pleasurable but also as askew and chaotic as the female equivalent that Walter and Tristram fear.

ENTHUSIASM, METHODISTS, AND

METAPHORS IN *THE SPIRITUAL QUIXOTE*

A S PART OF THE TRACT WAR that followed Samuel Foote's one-act anti-Methodist afterpiece *The Minor* (1760), two hieroglyphic epistles, titled *The Retort* (1760) and *Retort upon Retort* (1760) were published. Ostensibly an exchange between Foote and the Methodist preacher George Whitefield (who had been the target of satire in Foote's play), the epistles exchange objects for letters. The first *Retort* (figure 8), framed as a letter by Whitefield, conceptualizes Whitefield's heavily metaphorical Methodist discourse as a literal swapping of word for object. Misty G. Anderson observes: "The mocking graphic production presses up against the representational function of language and forces the reader to move back and forth from signified to signifier across representational registers."[1] While *The Female Quixote* might play with the close connections between viewing and reading (chapter 1), *The Retort* points to how reading print on a page and viewing pictures are uncomfortably different processes. Some objects are used to signify themselves, but others are also homonyms, impelling the reader to move between reading letters, deciphering pictograms, and registering the pictures of the objects as sounds, sometimes within a single printed word. Methodism, and its use of religious metaphor, seems to turn the printed word—and language itself—into a puzzle.

I begin with this hieroglyphic epistle because Richard Graves's novel *The Spiritual Quixote, or The Summer's Ramble of Mr. Geoffry Wildgoose* (1773) shares with *The Retort* both a strong sense of distinction between words and images and a concern with Methodist discourse's literality and its seeming capacity to bring sign and signifier, or word and image, in uncomfortably close proximity. For instance, in *The Spiritual Quixote*, Geoffry Wildgoose (the titular "Spiritual Quixote") attempts to "allegorize" after the model of Whitefield's language: "Wildgoose was devising with himself how to allegorize the different athletic exercises, which were usually practised on these occasions, and apply them to the best advantage"

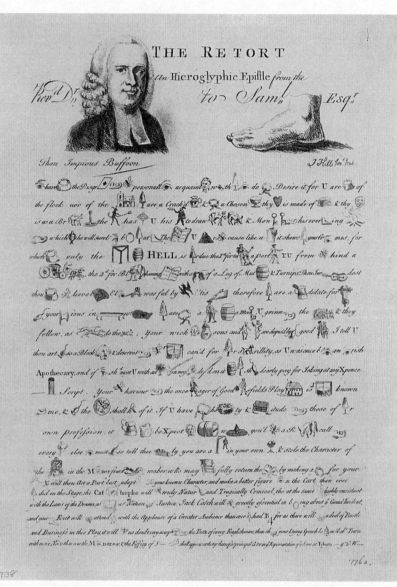

FIGURE 8 *The Retort*, 1760. Library of Congress, Prints and Photographs Division, LC-USZ62-137505.

(*SQ*, 50). He decides that for the wrestlers, he will "preach up the necessity of *struggling* against flesh and blood; against the world and the Devil; and also frequently to *wrestle* with God in prayer; as Mr. Whitfield so often did" (*SQ*, 50). The satiric relation between Geoffry Wildgoose and George Whitefield is suggested by the way they share initials. In one of many puns in the passage, where Wildgoose "allegorizes" a variety of sports, athletic wrestling is conflated with a spiritual struggle "against flesh and blood" (*SQ*, 50). This bathetic yoking of a spiritual struggle with a bodily activity is typical of Wildgoose's preaching style throughout the novel. His speeches involve numerous, comically inappropriate extended metaphors or religious allegories, suggesting an unsuitability to the embodied way he—and by extension, Methodist discourse—conceptualizes the spiritual. Like *The Retort*, Methodist discourse is presented as having a problem with metaphors.

In this respect, *The Retort* and *The Spiritual Quixote* are not alone. Throughout the mid- to late eighteenth century there are comments about Methodism and metaphors.[2] Horace Walpole to friend Horace Mann (July 24, 1749) characterizes Methodist discourse as "the old exploded cant of mystical devotion." He then ascribes Methodism's atavism to Methodist metaphorics: "For example, you take a metaphor; we will say, our passions are *weeds*; you immediately drop every description of the passions, and adopt everything peculiar to weeds: in five minutes a true Methodist will talk with the greatest compunction of *hoeing*—This catches women of fashion and shopkeepers."[3] There is an uncouth physicality and literality to the Methodist use of extended metaphor, a sense that Methodism runs away with language. This is also seen in Foote's play *The Minor*, where Sir George comments, in response to Mrs. Cole's quasi-Methodist discourse: "Ha, ha, what a hodge podge! How the jade has jumbled together the carnal and the spiritual; [. . .]. No wonder these preachers have plenty of proselytes, whilst they have the address, so comfortably to blend the hitherto jarring interests of the two worlds."[4] Foote, Walpole, Graves, and the anonymous author of *The Retort* register an anxiety about the apparent capacity for Methodist metaphors to paper over gaps between the sacred and the earthly.

Given the way "impressions" straddles the boundary between literality and metaphor, *The Spiritual Quixote* is a particularly appropriate novel to focus on. Not only does it, as we will see, situate quixotic impressions within eighteenth-century religious cultures; it examines metaphoricity itself, including metaphor's place within religious discourse. The novel describes Wildgoose's quixotism as an enthusiastic encasement within the textures and difficulties of figurative language. The novel's concept of enthusiasm, which it pointedly interweaves with the problem of quixotism, speaks to anxieties about linguistic embodiment and the limits of analogy.

The Spiritual Quixote was a popular novel, though it is now out of print and relatively understudied.[5] Clarence Tracy's early criticism stresses its autobiographical elements, and focuses on incidents in the novel that potentially draw on Graves's own life as an Anglican clergyman and on his family.[6] More recent work by Misty G. Anderson and Paul Goring productively situates *The Spiritual Quixote* among eighteenth-century cultural formulations of Methodism, sensibility, and enthusiasm. This chapter will build on both Anderson's and Goring's arguments, analyzing *The Spiritual Quixote*'s suggestive connections between the stereotypical quixotic female reader and the permeable Methodist body.

Methodism is persistently presented as imprinting, impressing, marking, and molding the characters of its converts in eighteenth-century print culture. Anderson argues that the believing Methodist was repeatedly represented within both Methodist and anti-Methodist discourse as penetrable, vulnerable, and feminine.[7] The porousness of the Methodist "self" that Anderson analyzes occurs alongside what this book has been tracking: the formulation of the quixotic novel reader as impressionable and feminine. *The Spiritual Quixote* takes these congruities as the basis for crafting and illuminating tightly woven connections between quixotic impressions, enthusiasm, Methodist metaphors, and print.

The Spiritual Quixote is set in the first half of the eighteenth century, when Methodism was just beginning "to spread into most parts of the nation" (*SQ*, 30). Methodism began in the late 1730s, led by the Anglican ministers John Wesley, Charles Wesley, and George Whitefield. In contrast to the orthodox Anglican Church, Methodism featured lay leaders and lay preachers, and also stressed a more personal, emotional approach to religion.[8] In *The Spiritual Quixote*, Wildgoose is transformed from a staid, eighteenth-century landed gentleman into an itinerant Methodist preacher by consuming a library's worth of dissenting theology and attending some Methodist meetings. He travels the English countryside, attempting to disseminate ideas he has absorbed from Methodist books and speeches, accompanied by the Sancho-esque Jeremiah Tugwell. The power of novels to impress their readers becomes congruous to Methodism's power to penetrate and newly "birth" its converts.

This is apparent from the full title of Graves's novel, *The Spiritual Quixote, or The Summer's Ramble of Mr. Geoffry Wildgoose, a Comic Romance*, which seems to place *The Spiritual Quixote* within the vexed category of "Romance." Both Tracy and Anderson read the label of "Romance" as distinguishing *The Spiritual Quixote* from a satire, and signaling it as something gentler.[9] Dragoș Ivana argues that "Comic Romance" also references another quixotic novel: Henry Fielding's *Joseph*

Andrews (1742), which Fielding describes in his preface as "a comic Romance" as well as a "comic Epic-Poem in Prose."[10] It is important to also note that Graves's reference to "Romance" occurs in the context of a title with a clear debt to Charlotte Lennox's *The Female Quixote* (chapter 1).[11] As well as placing *The Spiritual Quixote* within a growing canon of eighteenth-century British appropriations of *Don Quixote*, then, the title also suggestively associates quixotic romance-reading with Methodism. Within the novel, Methodism seems to share romance's capacity for simultaneously troubling empiricism and spawning feminized, quixotic consumption.

The phrase "comic romance" also invokes Voltaire's satirical, science-fictional work *Micromégas* (1752), published in English as *Micromegas: A Comic Romance. Being a Severe Satire Upon the Philosophy, Ignorance, and Self-Conceit of Mankind* (1753).[12] Voltaire's satire details the travels through the universe of a massive alien, the eponymous Micromégas. Similarly, the "Comic Romance" tag in *The Spiritual Quixote*'s title might serve to frame the work as a satire and position Methodism as a movement removed from everyday, eighteenth-century life, belonging with Voltaire's aliens, or the heroines in ancient history Arabella (chapter 1) concerns herself with. Methodism is thus potentially atavistic and romantic, situated in a strange and distant world, rather than in the temporal and spatial locality of *The Spiritual Quixote*'s publication.

ENTHUSIASM

Central to *The Spiritual Quixote*'s treatment of Methodism and quixotism is the concept of enthusiasm. Methodism, subject to a vehement and often violent backlash after its rise to prominence, was frequently branded as an "enthusiastic" religion.[13] Catholicism and many nonconformist Protestant sects were also frequently denigrated as "enthusiastic" in eighteenth-century Britain, a designation that categorized them as "false," corporeal modes of Christianity. The idea of "enthusiasm" colors *The Spiritual Quixote*'s description of Wildgoose's quasi-spiritual quixotic impressions as well as larger questions the novel poses about what it means to (quixotically) embody or perform text, how one might read or interpret an affectively impressed body, and what is at stake when doing so. "Enthusiasm" here refers to a specific religious error, where bodily transports with physical causes are mistaken for spiritual experiences. John Locke, for instance, describes enthusiasm as "founded neither on Reason, nor Divine Revelation, but rises from the Conceits of a warmed or over-weening Brain."[14] Discourse around and against enthusiasm relies on a sharp, Cartesian delineation between the somatic and the spiritual. For instance, Quakers are described as enthusiastic by the English writer John Trenchard (1709) because of the apparent mistake they make between their "Tremblings" and "Quakings" and "the immediate Spirit of God." Trenchard asserts that these "Transports" are instead "owing to Natural Causes."[15] Trenchard points to how the problem of enthusiasm is a problem with reading, specifically reading the ecstatically imprinted body, and determining whether its imprints stem from "Natural Causes" or the "immediate Spirit of God." *The Spiritual Quixote* contains several comic variations on this problem of reading somatic signs, for instance, when Jeremiah Tugwell, Wildgoose's servant and companion in his travels, interprets his own colicky "belly-ach" that he received from indulging in cider as originating from a spiritual cause (*SQ*, 231). Tugwell believes it is cured by Wildgoose's preaching and thus categorizes a bodily ill as a religious experience (*SQ*, 232).

The narrator of *The Spiritual Quixote* terms Wildgoose a "religious enthusiast" (*SQ*, 78) and by doing so presents Wildgoose's quixotic practice as springing from this blurring of spiritual and somatic impressions. By coalescing religious enthusiasm with quixotism, *The Spiritual Quixote* also draws on well-established associations. Samuel Butler's *Hudibras* (1662–77), for instance, a mock-heroic narrative poem, adapts *Don Quixote* to satirize Puritans and Calvinism.[16] By the mid-century, Methodism had been directly associated with quixotism. George Lavington wrote in his anti-Methodist tract *The Enthusiasm of Methodists and Papists Compared* (1749) that the "*Wind-mill* is indeed in all their Heads."[17] The anonymous *A Sovereign Remedy for the cure of Hypocrisy and Blind Zeal* (1764) opines that Methodists "are as really *Quixotes in Religion*, as the famous Knight was in *Chivalry*."[18] *The Spiritual Quixote* draws upon and reworks these established associations between enthusiasm, Methodism, and quixotism in its narrativization of a "spiritual quixotism."

Enthusiasm, like quixotism, could potentially denote an anachronistic relation to history. In ways redolent of the Countess telling Arabella "that we live in an Age in which the Customs, Manners, Habits, and Inclinations differ so widely" from that of romances (*FQ*, 326), the narrator of *The Spiritual Quixote* describes Don Quixote's key mistake as attempting to "revive that profession [of knighthood]; when the more perfect regulations of civil society had rendered it, not only unnecessary but unlawful" (*SQ*, 39).[19] The Methodist reformers are then described as being similarly out of time: "[They] have conjured up the powers of darkness in an enlightened age. [. . .] [T]hey are combating the shadow of Popery, where the Protestant religion is established" (*SQ*, 40). Anderson argues that the novel describes Methodism as being atavistic in an increasingly secularized world.[20] I would add that crucial to this is the novel's treatment of Methodist metaphor. Conal Condren, discussing the coincidence of metaphor and history, observes how at particular points in time new meanings are created through the analytic invention of the figurative. For example, Condren argues that the reformation redefined transubstantiation as "a metaphor that had been mistaken for a literal transformation."[21] *The Spiritual Quixote* represents Methodists—and on a larger level, enthusiasts and quixotes—as trapped in anachronism: literalizing what has been since relegated to the metaphorical.

This is apparent in the novel's description of Wildgoose's formative consumption of Puritanical literature. His reading is described as eating in an extended metaphor that persists for two chapters (*SQ*, 18–21). Wildgoose finds his "appetite" for reading Puritanical texts "increase by indulgence," but it is "crabbed food," and he is driven to read other nonconformist texts (*SQ*, 19). The theological works Wildgoose digests—all historical seventeenth-century books—have titles like "the Marrow of Divinity, Crumbs of Comfort, and Honey-combs for the Elect" (*SQ*, 19).[22] Wildgoose reads books that frame themselves as edible objects. While the books Wildgoose reads, and, for that matter, the Bible itself, take the trope of spiritual food seriously, *The Spiritual Quixote* does not. Beyond the description of Wildgoose's quixotic, appetitive reading, the novel elsewhere actively undermines any serious, spiritualized interpretation of the reading-as-eating metaphor. It deploys the trope in its prefatory material to self-consciously offer itself up as a meal for its readers. The fictive author of *The Spiritual Quixote*, "Collop" (a name that evokes food), dedicates his manuscript to a pastry cook in a dedication laden with puns on reading and eating, the majority of which are helpfully italicized for the reader.[23] Collop asks for the cook to "*preserve*" his works "from the attacks of the *sourest* criticks" (*SQ*, 7). The dedication classes *The Spiritual Quixote* as a frivolous and secular meal for its readers, suggesting that the reading-as-eating metaphor is only appropriate when used in a playful sense.

To seriously use a spiritualized eating-as-reading analogy, *The Spiritual Quixote* suggests, is to be as anachronistic as the literature Wildgoose consumes. The ostensibly outmoded nature of the spiritualized eating trope is inseparable from the reformation's redefinition of transubstantiation in terms of metaphor, to refer back to Condren's point. Changing conceptualizations of the Eucharist were part of increasing attempts to provide a "reasonable" religion applicable to everyday life.[24] Anglican conceptions of the Eucharist as a memorial were shaped by John Tillotson's *A Discourse against Transubstantiation* (1684), which describes mystical or spiritual understandings of the Eucharist as Catholic.[25] Despite John Wesley writing against transubstantiation and early Methodists' anti-Catholicism, Methodists were persistently accused of believing in transubstantiation.[26] In this light, the representation of Wildgoose's quixotic reading as spiritual eating, with the resultant echoes of transubstantiation, is a way of describing him as being enthusiastically and anachronistically trapped in out-moded religious language.

That said, Graves's description of appetitive reading is informed as much by the eighteenth-century literary marketplace (and anti-novel discourse) as it is by religious rhetoric. Take, for example, a review in Tobias Smollett's *Critical Review* (December 1763) of the novel *Each Sex in their Humour*, penned by a "Lady of Quality" and printed by "Mr. *Noble*'s novel *manufactory*." The review laments that "booksellers, those pimps of literature, take care every winter to procure a sufficient quantity of tales, memoirs, and romances for the entertainment of their customers, many of whom, not capable of distinguishing between good and bad, are mighty well satisfied with whatever is provided for them: as their female read-ers in particular have generally most voracious appetites and are not over delicate in the choice of their food, every thing that is new will go down."[27] Feminized genres ("tales, memoirs, and romances") are consumed by their "female readers" on a bodily rather than a cerebral level. The familiar trope of reading as sexual commerce, with circulating books described as circulating human bodies (and "booksellers" as "pimps," procuring goods for their customers) merges into another familiar metaphor: books as "food." The reviewer describes a mass of readers with an undiscriminating, "voracious" appetite, consuming vast quantities of print without judgment or thought, seeking out what is "novel." The book becomes a commodity for the mindless consumption of a feminized mass.[28] The description of Wildgoose's appetitive reading can be read along these lines: his feasting on "crude trash" with a "vitiated palate" suggests an analogous mode of consump-tion (*SQ*, 19).

The Spiritual Quixote's positioning of quixotism as a problem with metaphor is also exemplified in Wildgoose's conversation with Dr. Greville. The latter is rep-resented as an ideal clergyman in direct contrast to Methodists, possessing "sin-cere piety, sanctity of manners, and goodness of heart," and "really was what Mr. Wesley and his associates ought to have been" (*SQ*, 432). While Wildgoose recovers from a blow to the head, Dr. Greville wonders why Wildgoose "should be so strangely imposed upon by a spirit of enthusiasm, that had possessed his imagination" (*SQ*, 435). The subsequent passage plays with the word "spirit" and its potential religious, metaphorical, and physiological meanings.

Greville serves a similar function in *The Spiritual Quixote*'s narrative to the unnamed Johnsonian clergyman who lectures Arabella in *The Female Quixote*. Both men act as voices of masculine "reason" and, at the climax of the respective novels, are instrumental in the quixote's cure. Hence, Greville's metaphorical use of the word "spirit" is significant. Greville seems to strive for a language that is secular, and refers to the spiritual in a strictly metaphorical sense. We can read "spirit of enthusiasm" being deployed by Greville in the same manner it was used in other contemporaneous texts, as a figure of speech, and in this particular case, as a metaphor for Wildgoose's delusions (*SQ*, 435).[29] Wildgoose responds to Greville's figurative and secular use of "spirit" by restoring the word's religious charge. He defends the "*call* of the *spirit*," and the italics draw attention to its shift in meaning. Wildgoose's insistence on using "spirit" to refer to divine inspiration exemplifies his anachronistic use of religious metaphor. The passage then plays on "spirit" for the third time: "Dr. Greville was afraid of bringing on too violent an agitation of spirits, and of renewing the hæmorrhage" (*SQ*, 435). The word here refers to Wildgoose's animal spirits (the finest particles of the blood). Wildgoose's literal, *spiritual* interpretation of "spirit" as a connection to God is rebuked as anachronistic. In this conversation, the novel only acknowledges two meanings of "spirit": the metaphorical and the physical. Wildgoose's non-metaphoric, "spiritual" use of "spirit" threatens to be enthusiastic.

Through such instances as these, Wildgoose's discourse is presented as an enthusiastic version of Christianity and opposed to a "reasonable" one. "Reasonable Christianity" or "rational piety" was a cross-denominational goal in the eighteenth century, but there were differing ideas over what exactly was reasonable religion, or its discourse.[30] Wesley, for instance, appealed to reason as well as faith in his writings, and sought to express himself in a mode of English that would be readily intelligible no matter his audience's class, while also drawing extensively on biblical language.[31] However, in *The Spiritual Quixote*, the language of the Bible is described by the narrator as old-fashioned: the Old Testament has "quaint Hebraisms" and the apostles speak in "peculiar expressions" (*SQ*, 27). Wildgoose's use of scriptural language is repeatedly portrayed as the opposite to "the greatest simplicity of speech" (*SQ*, 34). Appended to a "harangue" of Wildgoose, which describes heaven in "luscious" and "sensual" expressions (*SQ*, 74), is a footnote by Graves that states: "Tho' these kinds of expression are used in scripture, in compliance with the carnal notions of the Jews, and have affected their common language—yet on moral subjects, I think, they have but an uncouth effect" (*SQ*, 481n74.3). So, though the Bible provides sensual descriptions of spiritual pleasures, Wildgoose's conflation of the sensual and the spiritual is yoked to anti-Semitic conceptions of Jewish carnality and produces an "uncouth effect."[32]

Through critiques like this, *The Spiritual Quixote* treads a fine line between mocking Methodism and mocking "religion." A letter by Graves to James Dodsley, his publisher, planning the second edition of the novel (October 13, 1777), registers Graves's concern that he might be giving "some little offence."[33] These convolutions drive Graves's self-conscious deployment of the novel form. Graves frames *The Spiritual Quixote* as a found manuscript and encloses it among an abundance of prefatory material. The resultant authorial distance and anonymity is crucial for a novel that—as the "Preface" is uncomfortably aware, apologizing as it does for the comic and "frequent allusions to Scripture"—is liable to be accused of blasphemy (*SQ*, 4). The third edition (1783) omits several of the biblical quotations included in the earlier editions. Where the quotations are kept, the capital letters, italics, and quotation marks that had originally marked passages of scripture are silently dropped.[34] In this way, *The Spiritual Quixote* is itself shaped by the problem of enthusiasm. That is to say, the difficulty of distinguishing between "Religion" and its enthusiastic parody means that the stated motive of the text, the "ridiculing" of "the ill-judged zeal of a frantic Enthusiast," blurs into a potentially controversial "ridiculing" of "Religion" itself (*SQ*, 3).

METHODISM IN THE MARKETPLACE

In chapter 2 we saw how the eighteenth-century novel and the eighteenth-century theater were rivals for the same audience, offering different, but related, experiences of character and sympathy. Sermons—printed and spoken—and religious texts in general were also textual forms that were popularly consumed, and Methodism, particularly through Whitefield's theatrical style of preaching, offered potentially gripping entertainment. *The Scheming Triumvirate* (1760; figure 9) is only one of many anti-Methodist satires that put Whitefield onstage.[35] It depicts Laurence Sterne (chapter 3) holding up *Tristram Shandy*, the Methodist preacher George Whitefield in the center, and the playwright Samuel Foote (Whitefield's interlocutor in the hieroglyphic letter with which we began), waving his anti-Methodist satire *The Minor*. The three men are presented selling equivalent wares to the same audience. Novels, Methodist sermons, and anti-Methodist theater are circulated and consumed on mass, and seduce their susceptible audiences into wasting their money. Each panel in the triptych involves women ogling the men on the dais: a woman admiring Sterne exclaims, "Another Touch of your Homunculus"; a female member of Whitefield's audience smilingly states, "I wish his Spirit was in my Flesh"; and a woman gazing adoringly up at Foote exclaims that he is "quite a Jewel of a Man." The verses at the bottom of the etching affirm the way economics drives these men's textual production. While Sterne might be a "Selfish Slave" to "bawdy Wit" and Foote someone who "Laughs at Religion," they are all preoccupied with gaining a large audience to market their novels, sermons, and farces, "Thus Disagreeing—they upon the Whole / Agree in this one Point."

The Spiritual Quixote builds on this cultural comprehension of novels, plays, and sermons as proximate commodities in the eighteenth-century media market-

FIGURE 9 *The Scheming Triumvirate*, 1760. © The Trustees of the British Museum.

place. In an argument between Wildgoose and Captain Gordon, Wildgoose, ever Whitefield-like, denigrates the theater, ranting "with great vehemence against Plays and Theatrical Entertainments," wondering how "any Play-houses were tolerated in a Christian country" (*SQ*, 244).[36] Captain Gordon retorts with: "[I]f a mere representation of vicious or immoral actions (though with a design to expose them, or to deter others from imitating them) be unlawful, how shall we defend the practice of the Sacred Writers themselves, both of the Old and New Testament, who have recorded many cruel, unjust, and some lewd actions, even of God's peculiar people?" (*SQ*, 244). Wildgoose responds by bristling at the comparison between the Bible and "modern scribblers" (*SQ*, 244). The Captain argues that "the Sacred Writers relate many *tragical*, and, with reverence be it spoken, some *comical* events" (*SQ*, 245). Scripture and secular forms of entertainment are suggested to be far from distinct. Wildgoose offers no counterarguments to the Captain, beyond reiterating (with a sneer) his position that all plays should be made illegal (*SQ*, 245). Captain Gordon is hardly an exemplary or moral character in the novel; for instance, he is eager for the attentions of the married Mrs. Culpepper. Yet his remarks serve to place Methodist meetings firmly alongside plays and novels as potentially suspect media when consumed uncritically, but far from always encouraging immorality.

This is especially the case as, according to Wildgoose's aesthetic position, *The Spiritual Quixote* itself would encourage blasphemy and enthusiasm. The epigraph to the first volume of the novel: "Romances are almost the only Vehicles of Instruction that can be administered to a refined and voluptuous People," a quote from Jean-Jacques Rousseau, playfully positions (comic) romances like *The Spiritual Quixote* as instructive, if only for those readers who cannot learn from anything else, supporting Captain Gordon's position that secular forms of entertainment are potentially educative.

Elsewhere in its front matter, *The Spiritual Quixote* self-consciously comments on its own ability to mark its readers. The "rough draft" of Collop's "Author's Preface" announces: "I am convinced that Don Quixote or Gil Blas, Clarissa or Sir Charles Grandison, will furnish more hints for correcting the follies and regulating the morals of young persons, and impress them more forcibly on their minds, than volumes of severe precepts seriously delivered and dogmatically inforced" (*SQ*, 3). Collop places *The Spiritual Quixote* in the tradition of Cervantine fictions and Richardsonian novels. Both genres, the "Apology" claims, "impress" ideas on the minds of their readers more successfully than overtly didactic texts, where precepts are "seriously delivered and dogmatically inforced" (*SQ*, 3).[37] The power of novels to "impress" their readers' minds becomes the ostensible motivation for *The Spiritual Quixote*'s novel form.

Wildgoose's failure to acknowledge that theater, like scripture and novels, can serve a didactic function when it represents "vicious or immoral actions" (*SQ*, 244) stems from his own quixotic tendencies to misread and overidentify. The catalyst for his Methodist conversion is hearing the Anglican vicar sermonize against hypocrisy. With narcissistic self-identification, Wildgoose presumes the sermon is directed solely at himself (*SQ*, 17). Wildgoose follows quixotic listening with quixotic reading. Not only does he "eat" his reading, as we have seen, but after consuming the works of "our primitive Reformers" and observing the way they wear their hair in the frontispieces of their books, he imitates their hairstyles "that he might resemble those venerable men, even in his external appearance" (*SQ*, 41). Echoing *The Female Quixote*'s conceptualization of quixotism as structured by the visuality of the printed book object (chapter 1), Wildgoose tries to look like a frontispiece. Puritanical texts alter his "external appearance"; they reprint and reproduce themselves on his body (*SQ*, 41). It follows, then, that Wildgoose presumes that the play-going audience is as quixotic as he is, and that they will embody whatever representations they see. He concludes that the theater, through the presentation of "base and villainous action[s]" is a "nursery of lewdness and debauchery," a venue for quixotic reproduction, breeding an audience of villains, who will be quixotically imprinted by whatever is depicted on stage (*SQ*, 244).

The Spiritual Quixote's analogies between participating in Methodist meetings and quixotically consuming novels are perhaps most emphatic in the narrative of Miss Townsend, a female misreader whom Wildgoose encounters during his travels. By categorizing Miss Townsend as a quixotic misreader, I differ here from Anderson, who interprets Miss Townsend as a good reader, in contrast to Wildgoose.[38] Certainly, when Wildgoose meets Miss Townsend she is no longer quixotic, but rational and regretful, and she tells Wildgoose of her experience and reformation. Yet Miss Townsend also relates to Wildgoose how she was convinced by her consumption of literature to leave her father's house. Through her inset narrative, *The Spiritual Quixote* reiterates the old trope that literature has the capacity to impress itself on its readers' characters to such an extent that daughters no longer belong to their parents. Like Lennox's Arabella (chapter 1), the absence of a mother's guidance provides an opportunity for ungoverned reading. Eventually, imitating the characters she reads about, Miss Townsend leaves her father's house. She narrowly escapes being raped by a gentleman who seems to offer her protection and is forced, like Arabella, to learn that "the world in reality was very different from what it appeared in poetry and romance" (*SQ*, 87). Miss Townsend's marriage to Wildgoose at the end of *The Spiritual Quixote* implicitly parallels the two characters, and encourages the reader to see similarities in their respective quixotisms. As Wildgoose's love interest, she plays an important role in the resolution to *The Spiritual Quixote*'s overarching plot, such as it is. Her reconciliation with her father and her romance with Wildgoose develop alongside Wildgoose's own story, suggesting how her novelistic quixotism can be read as a feminine reflection of Wildgoose's quixotic Methodism.

Wildgoose, then, like the Shandy men (chapter 3), offers a complex remasculinization of the feminized, novel-reading quixotic subject.[39] His gender is further complicated by his Methodist rhetoric, which is pervaded with images of himself as penetrable and ambiguously sexed.[40] However, Wildgoose's masculinity is less compromised than that of the Shandy men. It seems, despite the excesses of his rhetoric, his status as a gentleman prevents his androgynous discourse from entirely evacuating his masculinity. For instance, the narrator describes Wildgoose's skill at winning over female devotees as being due to his "expressive countenance" and "gentleman-like air" (*SQ*, 236). Despite being the butt of most of the jokes in *The Spiritual Quixote*, Wildgoose escapes with his dignity and heterosexual masculinity intact, and it seems it is his status as a "gentleman" that allows him to do so.

This is the case even when Wildgoose seems to portray himself, through allegory, as a male spouse of Jesus. When asked by his landlady if he slept well the previous night, Wildgoose answers, in a parody of Whitefield's writings, "I sweetly leaned on my Saviour's bosom; and *sucked out* of the *breasts* of his consolation; and I can truly say, the banner of his love was spread over me the whole night" (*SQ*,

114). Part of the humor comes from the inappropriateness of Wildgoose talking in dense spiritual allegory in response to a simple inquiry about his sleep. He inflates and eroticizes an established Christian trope, layering a series of conceptually confusing, but undeniably corporeal, images. Wildgoose draws on several biblical passages describing spiritual breast-feeding, a maternal God, and a feminized Christ. Like the motif of eating the Word, spiritual breast-feeding is a way the relationship between the corporeal and the divine can be conceptualized. There are numerous passages in the Bible where God or Old Testament patriarchs are described as nursing fathers, an image that also was deployed in different ways by James I, Charles I, Cromwell, and Anne to consolidate their authority.[41]

Yet Wildgoose's image is not just simply one of God as a mother but rather that of a feminized Christ. Here, and elsewhere, Wildgoose (like Whitefield) works with an established tradition of an eroticized, ambiguously gendered Christ.[42] Wildgoose draws on maternal images of Christ from several biblical passages, such as when John is said to be "leaning on Jesus' bosom" and "lying on Jesus' breast" (John 13:23–25). The "banner of his [Christ's] love" borrows from Songs of Solomon, in the Old Testament, a quintessential example of the sacred mingling with the sexual.[43] Wildgoose's allegory upsets any binaries of sex or gender: Christ has breasts, Wildgoose sleeps lovingly with a "he" and is also penetrable, imbibing Christ's milk, or whatever fluid might be envisaged as flowing from Christ's breasts (blood, with its resonances of transubstantiation, is another possibility).[44]

Breast-feeding, like reading, had the capacity in the eighteenth century to radically shape a person's identity. Babies could potentially imbibe via milk their nurses' bodily deformities, as well as their morals, speech, and beliefs.[45] Milk, like ink, then, became a means by which a person's character could be formed. Read along these lines, Wildgoose's multigendered, eroticized metaphor demonstrates on multiple levels how much he has become a receptacle for antiquated words and tropes.

In short, when Wildgoose proclaims he has "leaned on my Saviour's bosom; and *sucked out* of the *breasts* of his consolation," *The Spiritual Quixote* draws on the overdetermined nature of milk and religious breast-feeding: religious and political, to create an obscurely fleshly image. This passage is within a chapter facetiously titled "Spiritual Advice"; Wildgoose attempts to "impart some spiritual advice to his host and family" and does not reflect on the "improbability of his audience's not comprehending his allegorical meaning" (*SQ*, 114). Tugwell ends up attempting to translate Wildgoose's images to his audience, "imagining he could explain his Master's meaning" (*SQ*, 114). The joke is that Wildgoose's "meaning" is absolutely buried under the dense layers of connotations and symbolic resonances outlined above. He attempts to describe a close relationship between himself and

Christ, but ends up comically entangled in his outdated religious "jargon" (*SQ*, 114). The word "meaning" is repeated, reflecting how "meaning" becomes displaced and deferred in the disconcertingly, nebulously erotic image that appears at first glance to encase some kind of spiritual message.

Yet while Wildgoose's rhetoric destabilizes his masculinity, it does not completely undermine it. The landlady stares at Wildgoose "with astonishment," but her shock registers an upset in the boundaries of age, not gender. She is surprised to hear an adult or "jolly man" like Wildgoose "talk of sucking at the breast" (*SQ*, 114). The novel suggests and then quickly dismisses Methodism's threat to gender. Wildgoose's discourse threatens but does not upset his claim to be a "man," though it renders him penetrable and infantile.

The narrator of *The Spiritual Quixote* reserves the most scorn not for gentlemen turned Methodists, but for itinerant "plebeians," who, by forsaking "their lawful callings" and becoming "reformers and teachers of their brethren," aspire beyond their station (*SQ*, 31). Graves articulates the anxiety that Methodism, by providing a means for women and members of the working class to preach, to act as authorities in religion, and to travel as itinerant preachers, removed people—figuratively and literally—from their "proper" place.

Wildgoose's Methodist rambles are a gentleman's imprudent follies, rather than a plebeian's dangerous error. Yet for a worker, or a woman like Miss Townsend, the social transgressions prompted by quixotic enthusiasm have the potential to be more serious. She describes running away from her home as "the greatest misfortune of her life" (*SQ*, 78–79). Her quixotism threatens her sexual reputation as a woman; her blushes and tears when her abscondment from her father's house is alluded to signal the way the novel treats her transgressions with a solemnity that barely touches its description of Wildgoose's "Summer's Ramble" (*SQ*, 79). In Wildgoose's case, his gender and his class work to maintain the light tone and moderation of *The Spiritual Quixote*'s anti-Methodist satire.

Miss Townsend's story is only a small slice of the novel's extensive parallels between female quixotic novel readers and Methodists. Like *Tristram Shandy*, *The Spiritual Quixote* self-consciously anticipates its own consumption by female readers. A chapter epigraph describes in rhyme a luxuriously adorned "blooming nymph" entering "the shop of learned Bibliopole, / That vends his ware at Tunbridge or at Bath, / Retailing modern trash to saunt'ring beaux" (*SQ*, 77). When the chapter begins, the prose picks up where the satirical verse left off, the narrator presuming that if "any of my amiable country-women" have carried "home this trifling volume from some Circulating-library," they must be frustrated by the lack of a "love-tale" (*SQ*, 77). Graves draws on the stereotypical feminine consumption of novels as motivated by romance, even describing female novel reading itself as being a luxurious state of laziness. The woman reader is envisaged as "throwing herself negligently upon her settee or sopha—or even on the feet of her truckle-bed" (*SQ,* 77). Since a truckle bed is a smaller bed tucked under another, typically used by a servant, its reference suggestively aligns novel reading with working-class indolence. The narrator tells the female reader, looking for a love plot, to watch Wildgoose and "attend him a few pages further" and then proceeds to describe how Wildgoose is attractive to particular "female votaries" (*SQ,* 77). The stereotypical female reader seamlessly blurs into the sexualized spirituality of the female Methodist.

METAPHORS AND CONCRETIZING IMAGINATIONS

So far we could say that while *The Female Quixote, Polly Honeycombe,* and *Tristram Shandy* deploy, modify, and critique the gendering of the impressionable romance or novel reader, *The Spiritual Quixote* takes these tropes in a religiously inflected direction. It maps anti-novel discourse's concerns about a feminized, proliferating marketplace onto related anxieties about Methodism as a sexualized, spreading religion. This is seen in Wildgoose's congregation's response to his attempts to describe heaven. He tells his listeners, "Their souls were espoused to Christ: he shall [. . .] entertain them with sweet kisses from his *lily lips*" (*SQ,* 74), parodying Whitefield's sermon *Christ the Best Husband* (1740). Whitefield's sermon describes how his listeners will "be received into the nearest and closest Embraces of his [Christ's] Love."[46] In Wildgoose's version the potential sexuality of Whitefield's sermon is intensified. The phrase "*lily lips*" is inserted and "sweet" is reiterated to an excessive extent, "sweet kisses from his *lily lips*—more sweet than the sweet-smelling myrrh" (*SQ,* 74), bringing Wildgoose's language to the edge of sensual meaninglessness.

The reader is told that Wildgoose's amorous expressions "in the nuptial style" successfully gain the attention of the "lewd and lascivious" and, on the same page, that his kind of "language particularly charmed the female devotees" (*SQ,* 74), echoing the sexual innuendo that was often directed toward female Methodists and used to explain their prominence in the sect.[47] Then, the narrator follows a description of how Wildgoose's sensual similes charm his "female devotees" with a gendered distinction between affective transport and "understanding," between "similes" and reasoned argument: "[B]y this soothing eloquence, and the earnestness of his manner, Wildgoose softened those hearts, which, for some years, had resisted the admonitions of friends, and the suggestions of conscience; and made many converts to religion: at least he made them so long as the brightness of those similies continued to glow in their imaginations. But, their affections only being moved, and their understandings not enlightened, nor their reason convinced, too many of them soon relapsed into their former dissolute courses" (*SQ*, 74–75). Wildgoose's feminized audience is momentarily converted by sensuous "similies," but their "understandings" are not "enlightened" and their "reason" is not "convinced" (*SQ*, 75).

Relevant here is Dennis Todd's analysis of the eighteenth-century enthusiastic imagination's power to relentlessly materialize. Todd argues that the enthusiast is preoccupied with the "images" of corporeal things, to a point where the enthusiast is ensnared in the corporeal, where ideas are reduced "to their corporeal concomitants": "In the mind of an Enthusiast, an idea is so concretized as a physical image that the image no longer acts as a sign but as a thing itself. There is no ideational kernel; there is only the physical husk."[48] This suggests Wildgoose's language is enthusiastic not just because it draws on a superseded mode of embodied spiritual expression, but because—like the hieroglyphic *Retort*—it points to a discourse that replaces concepts with physical *things*, and in Wildgoose's case enthralling images take the place of concepts that might speak to his audience's "understandings" or "reason" (*SQ*, 75).

The narrator's stress on the concretizing imaginations of Wildgoose's feminized, enthusiastic audience is reminiscent of *Tristram Shandy*'s description of Madam's reading practice (chapter 3): "nothing but the gross and more carnal parts of a composition will go down" (*TS*, 1.20.66). In both *Tristram Shandy* and *The Spiritual Quixote*, feminized imaginations have the capacity to relentlessly materialize or concretize; they can reduce texts and language itself to matter (even to food), and strip away more cerebral components.

Just as anti-novel rhetoric paradoxically invests the novel with a formidable power to imprint and impress the female reader's imagination, character, and/or body, *The Spiritual Quixote*'s moderated deployment of anti-Methodist discourse acknowledges the affective potential of the religion's embodied rhetoric. At a time when elocutionists were lamenting the dryness of the typical Anglican preacher, the theatricality of Methodist rhetoric offered an intriguing alternative.[49] Goring argues that *The Spiritual Quixote* both critiques the "impoliteness" of Methodist oratory and suggests that some elements of Methodism's persuasive preaching methods should be deployed by the Church of England.[50] The narrator is attentive to Wildgoose's manner of speaking and the effect his oratorical devices have on his audience. Readers of the novel are positioned at a critical distance from his speeches, and are instructed to observe their effects: "[T]hat part of the congregation seemed most affected, and bestowed the most hearty benedictions on the Preacher, who did not understand a word of English. This, however, we ought not to attribute merely to affectation, but to the vehemence and apparent sincerity of the Orator, and the mechanical and infectious operation of an enthusiastic energy" (*SQ*, 269). The content of Wildgoose's harangue is demonstrably irrelevant to the effect it has on his audience. The Welsh-speaking part of the audience cannot understand "a word" of what is said but are alive to the affective power of Wildgoose's oratory, a position mirrored by the reader of this passage, who is supplied detailed descriptions of the reactions of Wildgoose's audience, but little information about what he actually says. Wildgoose's "vehemence and apparent sincerity" results in a Swiftian "mechanical" contagion, with "enthusiastic energy" spreading from body to body.[51]

The relentless, mechanical materialism of enthusiasm is aligned with the audience's fascination with the tonality and texture of words delivered, which the narrator distinguishes from an understanding of the lexical purport of Wildgoose's speech, or being able to "understand a word of English." The "meaning" of Wildgoose's harangue, such as it is, is enthusiastically located in signs apparently detached from their signifiers.[52] The harangue's affective power depends, then, on multiple impressionable bodies pressed together, sharing and spreading "enthusiastic energy." *The Spiritual Quixote* formulates enthusiasm as attentiveness to the material form of texts rather than their content: drawing a distinction that threatens to collapse from the very moment it is made.

In keeping with these enthusiastic preoccupations with the mediation of Wildgoose's words, the nascent power of Methodist sermons to inspire in their audiences "infectious" quixotic energy is attributed to the incongruous spaces within which they are delivered. When Wildgoose preaches outside the church in a barber's shop, the unusual locale is what gains him a large audience. A stranger preaching in a church, the narrator writes, might have attracted those "who happened not to have upon their hands any more agreeable Sunday's amusements" (*SQ*, 73). However, the setting of Wildgoose's sermon "at the Barber's upon a cydercask" and the manner in which he gives it, "leaning over the top of an old cheesepress" make the prospect of him speaking more entertaining, and the barber's house is "crowded with attendants from every quarter of the city" (*SQ*, 73). Adding to the sensational nature of the location is the fact that it is barely legal.[53] This was stressed in Edmund Gibson's *Observations upon the Conduct and Behaviour of a Certain Sect, Usually Distinguished by the Name of Methodists* (1744). Gibson writes: "they have had the Boldness to preach in the *Fields* and other open Places, and by publick Advertisements to invite the *Rabble* to be their Hearers" despite statutes to the contrary.[54] Historian David Hempton summarizes Gibson's concerns: "Methodists placed themselves in open defiance of government in Church and State; by engaging in itinerant preaching and extra-parochial communion, Methodists infringed the principles of territorial integrity upon which all established churches depended for their security; and by encouraging the 'rabble' to meet out of doors they were inviting, even instigating, social instability."[55] The social disruption Methodism seems to pose is embodied in the spatial violations that Gibson outlines; the Methodist outdoor preacher is literally outside the established church. Wildgoose's plebeian audience is "not capable of distinguishing nicely between his doctrine and what they heard at church; yet being delivered to them in a more familiar manner, and by a new teacher, and in a new place, it made a considerable impression upon them" (*SQ*, 26). Outdoor sermons seem to spur enthusiasm and quixotic impressions.

The apparent power of "field-preaching" led many anti-Methodist writers to condemn "field-preaching" as an evil in itself, regardless of the subject of the sermons. For example, William Warburton's *The Doctrine of Grace* (1763), which Tracy identifies as being obliquely mentioned in *The Spiritual Quixote* (*SQ*, 4), describes field preaching as being a "*fanatic manner* of preaching, [which] tho' it were the doctrine of an Apostle, may do more harm, to Society at least, than a modest revival of old speculative heresies, or, than the invention of new; since it tends to bewilder the imaginations of some, to inflame the passions of others, and, in the state of things, to spread disorder and disturbance throughout the whole Community. What for instance, does FIELD-PREACHING imply, but a famine of the Word, occasioned by a total neglect in the spiritual Pastors appointed by Law?"[56] The space beyond the church, then, is a sensational environment for preaching; it produces an audience more liable to have their imaginations "bewilder[ed]" and their passions "inflame[d]."

Warburton's words rely on the same close interconnections between the imagination, the passions, and the body that are present in contemporaneous anti-novel rhetoric. It is easy to find examples of anti-novel discourse in the 1770s that seem to share Warburton's turns of speech. Vicesimus Knox, in his essay "On Novel Reading" (1778), seems to almost directly quote Warburton when he writes that can "inflame the passions" of their vulnerable readers.[57] Similarly, John Gregory, in *A Father's Legacy to His Daughters* (1774), describes how books can "warm" the "imagination."[58] Looking back to chapter 1, in *The Female Quixote* Arabella is told by the Doctor toward the end of the novel that her reading serves to "inflame" her "Passions" and give them "new Fire" (*FQ*, 380). Like the quixotic female reader, then, the listeners to an outdoor sermon become in thrall to their "passions" and "warm" imaginations.

On a similar note, it is important to observe the intimate affinity between Methodism's emoting body and the weeping, blushing body of sensibility. G. J. Barker-Benfield argues that adherence to the ideologies of Methodism and sensibility is "demonstrated by the capacity to feel and to signify feeling by the same physical signs—tears, groans, sighs, and tremblings."[59] Graves yokes sensibility and Methodism together by making it clear that it is Wildgoose's eloquent body—more than the content of his speech—that moves his listeners. The narrator states that Wildgoose "had something naturally agreeable in his countenance, and also a very musical tone of voice: and though, in the vehemence of his harangues, he had a wildness in his looks, proceeding from the enthusiastic zeal which possessed his imagination, yet that very circumstance gave a more pathetic force to his eloquence. And he himself appearing so much in earnest, and affected with the subject, it had a proportionable effect upon his audience" (*SQ*, 73). Wildgoose impresses his audience's imagination through his tonal or analogously "musical" performance of feeling. His display of affect—he appears "so much in earnest, and affected by the subject"—results in the audience being "proportionabl[y]" marked with emotion. He creates a scene of emotional contagion and spurs the quixotic reproduction of affective impressions.

It is possible to say, then, that the Methodist body, like the body of the sentimental reader, is imprinted with legible impressions. The influential theorist on elocution, Thomas Sheridan, suggests how this might be the case. In *A Course of Lectures on Elocution* (1762), Sheridan strives to distinguish the eloquent, sensible body from the body of the religious enthusiast and the language of enthusiasm from the language of "believers." By doing so, he only emphasizes their similarities:

> [T]he fancied operations of the spirit, in the people called Quakers, manifested by the most unnatural signs; and in some other religious sects, by a certain cant, and extravagant gestures, produce powerful effects, on the imaginations of such hearers, as are bred up in the persuasion, that such signs are the language of the spirit: But it must be evident, upon observing both the preachers, and their auditory, that it is only the imagination, which is so wrought upon; as there is no discovering in their countenances, any signs which are the natural concomitants of the feelings of the heart. This sort of language of emotions therefore, is well calculated to make enthusiasts, but not believers.[60]

Sheridan defines enthusiastic rhetoric as only affecting the imagination, leading to bodily signs that do not stem from the "heart." He writes as though enthusiasm is easily distinguishable from heartfelt emotions through the reading of "signs" marking the body. However, the problem of enthusiasm is that the "sensible marks" the imagination makes on the body and those that stem from the "feelings of the heart" cannot be easily distinguished.

In fact, returning to the description of Wildgoose's oratory quoted above, although his bodily signs result from "the enthusiastic zeal which possessed his imagination," this enthusiasm is described as aiding his affective power, giving "a more pathetic force to his eloquence" (*SQ*, 73). Both sentimental and enthusiastic bodies, marked and molded by powerful imaginations, legibly embody, perform, and transmit affect. The "mechanical and infectious" operations of enthusiasm crucially involve a misreading of the impressed body, as imprinted by spiritual (rather than simply somatic) forces (*SQ*, 269). The body of the enthusiast thus complexly speaks to literary-cultural formations of the tropically marked quixotic body and the quixotic problem of distinguishing between experiential and imaginative impressions.

Through emphatic parallels between Methodism, reading, and theatergoing, structured around Wildgoose's "quaint" and quixotic use of metaphor, *The Spiritual Quixote* describes a Methodist body that—like the bodies of quixotic female readers—is impressionable and permeable and has the capacity for wayward "mechanical and infectious" reproduction.

THE NEW BIRTH

These concerns that I have been describing—impressionable Methodist bodies, concretizing imaginations, and problems around metaphorical language—come to a head with *The Spiritual Quixote*'s treatment of the Methodist stress on the importance of spiritual regeneration, or "new birth." For Methodism's detractors, the new birth exemplified the extent Methodism was a religion of enthusiasts, who mistook their physical tremors for spiritual experiences.[61] The analogies between spiritual conversion and giving birth were ridiculed: by comparing the effort of spiritual conversion to the work of giving birth, the allegory characterized Methodists as having pregnant bodies and ostensibly sexed all Methodists as female. For instance, Lavington in *The Enthusiasm of Methodists and Papists Compared*, sardonically states, "In order to attain this *New Birth*, in the *lower* or *higher* Sense, they are to undergo the Torments and Agonies of a *Woman in Travail*."[62] In what we can now recognize as a familiar trope in anti-Methodist rhetoric, Methodists are represented as aspiring to a "*higher* Sense" only be trapped in something "*lower*."

The Methodist new birth, like quixotic reading, involves a transformation that is explicitly gendered as feminine. As in *Tristram Shandy* (chapter 3), representations of impressionable, quixotic bodies coalesce with images of unruly female sexual reproduction. The theory of maternal impressions (marks on the fetus in utero, via the mother's imagination) again becomes analogized to a quixotic response to media. Specifically, in *The Spiritual Quixote*, the image of the new birth is used to evoke a comically chaotic collapse between words and bodies via a quasi-maternal imagination.

For instance, *The Spiritual Quixote* draws on the ready parallels between the new birth and quixotic impressions when a "poor fellow of a neighbouring hamlet (who used to be always quarreling with his neighbours, but who had been greatly affected by hearing Mr. Wesley preach two or three times)" gallops through the street on a little pony (*SQ*, 281). "[S]taring wildly, he rides up to Wildgoose, cry-ing out, "*Got* bless you! Master Wesley; hur is convinced of sin; and Got has given hur revelations, and visions, and prophecies; and has foretold, that hur shall be a king" (*SQ*, 281). The narration treats the "poor fellow" with a mixture of amuse-ment and pity, the transcription of his Welsh accent mocking his use of scriptural language. "[H]earing Mr. Wesley preach two or three times" has caused a radical transformation in this man's character (*SQ*, 281). He goes from being merely quar-relsome to being "almost mad" (*SQ*, 281). Wildgoose responds to the story of the "poor fellow" and his quixotic transformation with celebration, designating it as an instance of the new birth: "'Mad!' quoth Wildgoose; 'I wish all that hear me this day were not only *almost*, but altogether as mad as this poor countryman. No,' says he, 'these are the true symptoms of the New Birth; and he only wants the obstetric hand of some Spiritual Physician, to relieve him from his pangs, from these struggles between the Flesh and the Spirit'" (*SQ*, 281–282). When Wildgoose states that the poor, holy madman "only wants the obstetric hand of some Spiri-tual Physician" he clearly thinks of himself as this spiritual physician, and in this role encourages people to pray for the "poor countryman" (*SQ*, 281).

Wildgoose's self-portrayal as a kind of spiritual male-midwife contributes to a sense of him chaotically birthing ambiguously gendered bodies. His phrase "obstetric hand" has biblical roots; it appears in the Douay-Rheims Bible—the early Catholic translation of the Latin into English—which Graves's introduction to the novel refers to directly (*SQ*, 8), and hence aligns Methodist discourse with Catholicism.[63] That said, the Douay-Rheims Bible had grown unpopular during the eighteenth century, and it is likely most readers would have known the phrase "obstetric hand" from Alexander Pope's *Dunciad* (1742). The *Dunciad* describes a "second birth" of digested coins, with James Douglas, who was a man-midwife and involved in the Mary Toft affair (see chapter 3), lending his "soft, obstetric hand" to aid the anal delivery of the coins.[64] For his scatological image, Pope draws on the visceral suggestiveness of man-midwives using their hands to aid childbirth. Lisa Cody argues that the man-midwife was a fraught character in eighteenth-century cultures. As well as being sexualized due to his intimacy with birthing women's bodies, the man-midwife could both symbolize and catalyze a collapse in sexual difference.[65] Pope's evocative phrase reappears in Sterne's *Tristram Shandy* (see chapter 3), when the Catholic and incompetent man-midwife Dr. Slop is about to turn the doorknob and attend Mrs. Shandy's labor. Slop walks as if in slow motion toward the door, and the narrator exclaims, "Truce!—truce, good Dr. *Slop!*—stay thy obstetrick hand;—return it safe into thy bosom to keep it warm;—little do'st thou know what obstacles;—little do'st thou think what hidden causes retard its operation!" (*TS*, 2.11.126). Sterne, like Pope, uses "obstetric hand" to stress the visceral and violent realities of childbirth, as well as ironically point to the way Slop's hands are anything but skilled or appropriately "obstetrick." It would be safer for everyone involved in the birth if Slop kept his hands "warm" in his "bosom."[66]

So Wildgoose, by designating himself a "spiritual physician" with an "obstetric hand," becomes prey to all the negative associations I have outlined above: with Catholicism, with the sexually ambiguous role of the male midwife, and, more directly, with Dr. Slop's blundering incompetence and the grotesque image of Douglas fishing coins from anuses. The mad Methodist believer has a permeable body, which is metaphorically penetrated by Wildgoose's hands. Feminized and impressionable, the body of the Methodist believer and the body of the quixotic reader become sites of deviant reproduction, where identities are overwritten and reshaped via metaphors of penetration and propagation.

Elsewhere in the novel, the potential for double entendre around the new birth is duly exploited: "[A] little girl, who did not seem to be above thirteen years old, cried out from the midst of the croud, 'that she was pricked through and through by the power of the word.' This occasioned some confusion; but the people about her checked her zeal, and stopped the poor girl's outcries" (*SQ*, 250). Graves comically reworks an instance in Whitefield's journals, where Whitefield describes meeting "a little Girl of thirteen Years of Age, who told me in great Simplicity, 'She was pricked through and through with the "Power of the Word."'"[67] In *The Spiritual Quixote*, both the "confusion" the "poor girl's" words occasion and the anxiety of the crowd to silence her outcries emphasize the suggestiveness of her words (*SQ*, 250). Her outburst both plays upon the multiple meanings of "prick" and reiterates the trope of the penetrable Methodist body. When read in a purely metaphorical, secular sense, the girl's words are correct: she has been penetrated by the power of Wildgoose's language. His rhetoric has affected her so powerfully she shouts out to everyone nearby. However, she, like so many of Wildgoose's Methodist followers, enthusiastically mistakes the power of Wildgoose's oratory and the "infectious operation of an enthusiastic energy" for a transcendental experience (*SQ*, 269).

The girl and her mistake resurface later in the novel, when she and her mother privately meet with Wildgoose. The narration identifies her by her own confused metaphorics: "the poor girl that was pricked through and through, by the power of the Word, at his last preachment" (*SQ*, 256–257). At their meeting the girl has a hysterical fit. When Wildgoose attempts to assure the mother the girl is just manifesting symptoms of the new birth, the mother responds with "I wish it may be" but that she is "sadly afraid" her "poor girl is with child" (*SQ*, 257). A claim to be penetrated by the logos is bathetically paralleled by a more corporeal penetration and the symbolism of the new birth satirically becomes synonymous with an illegitimate conception. Yet the narration reveals that the girl's mother is lying, in the hope of motivating Wildgoose's charity. What seems initially to be a corporeal parody of the new birth becomes an imagined or fictive pregnancy. Methodists' embodied spiritual experiences, then, are by turn equated with imaginative delusions, illicit sex, and scams.

DIVINE ANALOGIES

The way fleshly depictions of Christ, and immediate, embodied encounters with the spiritual are mocked in *The Spiritual Quixote*, raises the question whether it is possible for the "joys of Heaven" to be described at all without drawing on "enthusiastic" discourse. In a published sermon, Graves states that "it is impossible for our limited capacities" to fully understand "the nature and essence of God, (as, indeed, they cannot of their own souls, or of any spiritual substance)."[68] Similarly, Warburton writes that humans, with fleshly senses can only obtain knowledge of God obliquely. "[T]he passages to the Soul" are "so clogged up in this incumbrance of flesh as to be unable to convey to the sensory any more than an oblique glimpse of the sovereign Good."[69] By this reasoning, to describe a direct spiritual experience is to fall into enthusiasm, and to confuse the spiritual with an "incumbrance of flesh."

Peter Browne, the Bishop of Cork and Ross, elaborates and theorizes a similar position to Graves and Warburton. According to Browne's philosophy, heavily indebted to Lockean epistemology, there is no way a mortal person can have an immediate consciousness of God. Browne believed that human faculties of knowledge and reason involved body as well as spirit, precluding any direct knowledge of God, who is pure spirit.[70] Therefore, the only possible approach toward the divine is through analogy and metaphor, with an awareness of the limitations of such analogies. Quoting Saint Hilary, Browne writes, in *Things Divine and Supernatural Conceived by Analogy With Things Natural and Human* (1733), "*[W]hen we make*

any Comparison from things human, we may be understood not to think of God accord-
ing to the Nature of things Corporeal; nor to compare Spiritual things to our Passions:
But to have applyed the Species of Appearances of things Visible, to the Understanding
or Apprehending things that are Invisible."[71] With his God unable to be adequately
described through human language, the figurative becomes a means of mediating
spiritual experience. Metaphors, once again, are theologically charged.

Wesley was an avid reader of Browne, writing a lengthy abstract on Browne's
treatise, as well as recommending it to his followers for private reading.[72] However, he disagreed with Browne's belief that a direct encounter with the spiritual
world is impossible on earth. He counters Browne's argument by adapting Lockean epistemology and positing that there are "spiritual senses," analogous to bodily
senses, belonging to the soul, which are able to perceive spiritual objects. This idea
seems to be parodied in *The Spiritual Quixote*, where Wildgoose describes a soul
that kisses, drinks, and eats (*SQ*, 74).

The novel also targets Wesley's notion of "the natural man," who relies solely
on bodily senses and lacks spiritual senses. According to Wesley, the natural man
"is alive unto the world, and dead unto God," because the Word of God is dis-
cerned "by that spiritual sense, which in him was never yet awakened."[73] *The Spiritual Quixote* describes a world decidedly without spiritual senses where the means
for a direct experience of God, of the kind that Wesley describes and Wildgoose
seeks, are absent. To believe that there exist any senses other than the bodily ones—
that spiritual experience is so directly analogous to sensory experience—is, in *The
Spiritual Quixote*, to be a quixotic enthusiast like Wildgoose, and to refuse to
acknowledge the limits of metaphor and analogy. It is, again, to confuse the material impressions on corporeal senses for spiritual experiences.

That said, numerous sightseeing digressions in *The Spiritual Quixote* represent spiritual experiences as not impossible, even if spiritual senses are designated
a fiction. The tellingly named Miss Sainthill argues that there are biblical grounds
for enjoying nature; for example, David "always speaks with rapture of the beauties of Nature; of the magnificence of the heavenly bodies" (*SQ*, 396). Graves's own
sermons demarcate an appreciation of nature as religious: "A plain man, of good
sense, on contemplating the beauty and harmony of the creation, with evident
marks of wisdom and design in everything around him, would find no difficulty,
one should suppose, in acknowledging some great, intelligent, First Cause of all
things; the Creator and Governor of the world."[74] Graves and Miss Sainthill both
use what was known as the argument by design, which posits that the systematic
order of nature establishes a proof of divine creation.[75] Graves renders this argument in poetic form in his "Poetical Essay" *The Love of Order*, published in the
same year as *The Spiritual Quixote* (1773).[76] In *The Spiritual Quixote*, Wildgoose,

as his name implies, is represented as being on a wild goose chase, attempting perpetually to inscribe the "spiritual" in his language, when there are "evident marks of wisdom and design" in the natural world around him.

Given Wildgoose's mimetic attention to the frontispieces of the Puritanical literature he consumes, it makes sense to take note of the frontispieces Graves proposed for *The Spiritual Quixote*. A sketch Graves drew for a frontispiece proposed for volume 1 of the second edition depicts Wildgoose as not facing the prospect but gazing away from it, suggesting his enthusiasm turns him away from appreciating the natural environment.[77] Significantly, Graves's proposed frontispiece for volume 3 also stressed the natural environment: "A view amongst the rocks, in Dovedale" (figure 10).[78] *The Spiritual Quixote*'s ecologically infused religiosity is also explicit in an impassioned passage, early in Wildgoose's travels:

> There was an extensive prospect of the rich vale of Evesham, bounded at a distance by the Malvern hills. The towers and spires, which rose amongst the tufted trees, were strongly illuminated by the sloping rays of the sun; and the whole scene was enlivened by the music of the birds; the responsive notes of the thrushes from the neighbouring haw-thorns, and the thrilling strains of the sky-lark, who, as she soared towards the heavens, seemed to be chanting forth her matins to the great Creator of the universe.
>
> Wildgoose was touched with a kind of sympathy: and a ray of true devotion darting into his soul, he broke out in the words of Milton, with whom he had been much conversant—
>
> These are thy glorious works, Parent of good,
>
> (*SQ*, 42–43)[79]

This description of natural beauty, framed by church "spires," evidences a building rapture in a long, unbounded sentence, finally climaxing in Wildgoose's quotation of John Milton's *Paradise Lost* (1667). He quotes the passage where Adam and Eve, in Eden, praise their maker.[80] This passage is a rare instance in *The Spiritual Quixote* of Wildgoose's "soul" being described by the narrator as affected, rather than Wildgoose enthusiastically asserting it is so. In this passage, "the great Creator" seems to be mediated through nature, rather than, as in the case of Wildgoose's rhetoric, the spiritual being embodied through metaphor and directly encountered.

These issues of religion, quixotism, nature, and metaphor climax when Wildgoose visits his friend, Mr. Shenstone. William Shenstone is a historical person, who, like Wesley and Whitefield, is included as a character in the novel. A poet, he was famous for his landscape gardening and was an intimate friend and correspondent of Graves. The Shenstone in *The Spiritual Quixote*, like the historical Shenstone, has a property that attracts visitors due to the way its natural beauty has been "improved." Readers are kept in momentary suspense as to Wildgoose's

FIGURE 10 Sketch in a letter from Graves to James Dodsley, dated October 30, 1773. Bath Record Office: Local Studies.

opinion of Shenstone's garden. From the end of one chapter through the next, the third-person narration shifts from its typical perspective—tracing Wildgoose's thoughts and actions—to Shenstone's point of view (*SQ*, 330–331). For a few pages, Wildgoose suddenly becomes more elusive and mysterious. Mr. Shenstone wishes Tugwell and Wildgoose "goodnight" (*SQ*, 330), and at the beginning of the next chapter, it is morning. Between these two scenes—during the night, or in the space between the two chapters—Wildgoose destroys Mr. Shenstone's carefully maintained landscape.

Like Shenstone, the reader is ignorant of what Wildgoose has done, and then reads, simultaneously with Shenstone, the letter Wildgoose leaves: "You have forsaken the fountains of the living Lord; and hewn you out cisterns, broken cisterns, that will hold no water" (*SQ*, 331). Shenstone then goes outside, and discovers Wildgoose has vandalized his gardens. The frontispiece to the third volume of the second and later editions of *The Spiritual Quixote* feature this episode, depicting Wildgoose and Tugwell destroying one of Mr. Shenstone's statues (figure 11).[81] The nakedness of the statue might suggest that Wildgoose is attacking it because of its nudity. Wesley himself, though he enjoyed Shenstone's gardens, critiqued others such as Stourhead for its "statues with nudities."[82]

As for Wildgoose, his main motive in destroying the gardens seems to be his desire to literalize the biblical metaphor of broken cisterns he includes in Shenstone's letter. By forcing open Mr. Shenstone's sluices and emptying his reservoirs, Wildgoose ensures his words to Mr. Shenstone have more than mere figurative force. His actions directly invoke the *Retort* print, which began this chapter: the "Whitefield" who "authors" the epistle calls Foote a "cracked pot and not a chosen vessel," using pictures of crockery to signify "pot" and "vessel." When Shenstone looks at his gardens he sees that Wildgoose "had forced open his sluices, and emptied his reservoirs, so that, in a literal sense, his *cisterns could hold no water*" (*SQ*, 331). Wildgoose, it seems, is more enthusiastically preoccupied with literalizing and embodying the "sluice" metaphor rather than concerned with what his allegory might signify.

Here, as elsewhere, Wildgoose's quixotism manifests itself as a blurring of the already fluid boundaries between the metaphorical and the literal, the symbolic and the actual, the image and its interpretation. In Graves's novel, Wildgoose's spiritual discourse appears anachronistically at odds with the growing tendency in the eighteenth-century Anglican Church to disseminate a "practical" religion applicable to everyday life and, with it, an increasingly metaphorical interpretation to the Bible.

Alongside this concern with metaphor, *The Spiritual Quixote* makes repeated parallels between the religious enthusiast and the stereotype of the female quixotic

FRONTISPIECE Vol 3.

S Pages 27 & 28,

S Wale del,

C Grignion Sc,

FIGURE 11 Frontispiece to volume 3 of the second edition of *The Spiritual Quixote*, 1774. Beinecke Rare Book and Manuscript Library, Yale University.

reader. It suggests both are preoccupied with the concretized "husk" of images evoked by a text. The interanimation between quixotism and enthusiasm explored by *The Spiritual Quixote* continues and expands into the later part of the eighteenth century, when enthusiasm was identified not just with quixotic religious zeal but with any kind of passion that seemed to threaten the orderliness of society.[83] Elizabeth Hamilton's *Memoirs of Modern Philosophers* continues this preoccupation with enthusiastic, materialist misreading. Wildgoose is quixotically preoccupied by images rather than their meaning, something that is also true of Bridgetina, a character in *Memoirs*. However, Bridgetina takes this kind of misreading one step further. She is not so much impressed by the images painted by metaphorical language, but is instead so enthusiastically entrapped in the corporeal that she cannot go beyond the material text, the form of the words and phrases. Rather than become lost in images, she becomes lost in clusters of words. Taken together, the two novels suggest religious enthusiasm and atheism are two sides of the same quixotic coin: both produce indulgent reading practices and quixotically conflate somatic and "spiritual" impressions.

CITATIONAL QUIXOTISM IN *MEMOIRS*
OF MODERN PHILOSOPHERS

BRIDGETINA BOTHERIM, the anti-heroine of Elizabeth Hamilton's satirical novel *Memoirs of Modern Philosophers* (1800), is a quixotic consumer of "modern philosophy" and sentimental novels. Reading a new novel and pleased with its style, Bridgetina memorizes passages from the book, and luxuriates in the sound of her spoken voice: "[A]nxious to dress her thoughts on the present occasion to the very best advantage, she had retired to refresh her memory with a few of the most striking passages; she now returned fraught with three long speeches, so ardent, so expressive, so full of energy and emphasis, that it would have grieved a saint to have had them lost" (*MP*, 216). Hamilton never provides the title of the novel Bridgetina reads, but Bridgetina's subsequent quotations from the work identify it as Mary Hays's controversial, semi-autobiographical novel *Memoirs of Emma Courtney* (1796). Yet, though Hays's novel is parodied pointedly, the elision of its title signals that the bulk of the satire is directed at Bridgetina's reading practice rather than the novel she consumes. Unlike the conventional silent novel reader, Bridgetina's reading is an act of memorization and performance; she gathers "striking passages" to voice, commit to memory, and voice yet again. In company, her talk is thick with quotation. For instance, at one point she peppers her conversation with words taken almost verbatim from William Godwin's *Enquirer* (1797). She repeats Godwin's description of an intelligent man walking down the street. Bridgetina states that the intelligent man "gives full scope to his imagination. He laughs and cries. *Unindebted to the suggestions of surrounding objects, his whole soul is employed. In imagination he declaims or describes; impressed with the deepest sympathy, or elevated to the loftiest rapture*" (*MP*, 256).[1] Here, as elsewhere in *Memoirs*, Hamilton uses italics to signal ostensibly direct quotations, and to highlight, typographically, the incongruity of particular quotations and citations. Bridgetina's interlocutor (or, more precisely, her audience) Mr. Sardon is impressed "at the fluency of her expression," but when he "begged to know" how the wise and dull man "were to be distinguished in the country [. . .] Bridgetina was soon run aground. She had gone to the very end of her lesson" (*MP*, 257). She is thus only able to repeat "her lesson" and recite phrases from Godwin's text, unable to grasp the basic principles of what she is saying and deduce how a "wise man" in the country might behave. Bridgetina's propensity for quotation is acknowledged by almost every critic who has written on *Memoirs*. Joe Bray, for instance, notes "[i]t is not so much what she has read which makes her a pitiful laughing-stock, as the way she has read," memorizing quotation after quotation with no ability to paraphrase or generalize the arguments of the texts she consumes.[2]

This chapter will build on these observations about the importance of quotation to Bridgetina's reading practice through examining what her citational quixotism says about quixotic impressions at the turn of the century. Bridgetina's quixotism is central to *Memoirs*: her character played a pivotal role in *Memoirs'* reception. The *Anti-Jacobin Review and Magazine*'s review of *Memoirs* (September 1800) characterizes Bridgetina as "the heroine" of the novel.[3] When the novel was translated into French, its title was *Bridgetina, ou les Philosophes Modernes* (1802). The translation's title proclaims the centrality of Bridgetina to *Memoirs* and *Memoirs'* popularity.[4]

Bridgetina's quixotic, quotation-impelled reading is also highly politicized, and fundamental to the novel's response to the French Revolution. It is through Bridgetina's citational reading practice that British radicalism is yoked to older formulations of religious enthusiasm. Here, atheism is characterized along similar lines to Methodism in Richard Graves's *The Spiritual Quixote* (chapter 4), as materialist and enthusiastic. In this way, *Memoirs* affirms Simon Schaffer's argument that anti-revolutionary writing used the ostensible materialism of radicals' philosophies of mind to associate radicalism with older "enthusiastic" superstitions: "New enlightenment was but old illumination."[5]

Charles Lucas's novel *The Infernal Quixote* (1801) is a case in point. This Minerva Press, anti-revolutionary novel explicitly depicts "modern philosophy" as the heir to Graves's portrait of Methodist "enthusiasm."[6] The very title of Lucas's novel signals its reworking of Graves's novel, and Lucas repeatedly parallels "irreligion" and "modern philosophy" with Methodism throughout. Rattle, a character in *The Infernal Quixote*, exclaims: "What says the Methodist? 'The blacker the sinner, the brighter the saint!' The modern Philosopher will tell you 'The greater the villain, the better the citizen.'"[7] Rattle continues, stating that "[t]he author of the Spiritual Quixote" spoke of "the religious enthusiasm, ere the irreligious was yet matured."[8] The narrative follows this remark with "RATTLE'S DOUBLE ORATION" (figure 12), an interpolation of a "paper" that Rattle takes from his pocketbook,

crats; Sinners Aristocrats; for Satan,
read Tyrants; and for more sacred
names, take Nature and so forth.

RATTLE'S DOUBLE ORATION.

" *Satan   and   his   imps   of*
" *Tyrants   and   their   ministers   of*
darkness   beloved
tyranny are on the watch, my *fellow*

Brethren,
Citizens, to fasten you in the eternal

Hell
chains of *Slavery.*   Rouse, be vigilant;

garments of Hope,
put on the *cap of Liberty,* seize on the

shield

FIGURE 12 Rattle's "Double Oration" in volume 2 of *The Infernal Quixote*, 1801.
Beinecke Rare Book and Manuscript Library, Yale University.

which takes up four pages of the first edition of the novel. "RATTLE'S DOUBLE ORATION" presents the discourse of Methodist "enthusiasm" and that of "modern philosophy" as interchangeable, differing only according to their preferred synonyms. They are two italicized oratory options, stacked vertically in the same speech: two registers on a single score. The "DOUBLE ORATION" is Rattle's final proof that religious enthusiasm and "modern philosophy" are two variations of the same tune.

A year earlier than Lucas, Hamilton makes a similar point through the characterization of the radical philosopher, Mr. Myope. Formerly a leader of multiple religious sects, he has little difficulty transposing his religious enthusiasm into zeal for reason and radical philosophy (*MP*, 145). The anonymously published *Memoirs* was even attributed to Graves, the author of *The Spiritual Quixote*. The *British Critic* (October 1800) speculates that *Memoirs* being printed in Bath, near Graves's rectory in Claverton, prompted this attribution.[9] Yet the ascription of *Memoirs* to Graves also suggestively frames *Memoirs* as a sequel of sorts to *The Spiritual Quixote*, and underscores structural resemblances between the two quixotic novels, including Hamilton's treatment of radical philosophy as a variant of religious enthusiasm.

Memoirs not only represents the French Revolution and atheism as signifying a societal relapse into enthusiasm but associates the "modern philosophers'" citational reading practice with their materialist enthusiasm. Key to this is a distinction *Memoirs* draws between the materiality of a word—its sound, its letters, its look—from its meaning(s). This is unlike *The Spiritual Quixote*, where numerous puns point to the difficulty of separating meanings from the material stuff of language. In *Memoirs*, Bridgetina is incapable of even Wildgoose's valorization of corporealized metaphors evacuated of spiritual "meaning" (chapter 4). Instead, she is preoccupied not with the images words evoke but with their visual and aural patterns.

Memoirs' strict distinction between the sign and the signified is pivotal to both its conceptualization of quixotic impressions and its decoupling of Bridgetina's quixotic reading practice from philosophical formulations of subjectivity. Although, or perhaps because, Bridgetina's quixotism is implicated in larger sociopolitical problems, *Memoirs* ultimately presents her citational quixotism as more of a politicized aberration than symptomatic of a broader problem of subjectivity or epistemology. Through their habit of quotation, the modern philosophers follow the "letter" of the texts they consume, rather than understanding the "spirit" of their reading. Extending beyond Wildgoose's confused Methodist metaphorics, the radical philosophers in Hamilton's novel are wholly preoccupied with the material textures of words.

Crucially, Bridgetina's quixotic citations can be read alongside developments in print technology. For the most part, during the eighteenth century, if a work sold well, the new edition needed to be set all over again in movable type, and once again proofed and corrected, with very few printers having enough type to set an entire text, and store it while printing another work.[10] Yet the end of the eighteenth century saw the commercial adoption of "stereotyping," or the casting of printing plates from plaster of paris molds. "Clichage" became the name for the same process applied to the duplication of wood-engraved illustrations and ornaments, and its result was a "cliché."[11] The "cliché," passing through metaphor, became, in French and English, a word for phrases repeated unthinkingly: an apt description of Bridgetina's quixotic practice. The printer's impression therefore is etymologically yoked to the cliché: set material that is stored and ready to quickly disseminate. Bridgetina's reproduction of memorized phrases comes from a point in time when the reduplication of set text was easier and cheaper than it had ever been.

QUOTATION AND QUIXOTIC REPRODUCTION

Bridgetina's reproductive reading practice evokes *Polly Honeycombe*'s analogies between quixotic performance and the process of extraction (chapter 2). As I argued in the second chapter of this book, Polly's character, dependent on the books she consumes, renders her analogous to an "extract," whether it be an extract from a list of novels available at a circulating library or the portion of the book she reads in the opening scene of the farce. Similarly, the extensive quotation of radical philosophical texts by modern philosophers in *Memoirs* signals the way their characters are bound to the symbolic systems of the material texts they consume. This is particularly the case for Bridgetina, who, in a potted autobiography she narrates to her fellow misreader, Julia, stresses how she is marked by imprints from fragmented texts: "My mother got a packet of brown snuff from London by the mail-coach; it was wrapped in two proof sheets of the quarto edition of the Political Justice. I eagerly snatched up the paper, and notwithstanding the frequent fits of sneezing it occasioned, from the quantity of snuff contained in every fold, I greedily devoured its contents. I read and sneezed, and sneezed and read, till the germ of philosophy began to fructify my soul. From that moment I became a philosopher and need not inform you of the important consequences" (*MP*, 176). Bridgetina's pronouncement that she becomes a "philosopher" after reading two sheets of wrapping paper rather than the whole book is fitting, given her tendency to privilege pieces of texts, rather than their entirety. Meanwhile, her description of her reading as sneezing, comically suggests how her reading involves an automatic absorption of the text, as though she has, without conscious will, inhaled the text through her nose like snuff. Bridgetina's imbibing of Godwin and self-proclaimed development into a "philosopher" becomes a process of mindless inhalation. Its corporeality is also emphasized through Bridgetina's use of the word "germ," which, Richard De Ritter notes, potentially draws on the word's connotations with venereal disease.[12]

Bridgetina's account characterizes the origins of her quixotism as both material and maternal. Her wet nurse had only just learned how to read, when "from one of those associations so natural to the human mind, she conceived a tender passion for her instructor" (*MP*, 175). The nurse quixotically conflates her passion for literature with her tutor in a situation that distinctly echoes one of Bridgetina's favorite texts, Jean-Jacques Rousseau's *La nouvelle Héloïse* (1761). This is one of the manifold ways *Memoirs* self-consciously responds to and rewrites *La nouvelle Héloïse*, with Hamilton drawing on Rousseauian sensibility's already established associations with French Revolutionary radicalism.[13] Bridgetina then portrays herself as imbibing quixotism via her wet nurse's milk: "With her milk I greedily absorbed the delicious poison which circulated through every vein; and love of literature, and *importunate sensibility*, became from thenceforth the predominant features of my character" (*MP*, 175). Within Bridgetina's description of her nurse's milk as forming her "character" she seems to echo her nurse's conflation of the intellectual and the erotic. *Memoirs* uses already established associations between the maternal and the quixotic (see previous chapters), and reworks these connections in Bridgetina's autobiographical description of a formative imbibing of a radicalized sensibility.

Throughout the novel, Bridgetina uses her citational reading practice to attempt to subvert gender roles. She proclaims, "[W]hy should there be any distinction of sex? [. . .] [A]re not women formed with powers and energies capable of perfectibility?" (*MP*, 101–102). Bridgetina's error here is not a denial of sex-specific virtues, for the exemplary Dr. Orwell states that Christ's "morality was addressed to the judgment without distinction of sex" (*MP*, 103). However, despite the requirement for men and women to cultivate both "purity and humility in the heart," Hamilton endorses the notion that domestic female duties are assigned to women "by nature and Providence" (*MP*, 103). Harriet Orwell, a model daughter and domestic woman, and an idealized counterpoint to the quixotic Bridgetina and Julia, ensures her reading does not interfere with her feminine tasks. She listens to David Hume's *History of England* (1754–62) read aloud, by an "orphan girl she had herself instructed," in the company of her aunt and sister: her reading practice is ostentatiously sociable, communitarian, and charitable. It is integrated, rather than separate from the "fulfilment of every social as well as every domestic duty" (*MP*, 73).[14] Contrastingly, Bridgetina reads instead of helping her mother cook (*MP*, 37). By the end of the novel, Bridgetina is forced to embrace what are represented as appropriate feminine duties. Instead of migrating to Africa as she planned, she remains in her mother's home and learns to enjoy "the consciousness of contributing to the happiness of a parent" (*MP*, 387). Her reformation *is* her re-integration to the domestic sphere. She attempts to use "modern philosophy" to escape the constraints imposed on her by her appearance and her gender, but such attempts are persistently frustrated.

Her quixotism instead connects her to long-standing female stereotypes: Patricia Parker states the "oldest topoi of misogyny is the fabled inability of women to keep that particular orifice [the mouth] shut."[15] Parker notes the long-standing cultural associations between the open female mouth and the vagina, and we can see this connection persisting in *Memoirs* through the link it forges between Bridgetina's copious speech and her sexual availability.[16] When she cries, "Ah! wretched woman, restrained by the cruel fetters of decorum" (*MP*, 102), Gary Kelly observes that she enacts her feminism by interrupting Henry, who has just been speaking, and undermines her own argument by hinting at her undeclared passion for Henry.[17] Bridgetina's act of speaking out of turn, as much as what she says, articulates her impatience with social "fetters" on her desire.

The link between Bridgetina's open mouth and her sexuality is further exemplified when she rehearses her speech to Henry, declaring her love. Bridgetina runs over

> a sort of index taken of the contents, which she thus read aloud, while the maid cleared the table after dinner. *Moral sensibility, thinking sensibility, importunate sensibility; mental sensation, pernicious state of protracted and uncertain feeling; congenial sympathy, congenial sentiment, congenial ardour; delicious emotions, melancholy emotions, frenzied emotions; tender feeling, energetic feeling, sublimised feeling; the germ, the bud, and the full-grown fruits of the general utility, &c. &c.* "Yes," cried she, in extacy, when she had finished the contents, "this will do! Here is argument irresistible."
>
> (*MP*, 308)

Here, lexical meanings are emptied into the "extacy" of literary effect; her list reduces her words to tonal units. Bridgetina concludes, "Here is argument irresistible," having no doubt that the words themselves, voiced by her, will put Henry in a state that mirrors her own orgasmic "extacy." That she receives an erotic pleasure from hearing herself speak philosophical jargon is also seen in the way the list ends in "*&c. &c.*," which could have potential bawdy implications (see chapter 2). After all, Bridgetina's speech to Henry involves her offering him her body. The "*&c.*" of course has other meanings, and its use here also suggests that the rest of the words are so formulaic that they do not even need to be repeated, and that Bridgetina's speech continues to such a length that it exceeds the page. Bridgetina's desire for Henry produces a seemingly unrestrainable array of words, especially as what she reads aloud is just "a sort of index" to her speech. In short, this passage forcefully conjoins female sexuality with feminized textual plenitude. Bridgetina's final phrases even suggest an engorgement: "*the germ, the bud, and the full-grown fruits of the general utility*" (*MP*, 308).[18]

Hamilton continues the association between textual proliferation and the female body in a footnote to Bridgetina's ecstatic list: "Note, for the benefit of Novel-writers.—We here generously present the fair manufacturers in this line with a set of phrases, which, if carefully mixed up with a handful of story, a pretty quantity of moonshine, an old house of any kind, so that it be in sufficient decay, and well tenanted with bats and owls, and two or three ghosts, will make a couple of very neat volumes. Or should the sentimental be preferred to the descriptive, it is only leaving out the ghosts, bats, owls, and moonlight, and the above phrases will season any tender tale to taste" (*MP*, 308n27). The copiousness of Bridgetina's speech is mirrored by the suggestion of a proliferation of novels springing from her list. Such satirical "recipes" were not uncommon in the period, targeting both formulaic novels and the female reader craving predictable sensations.[19] Novel writing in this passage is a feminized, commercial industry of "fair manufacturers" (*MP*, 308n27). These formulaic novels are implicitly contrasted to *Memoirs* itself—its prefatory material represents its publication as being motivated by a moral, rather than a commercial, imperative—it is written to forward the "cause of religion and virtue" (*MP*, 35).

Hamilton's condemnation of female novelists is necessarily complicated by her own gender. The lengthy, satirical footnote itself, regardless of its content, serves to separate *Memoirs* from the conventional novels—and Hamilton, from the women writers—it satirizes. W. M. Verhoeven argues that "the intrusive body of bibliographical reference, critical comments and polemical asides that the [anti-Jacobin] authors cram into the footnotes of their novels become part of a conscious strategy to undermine a 'suspension of disbelief,' or even any reading of their novels *as novels*."[20] The footnotes prevent the text being read simply as an absorbing narrative, and instead give the impression of something more than a novel. Footnotes, used predominantly in such "masculine" textual productions as edited classical texts, natural history, and classical history, become a strategy Hamilton uses to construct an unfeminine authorial persona, separating *Memoirs* from "mere" novels, and also from Bridgetina's citational monologues.[21]

In other ways *Memoirs* consistently foregrounds its own constructedness. Like *The Spiritual Quixote*, *Memoirs* is represented in the prefatory material as a found manuscript. An introduction by a fictive editor, Geoffry Jarvis, describes how he has found a dead author's manuscript at an inn and sets forth his reasons for publishing the novel. In the main text, Jarvis continues to speak to the reader via footnotes. Susan B. Egenolf has demonstrated the paradoxical centrality of the peripheral to Hamilton's two other novels, *Translation of the Letters of a Hindoo Rajah* (1796) and *The Cottagers of Glenburnie* (1808).[22] *Memoirs* similarly stresses textual peripheries. The main narrative does not begin until midway through chapter 5, as the manuscript's first fifty pages have "been torn off to kindle the morning fires" (*MP*, 35). This device overtly obstructs the reader's immediate immersion in the main narrative, as well as ironically drawing parallels between *Memoirs* and the incomplete texts that structure Bridgetina's quixotism. The "lost" opening chapters of *Memoirs* also stress the materiality of the written and printed page, and the multiple uses to which texts can be put. This preoccupation is continued through the main narrative's description of Bridgetina's fetishization of the sonic performativity of print.

Hamilton uses such paratextual devices to distance the authorial voice of *Memoirs* from both Bridgetina and the stereotypical "fair manufacturers" of novels. The prefatory material presents her work as masculine writing: originally written by a male author and found, edited, and mediated to the public by another man. Throughout *Memoirs* the reader is reminded of the ostensible maleness of the author. At one point, the narrator facetiously anticipates a housewife's response to the narratorial assertions about domestic organization: "[W]hat nonsense these *men authors* speak!" (*MP*, 73). So successful was Hamilton at ventriloquizing a male authorial voice that *Memoirs*—as I discussed above—was attributed to Graves. The first edition was published without any name on the title page, but with the prefatory material announcing Jarvis to be the editor. *Memoirs* therefore occupies a space between anonymity and (male) pseudonymity. Hamilton owned the authorship, and explained the reason for her anonymity in the advertisement to the third edition, writing that "prejudice against the known opinions, or even the *sex*, of a writer may unwittingly bias the reader's mind" (*MP*, 30).[23]

Throughout *Memoirs*, Bridgetina's citational reading is juxtaposed with the author's more adept use of quotation. The majority of the chapters are prefaced by epigraphs, which are used, Kelly and Claire Grogan note, to establish Hamilton's wide reading as opposed to Bridgetina's narrow consumption of "[n]ovels and meta-physics" (*MP*, 38).[24] For instance, Hamilton prefaces one chapter with a quote from Samuel Butler's anti-Puritan satirical mock-epic *Hudibras* (1662–77), which adapts Cervantes's *Don Quixote*. The epigraph reads, in part:

> "—He was a shrewd philosopher,
> "And had read every text and gloss over.
> "Whate'er the crabbed'st author hath,
> "He understood b'implicit faith.
> . . .
> "All which he understood by rote,
> "And as occasion serv'd, wou'd quote."
>   (*MP*, 316)

This quotation is about quotations. By referencing a seventeenth-century mock-epic about rebellion, Hamilton connects "English Jacobins" with Puritan rebels and regicides.[25] Importantly, the epigraph forges an association between Sir Hudi-bras and the modern philosophers through the way their reading centers on the act of quotation. Both Bridgetina and Hudibras do not understand what they read. Both have a misplaced, semi-religious "faith" in the text and use rote learning to disguise their lack of knowledge. Bridgetina's extensive quotations disrupt social gatherings, reduce conversations to monologues, and bore her interlocutors (*MP*, 45, 166, 286), and Hudibras is implied to have a Bridgetina-like propensity to quote "as occasion serv'd." The *Hudibras* quotation is carefully chosen to complement the chapter that follows, which concentrates on Bridgetina's pose of a "shrewd phi-losopher." Thus the chapter epigraph invites the reader to contrast Bridgetina's and Hudibras's quotational practice with the author's.

The problem with Bridgetina, then, is not simply that she quotes, but that she does so without comprehending what it is she is saying. Harriet states that the subjects Bridgetina and the modern philosophers speak of are topics "which the mind has never thoroughly mastered. They will be found to have been driven into that little corner of the brain, which is said to be the store-house of memory, by the arch witch imagination; and driven thither in such confusion too, in such hig-gledy piggledy order, that they have never passed under the close examination of judgment; and pop out they come again, just in the same manner that they got it" (*MP*, 166). Harriet draws upon the Lockean description of the eighteenth-century subject as a collector, accumulating experiences. Imagination is an "arch witch," preventing a jumbled collection of words from being examined by "judgment." It might seem paradoxical that the act of (mindless) quotation is blamed on the power of the imagination, but it makes sense given the traditional opposition of the imagination to reason and "reality" and its association with the corporeal. Harriet presents Bridgetina's manner of quotation as a somatic act, a kind of verbal excretion: "pop out they come again, just in the same manner that they got it" (*MP*, 166). The modern philosophers, in particular Bridgetina, are unable to subject their reading to critical scrutiny and are instead in thrall to the urges of their fallible bodies.

JACOBINISM, ANTI-JACOBINISM, AND QUIXOTISM

Before interrogating further the compelling ways *Memoirs* reacts against radical philosophy and uses and modifies particular anti-Jacobin tropes, the extent the anti-Jacobin label is applicable to *Memoirs* must be addressed. Much scholarship on *Memoirs* is focused on arguing whether *Memoirs* is or is not an anti-Jacobin novel. Anti-Jacobin novels were political novels, written in the aftermath of the French Revolution, ostensibly to counter the threat of radical politics, radicalized sensibility, and, above all, radical political novels. Given the vast range of different anti-revolutionary positions, the usefulness of the term "anti-Jacobin" is queried by critics such as Miriam L. Wallace, Claudia L. Johnson, and John Bugg. They contend that the labels "Jacobin" and "anti-Jacobin" risk engrafting a simplistic dichotomy onto a complex, shifting spectrum and, moreover, encourage a reading of these novels as political diatribes, rather than complex literary texts.[26] Yet M. O. Grenby asserts that the reception history of novels like *Memoirs* demonstrates a public awareness of two literary camps, conservative and radical.[27] Arguably, *Memoirs* both strategically adopts the form of an anti-Jacobin novel and contains politically progressive elements. It can be convincingly demonstrated, as Grogan does in consecutive chapters of the same book, that *Memoirs* is both anti-Jacobin and progressive.[28]

Despite its more ambiguous content, *Memoirs* has the outward appearance of an anti-Jacobin novel: its title identifies itself as such and invites its audience to class it among more unambiguously anti-Jacobin works, like George Walker's *The Vagabond* (1799), Jane West's *A Tale of the Times* (1799), Edward Du Bois's *St. Godwin* (1800), and Lucas's *The Infernal Quixote*. In other ways, it adopts the trappings of an anti-Jacobin novel, satirizing Godwin and Hays, caricaturing new philosophy, and attacking the French Revolution. It does so largely through quotation: a generic feature of the anti-Jacobin novel, as well as a vital part of the quintessential anti-Jacobin publication, the *Anti-Jacobin Review and Magazine*.[29] Anti-Jacobin novels often extract passages from what they identify as "Jacobin" texts to represent the strength and the dangerous nature of the "Jacobin" cause and thus establish the pressing need for anti-Jacobin writing, yet quotation in *Memoirs* has a centrality even exceeding that of a typical anti-Jacobin novel.[30]

Memoirs was identified as anti-Jacobin by many of Hamilton's contemporaries, for instance, the *Anti-Jacobin Review and Magazine* (September, December, 1800) published a lengthy two-part commendatory review, containing detailed summaries of the plot and extended excerpts from the novel.[31] A review in the *British Critic* (October 1800), asserts *Memoirs* has "the same design" as Walker's virulently anti-Jacobin *The Vagabond*, a comparison continued in the French edition of *The Vagabond*, where the translator expresses the hope that the same positive reception bestowed on Bridgetina will be granted to Walker's characters.[32] Hamilton's reasons for making *Memoirs* identifiably anti-Jacobin could include the way the genre provided a "screen of correctness" that allowed writers, and in particular female writers, to use patriotism and the desire to benefit the national cause as an excuse for authoring novels.[33] The conservative outlay of *Memoirs* aids Hamilton's respectability, but also gives Hamilton leeway to be more subversive within the book itself.[34] Perhaps more pertinently, by 1800, there was a clear market for anti-Jacobin novels, providing a commercial imperative for *Memoirs* to assume the appearance of an anti-Jacobin novel, whatever its inward complexities.[35] To recognize that *Memoirs* consciously situates itself among anti-Jacobin novels is not to deny *Memoirs'* complexity or occasional radicalism. Moreover, even the anti-Jacobin novels that are unambivalent in their politics are complex in their parody, recycling the words, characters, and plot devices of the "Jacobin" texts they satirize.

Anti-Jacobin novels share the deep suspicion of novel reading prevalent throughout the century, as well as the more historically specific contempt for Jacobinism. They persistently associate Jacobinism with novel reading: fiction has the power to convert the vulnerable reader to radicalism through appealing to their imagination.[36] Novel reading, already associated with seduction, corruption, and female domestic disobedience, becomes now directly tied to political instability. West, speaking of herself in the third person, writes in the anti-revolutionary novel *A Tale of the Times*: "[A]s the most fashionable, and perhaps most successful, way of vending pernicious sentiments has been through the medium of books of entertainment, she [the author] conceives it not only allowable, but necessary, to repel the enemy's insidious attacks with similar weapons."[37] Novels might be dangerous, spreading "pernicious sentiments," but they are necessary weapons in the war against Jacobin thought that West represents herself as fighting. Similarly, the introduction to *Memoirs* states that it is written to counter "[t]he ridiculous point of view in which some of the opinions [are] conveyed to the young and unthinking through the medium of philosophical novels" (*MP*, 36–37), and that *Memoirs* provides "an excellent antidote to the poison; calculated to make an impression upon those to whom serious disquisitions would have been addressed in vain" (*MP*, 37). West and Hamilton blame radicalism and immorality on novel reading, while claiming that both can be countered by their novels.

We have seen how a tension between the disparagement and an exploitation of a form is typical of quixotic narratives. *The Spiritual Quixote* is pervaded by the language of Wesley and Whitefield, while *The Female Quixote* is suffused with the discourse of romance. Anti-Jacobin novels are similarly built around the "Jacobin" tropes they ridicule.[38] Bridgetina's unsuccessful pursuit of Henry Sydney echoes *Emma Courtney*'s main plot (which, like *Memoirs*, was published by G. G. and J. Robinson), where Emma pursues the uninterested Augustus.[39] April London and Eleanor Ty both argue that this extensive intertextuality is an obstacle to successful satire.[40] Yet all parodies, by incorporating the discourses they critique, are dependent on what they seem to despise, for parody, as Linda Hutcheon puts it, is "repetition with critical difference."[41] The quotations may be "double-edged" and "paradoxical," but quixotic novels are paradoxical and double-edged by definition, and the resisting reader can always resist. More interesting, then, is the way the quotations are presented, the effect they have on the form of the book, and the way they are associated in *Memoirs* with a mechanical, secular thoughtlessness.

Emma Courtney's centrality to Bridgetina's quixotism is a case in point. Emma Courtney can herself be read as a quixotic reader, emulating sentimental literature, especially Rousseau's *La nouvelle Héloïse*.[42] Bridgetina, then, is implicated in an imitative chain, like that which Arabella proffers in *The Female Quixote* (chapter 1). While the example of Rousseau's heroine encourages Bridgetina to make sexual advances toward Henry, she uses *Emma Courtney* to guide her behavior when her advances are refused. Emma relentlessly pursues Augustus, so Bridgetina chases Henry with similar avidity. When, like Augustus, Henry returns her letters unanswered, Bridgetina speaks in the vocabulary of Hays's novel (*MP*, 310).[43] *Memoirs* pastiches and parodies "Jacobin" texts in a way that pointedly emphasizes how the misreading heroine mindlessly follows—and quotes from—characters' "bad" examples without interrogating what these examples might teach about morality, or, in Emma's case, about misreading.

The connections between quixotism and anti-Jacobinism are perhaps most overt in Lucas's *The Infernal Quixote*, where the villainous Marauder is the titular "Infernal Quixote." In a footnote, the narrator connects a "diabolist" type of modern philosopher to quixotry: "Some people, without Judge or Jury, condemn them at once as CACODÆMONS; perhaps the salving term of INFERNAL QUIXOTES may suit them, as it seems the fashion of the present day to rank all our assassins and self-murderers under the general name of MADMEN."[44] Here, "Quixote" becomes an ironically generous term to describe someone far worse. Grenby describes the title's designation of Marauder as a "Quixote" as ironic, given the way Marauder is not "naïve" or idealistic: "The novel might, with less irony, have been called 'The Infernal Machiavel.'"[45] Alternatively, Dragoş Ivana asserts Marauder possesses quixotic "rebelliousness."[46] While I would agree with Ivana that quixotism is more than an issue of naïveté or idealism, it is very difficult to categorize Marauder as a quixotic misreader. His vision of the world is not stamped by a particular philosophy, system, or genre. He mercurially moves between embracing aristocratic privilege and agitating for democracy, between being a Catholic and arguing against religion, depending on what best suits his quest for power and wealth.[47]

Instead, a more typical quixote exists in the character of Emily Bellaire, a young woman Marauder corrupts by recommending her to read Mary Wollstonecraft's *A Vindication of the Rights of Woman* (1792), "the celebrated works of Rousseau," and "[m]any other original French Novels."[48] Just as Marauder is a recognizable anti-Jacobin "type," the unscrupulous libertine who uses the language of radical philosophy to seduce vulnerable women, Emily becomes, through his reading recommendations, another such "type": the character who is duped by her reading and the rhetoric of the new philosophy, "[t]he emancipated girl convinced of her right to pre-marital sexual intercourse," who has to learn the error of her ways before the novel's end.[49] Marauder's reading recommendations, and his marking up of select passages, are part of his "ingenious stratagems" that render Emily vulnerable to seduction.[50]

Julia in *Memoirs* is a similar character to Emily. Her reading results in her viewing the world through a quixotic lens. She reads Rousseau's *La nouvelle Héloïse*, and the model of Rousseau's heroine, the similarly named Julie, prepares her for seduction by the French libertine Vallaton. The portrayal of Bridgetina's quixotism also draws on established anti-Jacobin and anti-novel tropes, but modifies and extends them. To a degree, Bridgetina's misreading has conventional results, including her refusal to conform to the role of the dutiful domestic woman and daughter. Yet, unlike Julia, Bridgetina's misreading stems from her narcissism. Katherine Binhammer accurately describes the issue: Bridgetina's "soliloquizing—living in a world in which only her own voice exists—figures the problem of the way she reads."[51] Bridgetina's reading is ultimately solipsistic rather than sociable. She seeks not an interlocutor, but an audience, and repeatedly proves to be incapable of having a conversation about her reading. She reads with the goal of regurgitating texts as quotations. Unlike Julia, and Lucas's Emily, whose views of the world are warped by their reading, Bridgetina reads to speak.

"A SLAVE TO THE LETTER AND A STRANGER TO THE SPIRIT": QUOTATION AND THE NEW TESTAMENT

The Christianity advocated in *Memoirs* fuels its anti-Jacobin stance, with the novel relentlessly reproving the atheism espoused by the modern philosophers. At the same time, the religion endorsed by the novel also problematizes its anti-Jacobinism because *Memoirs* advocates a broad Christianity invested in acts of practical benevolence and dismisses theological difference.[52] Contrastingly, Anti-Jacobinism generally involves a fervent loyalty to the established Church and a deep suspicion of dissenters. Tellingly, the *Anti-Jacobin Review* wrote repeatedly against dissenters, while *The Infernal Quixote*, as we have seen, represents Methodism as an earlier version of "Jacobinism."[53] However, though Hamilton also connects enthusiasm with "Jacobinism," she not only tolerates dissenters but represents them as being as virtuous, as pious, and as sensible as members of the Church of England.[54] The dissenting Dr. Orwell is as much an exemplary character as Mr. Sydney, an Anglican. The two clergymen enjoy a friendship "which received no interruption from the difference of their opinions in some speculative points" (*MP*, 43). Theological differences are unimportant, as both "reverend gentlemen" are "pious, unaffected, and sincere. The minds of neither were narrowed by party zeal" (*MP*, 43). Their respective children, Harriet and Henry, even marry at the end of the novel. Hamilton also differs tentatively from the typical anti-Jacobin treatment of women who have or are forced into sex outside marriage. Geraldine, for instance, in West's *A Tale of the Times*, is raped by Fitzosborne after he persuades her to leave home, and she dies from remorse afterward.[55] Grogan observes that Hamilton, unlike West, does not depict female transgressions as irreversible and ignominious deaths as inevitable.[56] For example, the character Mrs. Fielding founds a refuge for "destitute females," which offers cast-out women shelter and the opportunity to be rehabilitated into society (*MP*, 301).[57]

The New Testament's opposition between the "letter" and "spirit" of the law becomes a framework within which *Memoirs* opposes a stricter, more conservative treatment of the "fallen" woman and a more humane alternative. Though the pregnant Julia does eventually and conventionally die, Hamilton critiques those who would not help her, or other "destitute females." The "ruined" Julia says to Harriet, who is trying to comfort her,

> In retirement, deep retirement, will I bury myself from the notice of the world. Even from you, my kind, my estimable friend—even from you must I hide myself; lest your fair fame should suffer by your deigning to pity such a wretch as I. Oh, I am indeed a wretch!

"Have I not steep'd a mother's couch in tears,
"And ting'd a father's dying cheek with shame?"
Oh, for me there is no comfort.

(*MP*, 368)

Harriet answers indignantly:

And think you, Julia, that I am a slave to the *letter*, and a stranger to the *spirit* of virtue! That you have erred, I regret; but that you are sensible of your error, gives you a claim not only to my esteem, but my admiration. [. . .] Amply, I am assured, shall your future life compensate the fault of inexperienced youth.

(*MP*, 368)

When Harriet assures Julia that she will be welcomed back by her friends, by all who are good and virtuous, Julia answers Harriet with a quotation from an elegy by William Shenstone, titled "Describing the Sorrow of an Ingenuous Mind on the Melancholy Event of a Licentious Amour" (1764).[58] The poem describes a seduced woman's estrangement from the world and from nature. She eventually drowns and dies. Harriet will have none of this: "think you, Julia, that I am a slave to the *letter*, and a stranger to the *spirit* of virtue!" (*MP*, 368). Harriet commends Julia's remorse, but rejects the idea that her friend should be given up altogether. For Harriet, to abandon Julia would involve being a "slave to the *letter*," or respecting the appearance of virtue rather than being genuinely so.

The biblical origins of the italicized "*letter*" and "*spirit*" deserve a closer examination here. "[S]lave to the *letter*" implies a fidelity to an abstract, moral system of behavior, precisely what *Memoirs* accuses the modern philosophers of doing: they take quotation for thought. A representation of "modern philosophy" as being faithful to the "letter" rather than the "spirit" is also common to anti-Jacobin novels, where "Jacobin" thought, whether it be secular materialism or Dissenting theology, is represented as a cold, rigid system, followed by its adherents at the expense of both common sense and basic humanity.[59] Anti-Jacobins frequently cite the passages of Godwin's *Political Justice* that seem to demonstrate his philosophy as an unfeeling system.[60] *Memoirs* similarly portrays Godwinian philosophy as sacrificing virtuous affections for an abstract system through the philosophers' frequently articulated reverence for the "general good" versus familial bonds, or "this confined *individuality* of affection" (*MP*, 51). A critique of an abstract, rigid "system" even infuses *Memoirs* when it comes to narrative structure. Kelly argues that *Memoirs* "switches from one principal story to another or stops for one of the insets, creating for the reader the impression of a loose, complex, but interconnected structure of stories," thus portraying a world that is not governed by a single set of rigid rules. Narrative justice is dispensed "not by some abstract 'system' but by local charity and domestic virtues."[61]

This is mirrored by Harriet's idealized virtue not adhering strictly to conduct book dictums. Harriet, by visiting a fallen woman, violates rules of conduct that decree women should protect their reputations by choosing their company carefully. Her behavior instead follows the intuitive *"spirit"* of virtue; she bends social norms of decorum to help her friend. Elsewhere in the novel, in response to Bridgetina's queries, Julia states, "I have never heard Miss Orwell [Harriet] define the abstract nature of virtue; she rather appears to practice it from the spontaneous influence of her heart" (*MP*, 173). Rather than adhering to an abstract definition of virtue as Bridgetina does, Harriet shows an intuitive, "spontaneous" understanding of morality. Returning to Julia's poetic quotation, it both endorses the conventional belief that "fallen" women can do nothing except seclude themselves from the world and die and simultaneously aligns this morality with the act of quotation itself. Harriet repudiates Julia's conventional, quoted dictums of behavior, demonstrating an understanding of virtue that extends beyond a mere knowledge of its forms. In place of Julia's quotations, Harriet offers something akin to paraphrase.

Integral to both Hamilton's idea of Christian virtue and her approach to reading is a reading practice that opposes the "sense" of words to the material patterns of letters and the sounds that express this sense. This body/spirit bifurcation of language leads to a different formulation of being quixotically marked by a text than the other quixotic narratives this book has examined. *The Female Quixote*, *Polly Honeycombe*, *Tristram Shandy*, and *The Spiritual Quixote* derive much of their humor from troubling any neat distinction between imprinted body and imprinted mind, and likewise between metaphor and literality. In *Tristram Shandy* (chapter 3), reading minds are repeatedly and emphatically equated with bodily organs, book objects, and printing machines, while *The Spiritual Quixote* (chapter 4) suggests the problems in conceptualizing (at least on earth) an idea of "spirit" that is entirely abstracted from matter.

However, Hamilton's stress on a spiritual reading practice is key to her formulation of how texts change their readers. Ideally, the reader should internalize the "spirit" or "truth" of words. The morality a text teaches its reader should be internalized and habitualized to such an extent that it becomes "a spontaneous impulse of the heart" (*MP*, 173). The heart, mind, or soul should be shaped by a text's spiritualized "truth," as opposed to a reading body being physically marked by the material stuff of language. In short, a naturalization of the "spirit" of the text as opposed to a (false) ethics of recitation and repetition that Bridgetina espouses and embodies.

Harriet explicitly endorses an internalization of the "spirit" of the text, draw-ing on the religious connotations of "spirit," and opposes this "spirit" of the text to the act of remembering quotation, which she describes using the discourse of material impressions. Harriet states:

> Memory, though an original faculty, is capable of improvement. It will be strong in proportion to the strength of the impression made upon it, and the impression most frequently recurring will of course become the strongest. Thus it happens, that trifling people are found only to remem-ber trifles; that the vain and the selfish can so well recollect every minu-tiae of every circumstance in which they were themselves particularly con-cerned; and that even among those who pique themselves on superior taste, so many are found capable of retaining the *exact words* of a well-sounding author, while to the few is confined the more estimable power of impressing the *sense* and *substance* in the mind.
>
> (*MP*, 166–167)

This description of how more frequently occurring impressions will remain lon-ger in the memory is indebted to John Locke and Hume. It is difficult to deter-mine the extent "impressions" are used here metaphorically. Harriet's language is consistent with the theory of memory traces, the idea that "impressions" on the brain are fundamental to memory's retention of sensory information. However, Hamilton, in other writings such as *Letters on the Elementary Principles of Educa-tion* (1801), makes it clear that she uses "the word Impression, whenever it is applied" to denote a "mental operation" in a "figurative sense."[62]

This qualification draws on not only Locke, but "common sense" Scottish philosophers like Dugald Stewart.[63] Stewart describes the memory in terms of "impressions" on the mind while also repudiating literal impressions: "The vari-ous theories which have attempted to account for it [memory] by traces or impres-sions in the sensorium, are obviously too unphilosophical to deserve a particular refutation. Such, indeed, is the poverty of language, that we cannot speak on the subject without employing expressions which suggest one theory or another; but it is of importance for us always to recollect, that these expressions are entirely figurative, and afford no explanation of the phenomena to which they refer."[64] Stewart points to the impossibility of stripping metaphor from language and, simultaneously, reflects the growing rejection of literal "impressions" in late eighteenth-century descriptions of memory.[65] In *Memoirs*, Harriet's description of impressing "the *sense* and *substance*" of texts on the mind is a step removed from the image of scriptive, or printerly, quixotic reproduction this book began with. In Harriet's formulation, words themselves are not impressed on the mind; instead, their "sense" and "substance" is, even as Hamilton's italicization emphasizes the materiality of the words (*substance* in a different *sense*). Ultimately, the only "*substance*" worth retaining from reading, Harriet (and Hamilton) implies, is the "*sense*" of words, not their pattern and sounds.

The opposition Harriet poses between material letter and soul or spirit references several verses from the New Testament, where "spirit" and "letter" are used to contrast the law of the New Testament to that of the Old.[66] Hamilton writes in *Letters, Addressed to the Daughter of the Nobleman* (1806) that the Judaic law of the Old Testament enjoins duties that are largely external.[67] However, in the New Testament, "the test of obedience" consists not "in the mere observance of outward ceremonies, but in the inward purity and unsinning righteousness of the heart, the goodness of God."[68] In *Letters on the Elementary Principles of Education*, Hamilton approvingly quotes Hannah More's *Strictures on the Modern System of Female Education* (1799), that "the New Testament is not so much a compilation as a spirit of laws; it does not so much prohibit every individual wrong practice, as suggest a temper and implant a general principle with which every wrong practice is incompatible."[69] Once again, an internalized "general principle" is stressed over externalized specificities.

This is important because Hamilton's views on reading are shaped by a conception of the New Testament as a "spirit of laws." In what was intended to preface a commentary on Romans (dated 1802), Hamilton writes on "the danger and impropriety" of "taking any expression separately and apart," and that she herself, when having trouble interpreting a passage, "endeavour[s] to reconcile them" to "the general tenor and spirit of the author."[70] Hamilton also denigrates rote learning in her novel *The Cottagers of Glenburnie*, where Mr. Gourlay remarks that using "the truths of revelation" as "principles of action and motives or conduct" can never be effected "by a mere repetition of the words" and that "[t]he mere sound, without the sense, will do us no more good than a tune on the bagpipe."[71] Instead, the desirable way to read centers an overall understanding. Or, as Hamilton writes in *Letters, addressed to the Daughter of a Nobleman*: "[N]ever to lay down this or any book of instruction without fixing in your mind a summary of what you have been reading. Consider its purport and its tendency; reflect upon the arguments which have appeared to you most convincing, and treasure them in your heart."[72] Hamilton exhorts her readers to attend to the "spirit" of a work, to memorize its general ideas, rather than its exact phrases, and then treasure its morals "in your heart." This is reading as a form of inner transformation, akin to spiritual conversion, and not requiring any lexical impressions on the body.

The value of a generalized, internalized understanding of the "spirit" of a text is reiterated throughout *Memoirs*. Henry recounts his encounter with a young girl who was "taught" to repeat words of the Bible "to which it was impossible she could affix a single idea" (*MP*, 111). This gratifies the "teacher's pride," but he is adamant that it fails to serve "the real advantage of the pupil" (*MP*, 111). Those like Bridgetina, who merely repeat words without understanding "a single idea," are denied the moral improvement possible from an internalization of a work's "purport and tendency."

The modern philosophers rely on the texture of specific words and phrases to defend positions that are represented as selfish and unjustifiable. For instance, when Martha Goodwin, a virtuous elderly woman is dying, Bridgetina does not spare Martha a thought, being wholly preoccupied by her own desire for Henry: "The life of a *prejudiced* old woman was, in her estimation, of little value, when compared with the *importunate sensations of exquisite sensibility*" (*MP*, 183). The italicized words—"*prejudiced*" and "*importunate sensations of exquisite sensibility*," the latter a quote from *Emma Courtney*—are all the justification Bridgetina needs to disregard Martha's death. Similarly, when Julia urges Bridgetina not to follow Henry to London, Bridgetina replies by listing Julia's objections: "First, with regard to my character; secondly, in respect to my mother; and thirdly, in respect to Henry himself. These are your objections; they may all, however, be answered in one word—*general utility*" (*MP*, 217). Referring to the two-word phrase "general utility" as "one word" is part of Bridgetina's tendency to treat phrases gleaned from her reading as mysterious, powerful, indivisible units, and her reluctance to engage conceptually with the ideas the words might suggest. Her inability to look beyond her own desire for Henry coincides with her materialistic fetishization of the sound rather than "spirit" of words.

Bridgetina's and Julia's quixotism—their veneration of the "letter" of the text—is thus fundamentally linked to their atheism. According to Hamilton, only Christianity can save people from being quixotes. She writes in her private journal that people of a similar intellectual capacity disagree because they are unable to escape their own individual circumstances, "such as education, society, prosperity, adversity," and, further, that "[w]hatever state of mind these circumstances tend to produce, will, by the frequent recurrence of them, become habitual."[73] Hamilton again draws on Locke in her discussion of the ways that "habitual" thinking shapes a person's judgment and opinion. She states that, ultimately, "[n]ever can reason become pure and perfect, until corruption has put on incorruption; never can the mental habits, which are formed by circumstances in this mortal life, be completely reformed, till this mortal have put on immortality."[74] The fallibilities of human reason, in other words, can never be cured on earth, but the best way to counter quixotism is through Hamilton's brand of Protestantism. For instance, the novel represents the secularism of Julia's father—his encouraging her to "consult the dictates of her mind instead of the morality of the gospel"

(*MP*, 292)—as responsible for Julia's seduction. Mr. Sydney laments that "[h]ad a proper value for the morality of the Gospel, enhanced by its gracious promises and elevated views, been instilled into her tender mind, his [Julia's father's] child, his darling Julia, would not have brought the grey hairs of her father with sorrow to the grave" (*MP*, 313).[75] Quixotism becomes the inevitable result of following human reason unaided by "the morality of the gospel" (*MP*, 292).

BESTIAL DESIRE AND THE GODDESS OF REASON'S MONKEY

Central to Hamilton's satire on the limitations of secular reason is the character of Emmeline, a Frenchwoman, who is called "the Goddess of Reason" by both the narrator and the modern philosophers, due to her performing that role in the Festival of Reason. The Festival of Reason, celebrated in the Church of Notre Dame, was one of many festivals performed in revolutionary France to replace Christian rituals, where living women played the part of the Goddess of Reason. In Lucas's *The Infernal Quixote*, Marauder tells Emily the "pretty story of the Goddess of Reason" but omits the "catastrophe" that involves the woman who played the Goddess being guillotined.[76] Marauder's identification of Emily with the Goddess of Reason further affirms her as a female victim of Marauder and Jacobinism. In *Memoirs*, the persistent, facetious designation of Emmeline, a woman who is defined by her sexuality as "the Goddess of Reason" by the narrator, similarly signals the modern philosophers' enthusiastic conflation of reason and erotic desire. Emmeline is represented as anything but a goddess. The *Anti-Jacobin Review*'s response to *Memoirs* refers to the Goddess of Reason as a "strumpet."[77] She is the mistress of the modern philosopher Myope, whom she betrays for the profligate Vallaton, a man who is French, like her, and her equal in sexual duplicity.

The presence of these French libertines among the modern philosophers draws on the conventional anti-Jacobin correlation between British radicalism and France, and the association of both with an uncontrollable sexuality.[78] The publication of Godwin's *Memoirs of the Author of a Vindication of the Rights of Woman* (1798), which dealt frankly with Wollstonecraft's personal life, was "something of a Godsend to anti-Jacobin novelists" intent on making these correlations.[79] *Memoirs* builds on these associations, with the Goddess of Reason persistently characterized as both French and sexually available.

Just as *Memoirs* ties France to atheism, radicalism, and uncontrollable sexuality, it renders Christianity and British patriotism as inextricable. Jane Rendall argues that Hamilton believed "'genuine patriotism' was to be found in maintaining the Christian imperative, [. . .] in the unquestioned beliefs of her own white,

Christian and domestic civilization."[80] Similarly, Grogan argues that *Memoirs* forges an association between the modern philosophers' ideas and a foreignness that has the potential to contaminate Britain.[81] Yet the bulk of Bridgetina's quotations come not from French writers, but from the English writers Hays and Godwin. Both, however, are represented as writers as foreign to Britishness as Rousseau. I have already mentioned how Bridgetina's interpretation of Hays's *Emma Courtney* suggestively aligns Hays with Rousseau. As for Godwin, the narrator facetiously suggests that it is from the extravagant French household where Vallaton used to work that the Godwinian notion of perfectibility springs (*MP*, 54). Hays and Godwin are further coded as foreign through the way they are opposed, via Bridgetina's quotations, to the quotations of quintessentially British texts in chapter epigraphs, which Kelly observes, suggest that the author of *Memoirs*, unlike the modern philosophers, "speaks for the 'national' culture."[82] In contrast to this, Bridgetina's style of reading is a direct importation of foreign matter. Harriet describes how Bridgetina "give[s] you out [. . .] speech after speech from the author she has last read, without alteration or amendment, all *neat as imported*, as they say on the sign-posts" (*MP*, 166). "*[N]eat as imported*" here evokes goods, such as wine that has been imported and sold without being diluted. In the context of *Memoirs*' concern with transoceanic contamination, Bridgetina's style of reading is particularly dangerous because it involves the importation of alien ideas that have not been screened and evaluated by a thinking—and in *Memoirs* that is synonymous with a Christian—mind. Like a plaster of paris "stereotype," Bridgetina's reading involves the mechanical reiteration of previously printed matter with all its potential "foreign" force.

Godwin's philosophy is depicted as African as well as French. Similarities between the tribal society of the "Hottentots" portrayed by François Le Vaillant in *Voyage dans l'intérieur de l'Afrique* (1790) and the society Godwin advocates are noted satirically by both the modern philosophers and the "editor" of *Memoirs*, with a footnote stating that "[t]he curious reader may, if he please, compare the passage quoted from Vaillant with the eighth chapter of the eighth book of Political Justice, vol. ii. octavo edition" (*MP*, 142n140). "Hottentot" was the racially derogatory epithet used by Europeans from the seventeenth century to refer to the South African Khoikhoi. The "Hottentots" were envisaged as quintessential savages, the antithesis to European sexual mores and beauty, the lowest rung on the chain of being.[83] In *Memoirs*, the modern philosophers view the "Hottentots" as the glorious embodiment of their philosophy. Mr. Glib describes the "Hottentots" as "a whole nation of philosophers, all as wise as ourselves!" (*MP*, 141). Grogan observes that *Memoirs*' ironic representation of "Hottentots" as a fulfillment of Godwinian philosophy serves to further align the modern philosophers with alterity.[84] Grogan argues that the "most important connection Hamilton makes between New Philosophers and Hottentots is based upon their sexuality."[85] Most of Hamilton's readers "knew" about the "Hottentots" through reports of their outlandish sexual organs and practices.[86]

An important example of the construction of an exotic "Hottentot" sexuality is the way Sara Baartman was exhibited through Europe as the "Hottentot Venus."[87] A decade after the publication of *Memoirs*, she was toured through England and France. A famous aquatint by Frederick Christian Lewis (figure 13), commissioned by Alexander Dunlop to advertise the exhibition of Baartman in London, depicts Baartman in exotic apparel that serves to frame, rather than hide, her naked body. One of her breasts is visible, and her rear is placed at the center of the picture. Quite clearly, the representation of her body places an emphasis on her sexuality. Early nineteenth-century scientists studied the "Hottentot" backside and genitals, believing that pronounced "bodily enticements to procreation" signaled primitiveness and hypersexuality.[88] In *Memoirs*, Hamilton associates the French Goddess of Reason in particular with these constructions of "Hottentot" sexuality and has her speak in pidgin English, rather than with a French accent.[89]

While critics such as Grogan have persuasively described *Memoirs'* evocation of the "Hottentot," Mr. Pug, the Goddess of Reason's pet monkey, demands more attention. Mr. Pug is introduced at the same time as the Goddess of Reason is: "the Goddess of Reason [. . .] lolling in the easy chair, caressing that favourite monkey who acted such a conspicuous part at the Apotheosis of her Goddessship at Paris" (*MP*, 48). Monkeys have a long association with lechery, and Erwin Panofsky, writing about medieval and early modern painting, argues that the monkey, lacking reason but resembling a human, represents all that is lustful, or potentially bestial in humanity.[90] A visual example of the monkey representing lust and shamelessness is plate 2 of William Hogarth's *A Harlot's Progress* (1732), "The Quarrel with her Jew Protector," portraying Moll Hackabout as a kept woman and the owner of a monkey (figure 14). Moll is depicted in the foreground alongside the man who is keeping her. Her second lover can be seen tiptoeing out of the room. Midway between the feet of Moll's two lovers is her pet monkey; like the second lover, it is fleeing the scene and moving to the left, a movement that links it to secretiveness and sexual guilt. At the same time, the position of the monkey's head and its expression parallels that of her "protector." The monkey seems to be inscribed with its owner's sexual history.

In *Memoirs*, the interspecies relationship between the Goddess of Reason and Mr. Pug is represented in sexual terms, conflating the carnality the monkey symbolizes with the conceptualization of "reason" that the modern philosophers embrace and the Goddess of Reason embodies. The sexuality in the representation

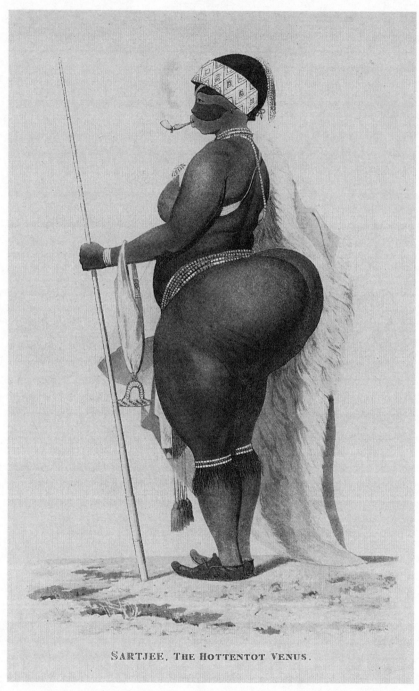

SARTJEE, THE HOTTENTOT VENUS.

FIGURE 13 *Sartjee, the Hottentot Venus*, 1810. © The Trustees of the British Museum.

FIGURE 14 William Hogarth, *A Harlot's Progress*, plate 2, 1732. The Metropolitan Museum of Art, New York, Harris Brisbane Dick Fund, 1932.

of the Goddess of Reason's relationship to her monkey is not so much subtext as text. The narrator describes her as "caressing" the monkey, "hugging" him "close to her bosom" (*MP*, 48). He is her "lovey" and her "favourite" (*MP*, 48). That the monkey is a sign of his owner's transgressive sexuality is further emphasized by his name, "Pug," which, while it could refer simply to a monkey, has other connotations: earlier in the century it was synonymous with whore.[91] Hamilton draws wryly upon the word's older significations.

The bestial sexuality Mr. Pug evokes is crucially racialized. During this period, monkeys and hominoid apes were rarely distinguished from each other, and Baartman, the "Hottentot Venus," was compared to a monkey by the anatomist Baron Georges Cuvier, who dissected her body.[92] Racist comparisons between Africans and monkeys were frequent in eighteenth-century travel writing.[93] Le Vaillant's *Voyage*, consumed by Mr. Glib (*MP*, 141), contains a relatively "sympathetic" portrayal of the "Hottentot," but even so, Ingrid H. Tague argues that Le Vaillant implicitly compares the baboon Kees to the "Hottentots."[94] Edward Long, in his *History of Jamaica* (1777), is more explicit. He describes a hierarchy from monkey to "perfection" in the "pure" white man, with the "negro" in between and stresses the similarity between "Hottentots" and monkeys, a similarity forged on the basis of the supposed abnormal sexuality of the "Hottentot" female.[95] Discussing the "Hottentot" female's "commerce with the other sexes," he writes: "[I]n these acts they are libidinous and shameless as monkies, or baboons. The equally hot temperament of their woman has given probability to the charge of their admitting these animals frequently to their embrace."[96] He also states, "Ludicrous as the opinion may seem, I do not think that an oran-outang husband would be any dishonor to an Hottentot female."[97] Long's insinuation of intercourse between the "Hottentot" female and orangutans was neither unusual nor without precedent.[98] The relationship between the Goddess of Reason and her monkey both implies a "Hottentot" lasciviousness and couples the modern philosophers' conception of reason with a "savage" sexuality.

Bridgetina is also aligned with the "Hottentot" through her interaction with Mr. Pug. Shortly after Mr. Pug is introduced to the reader, he embraces Bridgetina and "putting out his chin, chattered in her face in such a manner, that poor Miss Botherim, who was not accustomed to this sort of jargon, uttered a scream of terror" (*MP*, 48). The narration, describing the monkey's chattering as a "sort of jargon," bitingly compares the chatter of the monkey to Bridgetina's own quotation-laden speech. Human eyes meet monkey eyes, suggesting a mirror scene.[99] Laura Brown argues that similar depictions of monkey/human encounters raise questions about human identity.[100] However, in *Memoirs*, there is no suggestion of a general closeness between humanity and monkeys, but rather a specific intimacy between Bridgetina and monkeys. The comparison between Bridgetina's and the monkey's "jargon" implies that Bridgetina's attempt at philosophizing is failed mimicry; she attempts to be learned but can only "monkey" learning. This comparison is particularly poignant, given how several thinkers, including the French naturalist Georges-Louis Leclerc, Comte de Buffon, and the British writer Oliver Goldsmith, argued that the difference between human and nonhuman animals was the former's ability to reason.[101] Mr. Pug, Bridgetina, and the Goddess of Reason together are presented as offering apish parodies of "human" reason.

Female scholars were already associated with monkeys as early as 1708, when Edward Ward writes in *The Modern World Disrob'd* of the "*Learned Lady*": "She is the Mimick of a Scholar, as a Monkey is of a Man, and apes him in every Thing as near as possible, on Purpose to be thought as rational a Creature."[102] Bridgetina's mimetic response to both Hays's Emma and Rousseau's Julie has already marked her as a failed mimic, and her encounter with Mr. Pug builds on this. The comparison between Bridgetina's philosophizing and Mr. Pug's chatter suggests how Bridgetina can only "Mimick" or ape reason. Female would-be scholars like Bridgetina are in the same symbolic position as Mr. Pug: comically unsuccessful imitators of men.

Mary L. Bellhouse writes that through reiteration, terms such as "monkey," "non-European," "dark skin," and "mimic" became conflated and gradually constructed the nineteenth-century stereotype of the "colonial subject as failed mimic."[103] Coming back to Hogarth's engraving, we can see that Moll's monkey points to Moll's desire to "ape" gentility (she has a maid, takes a lover, and has a monkey as a pet) and, more generally, the way those in the engraving mimic the class or race with more power. Ronald Paulson observes how Moll's Jewish keeper "apes" a Christian; he has shaved his beard, taken a Christian woman as his mistress, and collects old master paintings.[104] Similarly, the enslaved child, in the periphery of the frame, is dressed as an English gentleman. The mirror, the mask, and most notably the monkey, wearing its piece of stolen finery, symbolize this widespread mimicry. In *Memoirs*, the racist caricature of the colonial subject, the monkey attempting to speak, chatters in the face of Bridgetina, the ugly woman attempting to be a sentimental heroine, attempting to be equal to a man, and attempting to be a philosopher. Both Mr. Pug and Bridgetina are failed mimics. Bridgetina tries to be learned, but all she can do is disconcert her company by lengthy quotations she does not understand. Her attempts to woo Henry and even her attempts at mobility are disrupted by her "ugliness and decrepitude" (*MP*, 218), her apparent repulsiveness denying her even the sentimental, tragic ending of Julia. Despite her assertions that mind is superior over matter, she is emphatically trapped in her own flawed, female body. Her reading practice only emphasizes this entrapment in the material.

At a time when the new technology of the "stereotype" and the "clichage" rendered the reproduction of typeset text cheaper and easier than ever before, Hamilton presents quixotism as a mechanical reiteration of set phrases. She forges a complex web of associations between Christianity, reason, Britishness, and an ideology of reading that stresses a text's "basic principles" over the way these principles are phrased. Opposed to these "virtues" are the established anti-Jacobin correlations between the "modern philosophy," atheism, alterity and an unmanageable sexuality, all of which Hamilton links to a reading practice that involves memorization and repetition at the expense of comprehension. The modern philosophers are trapped in the corporeal, not only through the way they repeatedly confuse the intellectual with the erotic, but through the way they are unable to get beyond the form of the words they read or speak. Bridgetina quixotically attempts to act out Godwinian philosophy, and live her life by it, but all she can do is parrot the words she has read. She apes scholarship through extensive quotation within a novel that describes "correct" reading as involving an ability to paraphrase and generalize.

What is more, Bridgetina's citational reading practice—her embrace of the sign of the signified—is ultimately presented as symptomatic of her position at the boundary of white/British/Christian "humanity." *Memoirs* presents being "marked" by the words of texts as a specific defective mode of reading rather than a potentially universal model of subjectivity. The impressionable quixote, corporeally reproducing literature—always a potential problem—is now overlain by Bridgetina's alterity. Quixotic reading becomes less of an epistemological question and instead has the quality of a politicized aberration.

CONCLUSION

Quixotic Impressions in the Nineteenth Century

FOR DAVID HARTLEY, in *Observations on Man* (1749), all sense impressions produce vibrations in the nerves, which then travel to the brain and prompt similar vibrations in the brain's "medullary substance."[1] Hartley's theory, Alex Wetmore notes, "consistently relies on analogies between cognitive and linguistic structures."[2] Ideas link to other ideas in ways "analogous, in Languages" to how "the Letters of Words" and "the Words of Sentences" build associative meanings.[3] Thought is like language, sensation is like print. Yet as the century progressed and turned away from neurophysiology, Hartley's theory, with its materialist vision of cognition insistently analogized with lexical forms, looked increasingly out-of-date.[4]

As I indicated in the previous chapter, late eighteenth-century philosophy and theories of cognition moved away from literal, physical formulations of impressions. Thomas Reid, in *Essays on the Intellectual Powers of Man* (1785), rejects Hartley's notion that physiological impressions on the brain reproduce what is perceived (or read): "The brain has been dissected times innumerable by the nicest Anatomists; every part of it examined [. . .] but no vestige of an image of any external object was ever found. The brain seems to be the most improper substance that can be imagined for receiving or retaining images, being a soft moist medullary substance."[5] Reid repudiates any notion that experience leaves physiological traces and argues for Locke's repository model of the mind as being solely metaphorical.[6] He draws a sharp distinction between "mind" and "brain" and asserts that the use of "impression" to describe perception at all is a misnomer, implying a passivity that the mind does not possess: "[I]t appears, that to give the name of an impression to any effect produced in the mind, is to suppose that the mind does not act at all in the production of that effect. If seeing, hearing, desiring, willing, be operations of the mind, they cannot be impressions."[7] Reid was not alone in reacting against Hartley and relegating impressions to an inadequate metaphor. Samuel Taylor Coleridge, in *Biographia Literaria* (1817), likewise rejected Hartley's and Descartes's "fanciful hypothesis of *material ideas*, or certain configurations of the brain, which were as so many moulds to the influxes of the external world."[8] Coleridge similarly dismisses Hobbes's theories of "living and intelligent fluids, that etch and re-etch engravings on the brain."[9]

Yet, despite the early nineteenth-century philosophical turn toward the transcendental, and a growing unpopularity of Cartesian theories of mind that articulate—even in metaphorical terms—a subject being somatically inscribed or imprinted by the "characters" of their experience, there is no shortage of representations of imprinted readers in early nineteenth-century print.[10] We have so far registered in this book how the concern with quixotic reading proliferated and intensified as the eighteenth century progressed, but this momentum continues into the nineteenth century. For instance, the *Quarterly Review*'s account of Maria Edgeworth's *Tales of Fashionable Life* (August 1809) states: "[N]ot only that a novel even of the lowest order always finds more readers than a serious work, but that it finds readers of a more ductile cast, whose feelings are more easily interested, and with whom every impression is deeper, because more new."[11] Feminized literature attracts readers of a "ductile cast," readers that the literature itself then affectively "cast[s]" with "new" impressions.

These treatments of the impressionable reader evidence both sensibility's formulation of a legible, affected body and the politicization of sensibility at the turn of the century. We saw this with Elizabeth Hamilton's *Memoirs of Modern Philosophers*, and the trend continues into the nineteenth century, in works such as Sarah Green's *Romance Readers and Romance Writers: A Satirical Novel* (1810). Though written after the high point of the anti-Jacobin novel, Green's work is as concerned with the seductive nature of French literature as *Memoirs*, a concern lent new urgency through the Napoleonic Wars.[12] The naïve Margaret reads Jean-Jacques Rousseau's *La nouvelle Héloïse* (1761) and Germaine de Staël's *Delphine* (1802) under the dangerous guidance of the worldly Lady Isabella. The narrator states: "[T]he weak mind of an inexperienced country girl may be softened and easily warped, which never was wicked, or in any degree *corrupt*. Margaret read these works with avidity; she laughed at, she ridiculed herself, and her former taste!"[13] Margaret's waxlike mind is "warped" and "softened" by the books she reads. The result is a stark delineation between Margaret before her reading and a Margaret afterward, who laughs at her former self and "her former taste." Impressions from "*corrupt*" literature bend Margaret's "easily warped" subjectivity. Like Julia's reading in *Memoirs*, Margaret's consumption of French literature has conventionally unhappy results; before the end of the book she is both pregnant and suicidal.

Margaret is one of innumerable quixotic female readers whose literary consumption seems to potentially spell political and national, as well as personal, disaster.[14] In Eaton Stannard Barrett's *The Heroine* (1813), Stuart, the love interest of Cherubina, a quixotic reader of sentimental and gothic romances, subjects her to a lecture where he sutures novel production to national health: "In a country where morals are on the decline, novels always fall several degrees below the standard of national virtue: [. . .] Thus, since France became depraved, her novels have become dissolute."[15] Stuart continues, "[A]s your ideas of real life are drawn from novels; and even as your manners and language are vitiated by them, I would recommend you to mix in the world, to copy living instead of imaginary beings."[16] Previously, impressionable reading was certainly a problem—a philosophical, economic, and literary one—but after the French Revolution and the "crisis of sensibility," it potentially catalyzes a national catastrophe.[17] What this means, then, is that while the quixotic reader becomes more insistently gendered, more of a political problem, the inscribable subject simultaneously becomes less universal.

Sentimental literature, Wetmore argues, persistently connects the expressive materiality of the book object with the imprinted, legible body of the person of sensibility. Wetmore's argument about sentimental literature's "embodied self-reflexivity" stands up to scrutiny, and so too does Wetmore's assertion that this embodied self-reflexivity became less prevalent at the turn of the century.[18] We can now connect this diminishment not just to the cultural crisis around sensibility but to philosophy's growing resistance to articulating subjectivity in terms of physical imprinting.

Such shifts also align with transformations in book production and print technology. In the nineteenth century, while the manufacture of paper objects still involved imprinting materials, this imprinting became increasingly industrialized. The nineteenth century saw the automation of printing, first with the development of iron presses that offered more consistent impressions, then later, steam presses and rotary presses.[19] Paper manufacture followed suit, with new, continuous papermaking machines draining the fiber through a moving mesh, then pressing, drying, and reeling it into an unbroken moving web.[20] Imprinting becomes an industrial rather than an artisanal process, implicating the imprinted reader within a matrix of national industry, mass production, and consumption. I suggested in chapter 1 that David Hume draws on the variability of eighteenth-century print technology in his formulation of belief, with heavier, darker impressions of the printing plate on paper equated with stronger assurance. This analogy becomes less relevant into the nineteenth century, with new printing machines offering more consistent impressions. The industrialization of print technology makes it a less resonant model for subjectivity.

At the same time, with the advent of new printing technology, aberrant impressions become more aberrant than ever before. To be precise, at the end of the century, while impressionable bodies are even more frequent in literature, they are also less associated with issues around subjectivity, epistemology, and the way the self might or might not be constituted by legible, imprinted, paperlike surfaces. Instead, like Bridgetina, Julia, Margaret, and Cherubina, they become increasingly marked as deviant and dangerous for national health and national stability.

Jane Austen reworks and reflects upon the fraught tropes of female quixotism, sensibility, and impressionability. If *Sense and Sensibility* (1811) retells on one level, through Marianne, the story of a female quixote with an "excess" of sensibility who must learn the error of her ways, it also, Sarah Raff notes, does more.[21] More explicitly, in *Northanger Abbey* (posthumously published in 1818), Austen reworks the tropes of the quixotic narrative to defend the pleasures of novel writing and novel reading. Henry Tilney's exhortation to Catherine, the enthralled consumer of Gothic novels, to remember "the country and the age" in which she lives, is redolent of the Johnsonian clergyman's injunctions in *The Female Quixote* (chapter 1).[22] However, Catherine comes to realize that in quixotically "suspecting General Tilney of either murdering or shutting up his wife, she had scarcely sinned against his character, or magnified his cruelty."[23] Catherine is a quixotic reader whose interpretation of the world, marked by her reading of Gothic fiction, allows her to see truths about General Tilney's tyranny. If Catherine is a female novel reader whose quixotism aids her reading of the world, Austen's male quixotes are a different story. There is Edward in *Love and Freindship*, whose father responds to him speaking "unmeaning Gibberish" by asserting, "You have been studying Novels I suspect"; and Captain Benwick of *Persuasion* (1818), a quixotic reader of Byron, whose "tremulous feeling" in his poetry recitation prompts Anne to take the role of Lennox's Johnsonian Doctor in *The Female Quixote*, and recommend him remedial reading.[24]

Austen's inversion of the feminized late eighteenth-century quixote is perhaps most striking in her unfinished fragment *Sanditon* (written 1817, published 1932), where the reader meets Sir Edward, who, like Arabella, had been "confined very much to one spot" by circumstance, and, like Bridgetina "had read more sentimental Novels than agreed with him."[25] Sir Edward, then, is a masculine version of the impressionable female reader of sentimental literature who pervades novels at the turn of the century. Like Polly Honeycombe, Sir Edward's "fancy had been early caught by all the impassioned and most exceptionable parts of Richardson's; and such Authors as had since appeared to tread in Richardson's steps."[26] His sympathy with Richardsonian villains—particularly Lovelace in *Clarissa*— has "formed his Character."[27] Sir Edward flips the tropes of Richard Allestree's romance reader: rather than his reading leading to his seduction, he unsuccessfully (in the fragment that we have at least) seeks to "seduce" women. Austen, through characters like Catherine, Marianne, Captain Benwick, and Sir Edward, simultaneously reworks and inverts the politicized literary tropes that, by the late eighteenth century, have attached themselves to female quixotism, sensibility, and impressionability.

This said, by the middle of the nineteenth century gendered constructions of reading—conceptualizing male readers as "active" and female readers as malleable and impressionable—were, Kate Flint argues, more forceful than they had ever been.[28] A review in the *Church of England Quarterly Review* (April 1842) opines: "The great bulk of novel readers are females; and to them such impressions are peculiarly mischievous: for, first, they are naturally more sensitive, more impressible, than the other sex; and, secondly, their engagements are of a less engrossing character—they have more time as well as more inclination to indulge in the reveries of fiction."[29] Novels are *still* molding and corrupting female readers, who absorb "sentiment passively like a sponge" to the point of imitating texts' examples.[30] Narratives about quixotic "impressible" readers persist, more feminized than ever before, and build on eighteenth-century tropes.

The impressionable reading body makes a *mark* on representations of quixotic, reproductive reading even after somatic markings had less valence in philosophical formulations of subjectivity. Into the nineteenth century, literal physiological impressions on the brain are increasingly described as impossible and advances in printing technology complicate the deployment of print as a model for subjectivity. Yet still, the gendered and political resonances of impressions remain stronger than ever. The impressionable, quixotic reading body is used less and less by writers to pose universal epistemological quandaries. Instead, in the early nineteenth century, the impressionable reader is more feminized, more politicized, and more aberrant.

However we read these readers, we can find no straight, progressive A-to-B line from literal to metaphorical impressions, from Allestree's reader to Austen's. We have been thrown, instead, down some nonlinear route, dragged up and tugged along by philosophical, religious, and geopolitical tectonics. For throughout the mid-to late eighteenth century, from Arabella's blushing body in *The Female Quixote* to Bridgetina's readerly regurgitation of philosophical jargon, and all those other unlikely examples born out in between these two, a host of epistemological, affective, and sexual conceptualizations of imprinting and impressions structures the text that is the quixotic book-like reader. This is how we now read down that fraught line from feminized literary consumption to (re)production; that is, how we now do *quixotic reading*.

ACKNOWLEDGMENTS

It is a delight to be able to type these words, and to be able to thank the people who need to be thanked. First, Nicola Parsons, with the deepest sense of gratitude for her boundless intellectual and personal generosity, and scrupulous critical attention; for her advice, for her ideas, for her questions, then and now. This book is dedicated to you.

There are so many friends and colleagues to whom I—and this book—are indebted, but I shall attempt to list some of them anyway. This project began at the University of Sydney and would have been impossible without the support of its English department, especially Kate Lilley, Liam Semler, Huw Griffiths, and Vanessa Smith. It is intellectually indebted to my dear friends and co-conspirators in the long eighteenth-century reading group at the University of Sydney, among them Elias Greig, Olivia Murphy, Shane Greentree, Jessica Sun, Judy Barbour, Alexandra Hankinson, and Ursula Potter, who read and heard me present on countless iterations of this material. A great deal of thanks is also due to Paul Goring, Aaron R. Hanlon, Will Christie, Jennifer Milam, Meegan Hasteed, Michael Falk, Jessica Hamel-Akré, Sarah Comyn, Clara Tuite, Catherine Jaffe, Judith Hawley, Jane Spencer, Gillian Russell, Darren Bevin, Emma Gleadhill, Richard De Ritter, Danielle Spratt, Adela Gato, Heidi Thomson, Lyndal Kelly, Brian Dale, Jane Wessel, Tonya Moutray, Douglas Murray, Eric Parisot, anonymous readers, and many others for their keen eyes, productive comments, suggestions, questions, help, and support for this project along its various stages. A big thanks to all my students who teach me, and especially my 2016 class for the "Eighteenth-Century Novel: Theory and Example" course, who have helped me read these texts anew.

I had the pleasure of completing this book in Shanghai, a move that has proved productive due to the kindness of many. Gratitude is particularly due to Wang Guanglin and Chen Beibei and to my colleagues in the School of Foreign Languages at Shanghai University of International Business and Economics (SUIBE), including Zhou Xiaojin, A. J. Carruthers, Ouyang Yu, Wen Jianping, and Si Yaolong, for their support, personal and professional. Being part of SUIBE has been a delightful experience.

Those writers whose work I have read and loved, your name is in these pages. Thank you to Greg Clingham and Pam Dailey at Bucknell University Press. Thank you also, to Bucknell's anonymous reader for their scrupulous reading and excellent advice and to Jane Lichty for her invaluable copyediting. But, to reiterate a necessary, if often repeated, acknowledgment formulae: the errors on these pages are mine and no one else's.

This book has been supported by a Chawton House Library fellowship; an Australian Academy of the Humanities traveling fellowship; an Associate Investigator Grant from the ARC Centre of Excellence for the History of Emotions in Europe: 1100–1800, CE110001011; the Australian Studies Centre at Shanghai University of International Business and Economics; and the Department of English at the University of Sydney. Some of what is published here has had previous incarnations: "Dolly's Inch of Red Seal Wax, or, Impressing the Reader in *Tristram Shandy*," in *Sterne, Tristram, Yorick: Tercentenary Essays on Laurence Sterne*, edited by Melvyn New, Peter de Voogd, and Judith Hawley (Newark: Delaware University Press, 2015), and "'Acting It as She Reads': Affective Impressions in *Polly Honeycombe*," in *Passions, Sympathy and Print Culture: Public Opinion and Emotional Authenticity in Eighteenth-Century Britain*, edited by Heather Kerr, David Lemmings, and Robert Phiddian (Basingstoke: Palgrave Macmillan, 2015).

INTRODUCTION

1. Also attributed to John Fell, Dorothy Pakington, Richard Sterne, and others. The English Short Title Catalogue has records of *The Ladies Calling* being published in the years 1675, 1676, 1677, 1682, 1684, 1687, 1693, 1695, 1700, 1704, 1705, 1713, 1717, 1720, 1723, 1727, 1763, 1765, and 1787. English Short Title Catalogue, British Library, http://estc.bl.uk (accessed May 3, 2017). Richard Allestree, *The Ladies Calling*, 2nd ed. (Oxford: Printed at the Theater, 1673), 2:9.

2. Plato, *Complete Works*, ed. John M. Cooper (Indianapolis: Hackett Publishing Company, 1997), 212.

3. Aristotle, *Complete Works of Aristotle: The Revised Oxford Translation*, ed. Jonathan Barnes (Princeton, N.J.: Princeton University Press, 2014), 1:715.

4. Douwe Draaisma, *Metaphors of Memory: A History of Ideas about the Mind*, trans. Paul Vincent (Cambridge: Cambridge University Press, 2000), 25.

5. René Descartes, *Rules for the Direction of the Mind*, trans. Dugald Murdoch, in *The Philosophical Writings of Descartes* (Cambridge: Cambridge University Press, 1985), 1:40.

6. Descartes, *Rules for the Direction of the Mind*, 1:40.

7. Descartes, *Rules for the Direction of the Mind*, 1:40.

8. Descartes, *Rules for the Direction of the Mind*, 1:42.

9. Descartes, *Rules for the Direction of the Mind*, 1:42.

10. Brad Pasanek identifies how the metaphoricity of impressions is connected to the mind-body distinction, asking "in what sense are some impressions literal and others figurative? Are sense impressions left in the brain *literal* impressions, and impressions left in the mind *figurative*?" Brad Pasanek, *Metaphors of Mind: An Eighteenth-Century Dictionary* (Baltimore: Johns Hopkins University Press, 2015), 139.

11. Descartes, *Rules for the Direction of the Mind*, 1:41–42.

12. Sigmund Freud, "A Note Upon the 'Mystic Writing-Pad,'" trans. James Strachey, in *The Standard Edition of the Complete Psychological works of Sigmund Freud* (1961; repr., London: Vintage Books, 2001), 19:228.

13. Freud, "A Note Upon the 'Mystic Writing-Pad,'" 19:229.

14. Jacques Derrida, *Writing and Difference*, trans. Alan Bass (1978; repr., London: Routledge, 2001), 278–279; Freud, "A Note Upon the 'Mystic Writing-Pad,'" 19:229.

15. Draaisma, *Metaphors of Memory*, 9.

16. Derrida, *Writing and Difference*, 278–279.

17. Sara Ahmed, *The Cultural Politics of Emotion* (Edinburgh: Edinburgh University Press, 2004), 6.

18. Pasanek, *Metaphors of Mind*, 141–142.

19. Draaisma, *Metaphors of Memory*, 26.

20. Michael F. Suarez, S.J., and H. R. Woudhuysen, eds., *The Oxford Companion to the Book* (Oxford: Oxford University Press, 2010), 2:814.

21. Suarez and Woudhuysen, *The Oxford Companion to the Book*, 2:815.

22. Joseph Addison, *Dialogues Upon the Usefulness of Ancient Medals. Especially in Relation to the Latin and Greek Poets* ([n.p.]: 1726), 20.

23. Lothar Müller, *White Magic: The Age of Paper*, trans. Jessica Spengler (Cambridge: Polity Press, 2015), 72.

24. Müller, *White Magic*, 72.

25. John Locke, *The Clarendon Edition of the Works of John Locke: An Essay Concerning Human Understanding*, ed. Peter H. Nidditch (Oxford: Clarendon Press, 1975), 81.

26. Deidre Lynch, *The Economy of Character: Novels, Market Culture, and the Business of Inner Meaning* (Chicago: University of Chicago Press, 1998), 34.

27. Margreta de Grazia, "Imprints: Shakespeare, Gutenberg, and Descartes," in *Printing and Parenting in Early Modern England*, ed. Douglas A. Brooks (Aldershot: Ashgate, 2005), 32–38; Wendy Wall, *The Imprint of Gender: Authorship and Publication in the English Renaissance* (Ithaca, N.Y.: Cornell University Press, 1993), 2–3.

28. De Grazia notes that the analogy between wax and women was more than a metaphor; women were actually seen as capable of engendering "because they are impressionable, like wax. [. . .] Midwifery manuals maintain that a matrix needs to be kept warm in order to avoid barrenness, just as wax needs warming before receiving an impression." De Grazia, "Imprints," 36.

29. Elizabeth Grosz, *Volatile Bodies* (St. Leonards, N.S.W.: Allen and Unwin, 1994), 4.

30. For the history of maternal impressions, see Marie-Hélène Huet, *Monstrous Imagination* (Cambridge, Mass.: Harvard University Press, 1993), 12–102.

31. Kiran Toor, "'Offspring of His Genius': Coleridge's Pregnant Metaphors and Metamorphic Pregnancies," *Romanticism* 13, no. 3 (2007): 258–259.

32. Jacques Du Bosc, *The Accomplish'd Woman. Written in French by M. Du Boscq* (London: Printed by and for J. Watts, 1753), 1:17. Several translations of Du Bosc's *L'honneste femme* had appeared by this time. I am quoting the one closest to the relevant dates of this book.

33. Mary Hays, *Memoirs of Emma Courtney*, ed. Eleanor Ty (1996; repr., Oxford: Oxford University Press, 2009), 23.

34. Allestree, *The Ladies Calling*, 2:10.

35. See Thomas Laqueur, *Solitary Sex: A Cultural History of Masturbation* (New York: Zone Books, 2004), 302–358.

36. Michael McKeon, *The Secret History of Domesticity: Public, Private, and the Division of Knowledge* (Baltimore: Johns Hopkins University Press, 2005), 296; *Onania; or, The Heinous Sin of Self-Pollution, and All Its Frightful Consequences, in Both Sexes, Considerd, with Spiritual and Physical Advice to those, who have already injur'd themselves by this abominable Practice. And seasonable Admonition to the Youth of the Nation, (of Both Sexes) and those whose Tuition They are under, whether Parents, Guardians, Masters, or Mistresses*, 8th ed. (London: Printed by Eliz. Rumball, for Thomas Crouch, 1723), 10, 21.

37. Paul Goring, *The Rhetoric of Sensibility in Eighteenth-Century Culture* (Cambridge: Cambridge University Press, 2005), 5.

38. John Mullan, *Sentiment and Sociability: The Language of Feeling in the Eighteenth Century* (Oxford: Clarendon Press, 1990), 16.

39. George Cheyne, *The English Malady, or, A Treatise of Nervous Diseases of All Kinds* (London: G. Strathan and J. Leake, 1733), 63.

40. Cheyne, *The English Malady*, 63–64.

41. Cheyne, *The English Malady*, 71.

42. Alex Wetmore, *Men of Feeling in Eighteenth-Century Literature: Touching Fiction* (Basingstoke: Palgrave Macmillan, 2013), 1–3.

43. Dror Wahrman, *The Making of the Modern Self: Identity and Culture in Eighteenth-Century England* (New Haven, Conn.: Yale University Press, 2006), 13.

44. Jane Barker, *The Lining of the Patch-Work Screen; Design'd for the Farther Entertainment of the Ladies* (London: Printed for A. Bettesworth, at the Red Lion in Pater-Noster Row, 1726), 106. Galesia in *Love Intrigues: Or, The History of the Amours of Bosvil and Galesia* (1713) is another example from Barker.

45. *The World* 79 (July 4, 1754): 475–476.

46. *The World* 79 (July 4, 1754): 476. The trope of the well-born quixote, whose reading leads her to sexual transgressions with a servant, continues through the century. In Tabitha Gilman Tenney's American novel *Female Quixotism* (1801), the quixotic Dorcasina behaves with increasing familiarity to John Brown. See Tabitha Gilman Tenney, *Female Quixotism: Exhibited in the Romantic Opinions and Extravagant Adventures of Dorcasina Sheldon*, ed. Jean Nienkamp and Andrea Collins (Oxford: Oxford University Press, 1992), 237–239.

47. See, for instance, John Brewer, *The Pleasures of the Imagination: English Culture in the Eighteenth Century* (London: HarperCollins, 1997), 194–197; Jacqueline Pearson, *Women's Reading in Britain, 1750–1835: A Dangerous Recreation* (Cambridge: Cambridge University Press, 1999), 122–151; Jane Fergus, *Provincial Readers in Eighteenth-Century England* (Oxford: Oxford University Press, 2006), 40–74; William St. Clair, *The Reading Nation in the Romantic Period* (Cambridge: Cambridge University Press, 2004), 226–232.

48. Pearson, *Women's Reading in Britain*, 1. See also William Warner, "Staging Readers Reading," *Eighteenth-Century Fiction* 12, no. 2–3 (2000): 391–416.

49. Catherine Ingrassia, *Authorship, Commerce, and Gender in Early Eighteenth-Century England: A Culture of Paper Credit* (Cambridge: Cambridge University Press, 1998), 47; Emma Clery, *The Feminization Debate in Eighteenth-Century England* (Basingstoke: Palgrave Macmillan, 2004), 1. For more on anxieties around female reading, see William Warner, *Licensing Entertainment: The Elevation of Novel Reading in Britain, 1684–1750* (Berkeley: University of California Press, 1998); Pearson, *Women's Reading in Britain*; Richard De Ritter, *Imagining Women Readers, 1789–1820* (Manchester: Manchester University Press, 2014), 17–54.

50. De Ritter, *Imagining Women Readers*; Joe Bray, *The Female Reader in the English Novel: From Burney to Austen* (New York: Routledge, 2009).

51. J.A.G. Ardila, "The Influence and Reception of Cervantes in Britain, 1607–2005," in *The Cervantean Heritage: Reception and Influence of Cervantes in Britain*, ed. J.A.G. Ardila (London: Legenda, 2009), 10.

52. David A. Brewer, *The Afterlife of Character, 1726–1825* (Philadelphia: University of Pennsylvania Press, 2005), 12–13. For an account of Don Quixote within world literature, see Aaron R. Hanlon, "Quixotism as Global Heuristic: Atlantic and Pacific Diasporas," *Studies in Eighteenth-Century Culture* 46 (2017): 49–62.

53. Allestree, *The Ladies Calling*, 2:10.

54. Aaron R. Hanlon, "Toward a Counter-Poetics of Quixotism," *Studies in the Novel* 46, no. 2 (2014): 143. Texts with "Quixote" in the title include *Tarrataria; or Don Quixote the Second* (1761); *Fizgig, or The Modern Quixote* (1763); Richard Graves, *The Spiritual Quixote* (1773); *The Philosophical Quixote* (1782); *The Country Quixote* (1785); *The City Quixote* (1785); *The Amicable Quixote* (1788); Jane Purbeck, *William Thornborough, the Benevolent Quixote* (1791); *The History of Sir George Warrington; or, The Political Quixote* (1797); and Charles Lucas, *The Infernal Quixote* (1801). These are only some of several. For more examples, see Ardila, "The Influence and Reception of Cervantes in Britain," 12–13.

55. Hanlon, "Toward a Counter-Poetics of Quixotism."

56. April Alliston, "Female Quixotism and the Novel: Character and Plausibility, Honesty and Fidelity," *The Eighteenth Century* 52, no. 3–4 (2011): 249–269; Scott Paul Gordon, *The Practice of Quixotism: Postmodern Theory and Eighteenth-Century Women's Writing* (Basingstoke: Palgrave Macmillan, 2006), 11–40; Wendy Motooka, *The Age of Reasons: Quixotism,*

Sentimentalism and Political Economy in Eighteenth-Century Britain (London: Routledge, 1998), 2–6.

57. Bray, *The Female Reader in the English Novel*, 24.

58. Gordon, *The Practice of Quixotism*; Motooka, *The Age of Reasons*.

59. Allestree, *The Ladies Calling*, 2:9–10.

60. Francis Bacon, *The Instauratio Magna Part II: Novum Organum and Associated Texts*, ed. Graham Rees and Maria Wakely, vol. 11 of *The Oxford Francis Bacon* (Oxford: Oxford University Press, 2004), 35.

61. Francis Bacon, *The Instauratio Magna Part III: Historia Naturalis et Experimentalis: Historia Ventorum and Historia Vitæ & Mortis*, ed. Graham Rees and Maria Wakely, vol. 12 of *The Oxford Francis Bacon* (Oxford: Oxford University Press, 2007), 9.

62. Gordon, *The Practice of Quixotism*, 16.

63. Gordon, *The Practice of Quixotism*, 19–20.

64. Sean Silver, *The Mind Is a Collection: Case Studies in Eighteenth-Century Thought* (Philadelphia: University of Pennsylvania Press, 2015); Pasanek, *Metaphors of Mind*; Wall, *The Imprint of Gender*.

65. Eve Tavor Bannet, "Quixotes, Imitations, and Transatlantic Genres," *Eighteenth-Century Studies* 40, no. 4 (2007): 553–569; Jodi L. Wyett, "Quixotic Legacy: *The Female Quixote* and the Professional Woman Writer," *Authorship* 4, no. 1 (2015): 1–19; Jodi L. Wyett, "Female Quixotism Refashioned: *Northanger Abbey*, the Engaged Reader, and the Woman Writer," *The Eighteenth Century* 56, no. 2 (2015): 261–276. Other recent work on British quixotic narratives includes Aaron R. Hanlon, "Maids, Mistresses, and 'Monstrous Doubles': Gender-Class Kyriarchy in *The Female Quixote* and *Female Quixotism*," *The Eighteenth Century* 55, no. 1 (2014): 77–96; Hanlon, "Toward a Counter-Poetics of Quixotism"; Ardila, "The Influence and Reception of Cervantes in Britain."

66. Rebecca Tierney-Hynes, *Novel Minds: Philosophers and Romance Readers, 1680–1740* (Basingstoke: Palgrave Macmillan, 2012), 4.

67. Tierney-Hynes, *Novel Minds*; Lynch, *The Economy of Character*; Wahrman, *The Making of the Modern Self*.

68. Lynch, *The Economy of Character*; Silver, *The Mind Is a Collection*.

CHAPTER 1 — MARKING THE EYES IN *THE FEMALE QUIXOTE*

1. Norma Clarke asserts, "There is no doubt that this novel belongs with *Clarissa* and *Tom Jones* and *Roderick Random* as one of the defining texts in the development of the novel." Norma Clarke, *Dr Johnson's Women* (London: Hambledon and London, 2000), 92.

2. Mary Patricia Martin, for instance, writes that Lennox exposes "the gendered rhetoric central to accounts of the new fiction. Using romance strategically to critique the definitive terms of the new genre, Lennox claims the novel, too, as 'women's writing.'" Mary Patricia Martin, "'High and Noble Adventures': Reading the Novel in *The Female Quixote*," *Novel: A Forum on Fiction* 31, no. 1 (1997): 46. According to Ruth Mack, *The Female Quixote* can itself be read as a history of the novel. Ruth Mack, "Quixotic Ethnography: Charlotte Lennox and the Dilemma of Cultural Observation," *Novel: A Forum on Fiction* 38, no. 2–3 (2005): 199. Laurie Langbauer argues that this novel "demonstrates the way gender underlies our constructions as critics of literary history." Laurie Langbauer, *Women and Romance: The Consolations of Gender in the English Novel* (Ithaca, N.Y.: Cornell University Press, 1990), 62.

3. James Engell, *The Creative Imagination: Enlightenment to Romanticism* (Cambridge, Mass.: Harvard University Press, 1981), 14–15. Wolfgang Iser argues that from John Locke's *An Essay Concerning Human Understanding* (1689) onward, "we can trace the growing impor-

tance of the imagination as it first—almost illegally—occupies the empty space, and then rises in association psychology [. . .] to become the recognized agent responsible for combining ideas." Wolfgang Iser, *The Fictive and the Imaginary: Charting Literary Anthropology* (Baltimore: Johns Hopkins University Press, 1993), 174–175.

4. Thomas Hobbes, *Leviathan: The English and Latin Texts*, ed. Noel Malcolm, vols. 4 and 5 of *The Clarendon Edition of the Works of Thomas Hobbes* (Oxford: Clarendon Press, 2012), 1:26.
5. Hobbes, *Leviathan*, 1:30.
6. Rebecca Tierney-Hynes, *Novel Minds: Philosophers and Romance Readers, 1680–1740* (Basingstoke: Palgrave Macmillan, 2012), 5; Ronald Paulson, *Don Quixote in England: The Aesthetics of Laughter* (Baltimore: Johns Hopkins University Press, 1998), 8.
7. Hobbes, *Leviathan*, 1:22. Similar references to palinopsia to describe cognition and experiential impressions persist throughout the century. Joseph Priestley, writing on David Hartley's theories, states: "If I look upon a house, and then shut my eyes, the impression it has made on my mind does not immediately vanish; I can contemplate the idea of the house as long as I please." Joseph Priestley, *Hartley's Theory Of The Human Mind, on the Principle of the Association of Ideas; With Essays Relating To The Subject Of It* (London: J. Johnson, 1775), xxxix.
8. Hobbes, *Leviathan*, 1:22.
9. Adrian Johns, *The Nature of the Book: Print and Knowledge in the Making* (Chicago: University of Chicago Press, 1998), 389.
10. John Locke, *The Clarendon Edition of the Works of John Locke: An Essay Concerning Human Understanding*, ed. Peter H. Nidditch (Oxford: Clarendon Press, 1975), 43.
11. Richard Rorty, *Philosophy and the Mirror of Nature* (1979; repr., Princeton, N.J.: Princeton University Press, 2009), 50.
12. David Hume, *An Enquiry Concerning Human Understanding*, ed. Tom L. Beauchamp (Oxford: Oxford University Press, 2000), 50.
13. David Hume, *A Treatise of Human Nature*, ed. David Fate Norton and Mary J. Norton, vol. 1, *Texts* (Oxford: Oxford University Press, 2007), 8.
14. Hume, *A Treatise of Human Nature*, 8.
15. Hume, *A Treatise of Human Nature*, 7.
16. Christina Lupton, *Knowing Books: The Consciousness of Mediation in Eighteenth-Century Britain* (Philadelphia: University of Pennsylvania Press, 2012), 74–75.
17. Hume, *A Treatise of Human Nature*, 127.
18. Michael McKeon, *The Origins of the English Novel, 1600–1740* (1987; repr., Baltimore: Johns Hopkins University Press, 2002), 274.
19. McKeon, *Origins*, 275–276.
20. McKeon, *Origins*, 276. See also Johns, *The Nature of the Book*, 30.
21. Hume, *A Treatise of Human Nature*, 68.
22. Hume, *A Treatise of Human Nature*, 68–69.
23. Hume, *A Treatise of Human Nature*, 68–69.
24. David Hume, "Of the Study of History," in *Essays, Moral and Political*, 3rd ed. (London: Printed for A. Millar, over against Catharine Street in the Strand; and A. Kincaid in Edinburgh, 1748), 53.
25. Hume, "Of the Study of History," 54.
26. Tierney-Hynes, *Novel Minds*, 134.
27. Tierney-Hynes, *Novel Minds*, 5.
28. Hume, *A Treatise of Human Nature*, 84.
29. For a discussion of Hume as a quixote, see Wendy Motooka, *The Age of Reasons: Quixotism, Sentimentalism and Political Economy in Eighteenth-Century Britain* (London: Routledge, 1998), 19–20.

30. Michael F. Suarez, S.J., and H. R. Woudhuysen, eds., *The Oxford Companion to the Book* (Oxford: Oxford University Press, 2010), 2:814.

31. Hume, *An Enquiry Concerning Human Understanding*, 46–47.

32. Hume, *A Treatise of Human Nature*, 239.

33. There are, of course, other romance-reading female quixotes who precede Arabella. As well as Jane Barker's Dorinda, discussed in the introduction, there is the romance-reading Biddy, a "perfect *Quixot* in petticoats," in Richard Steele, *The Tender Husband* (London: Printed for Jacob Tonson, 1705), 26.

34. Adrien-Thomas Perdou de Subligny, *The Mock-Clelia: Being A Comical History of French Gallantries, and Novels, in Imitation of Dom Quixote* (London: Printed for L.C., 1678), 15. For a detailed account of Subligny's work, see Nicholas Paige, *Before Fiction: The Ancien Régime of the Novel* (Philadelphia: University of Pennsylvania Press, 2011), 62–89.

35. Clarke, *Dr Johnson's Women*, 93.

36. Marta Kvande, "Reading Female Readers: *The Female Quixote* and *Female Quixotism*," in *Masters of the Marketplace: British Women Novelists of the 1750s*, ed. Susan Carlile (Bethlehem, Pa.: Lehigh University Press, 2011), 229.

37. Kvande, "Reading Female Readers," 229.

38. This trope, of illness erasing quixotic imprints, and thus providing a "cure" for quixotic impressions, originates in Don Quixote's deathbed "recovery." It also occurs in other eighteenth-century quixotic narratives. For instance, in Richard Graves's novel *The Spiritual Quixote* (1773) (chapter 4), Wildgoose has his quixotism cured after he is hit on his head by a rock, suggesting his quixotism also has physical origins.

39. Helen Thompson, "Charlotte Lennox and the Agency of Romance," *The Eighteenth Century* 43, no. 2 (2002): 91.

40. Thompson, "Charlotte Lennox and the Agency of Romance," 91–92.

41. Anna Viele, "Plotting the Coquette: Gender and Genre in the Eighteenth-Century British Cultural Imagination" (PhD diss., University of California, Santa Barbara, 2007), 195–196.

42. Viele, "Plotting the Coquette," 196.

43. Charlotte Lennox, *The Lady's Museum* (London: J. Newbery in St. Paul's Church-Yard, 1760–61), 1:2.

44. Lennox, *The Lady's Museum*, 1:2.

45. The quotation is identified by Manushag N. Powell, "See No Evil, Hear No Evil, Speak No Evil: Spectation and the Eighteenth-Century Public Sphere," *Eighteenth-Century Studies* 45, no. 2 (2012): 271.

46. Alexander Pope, *Letters of Mr Pope, and Several Eminent Persons, From the Year 1705, to 1735* (London: Printed for T. Cooper, at the Globe in Pater-Noster-Row, 1735), 1:127.

47. Powell, "See No Evil," 271.

48. Lennox, *The Lady's Museum*, 1:2.

49. Lennox, *The Lady's Museum*, 2:561.

50. S. Cailey Hall, "'All the Bright Eyes of the Kingdom': Charlotte Lennox's Discursive Communities," *Eighteenth-Century Life* 41, no. 2 (2017): 100.

51. Susan Carlile, *Charlotte Lennox: An Independent Mind* (Toronto: University of Toronto Press, 2018), 177.

52. Norbert Schürer, ed., *Charlotte Lennox: Correspondence and Miscellaneous Documents* (Lewisburg, Pa.: Bucknell University Press, 2012), xxxv–xxxvi; Duncan Isles, "The Lennox Collection (Part One)," *Harvard Library Bulletin* 18, no. 4 (1970): 335; William M. Sale, *Samuel Richardson: Master Printer* (Ithaca, N.Y.: Cornell University Press, 1950), 118–119; Keith Maslen, *Samuel Richardson of London, Printer: A Study of His Printing Based*

on Ornament Use and Business Accounts (Christchurch, New Zealand: University of Otago, 2001), 102.

53. Janine Barchas, *Graphic Design, Print Culture, and the Eighteenth-Century Novel* (Cambridge: Cambridge University Press, 2003), 117.

54. Maslen, *Samuel Richardson of London*, 47.

55. Maslen, *Samuel Richardson of London*, 47.

56. Maslen, *Samuel Richardson of London*, 46, 102.

57. Maslen, *Samuel Richardson of London*, 49.

58. Maslen, *Samuel Richardson of London*, 102, 314, 357; Charlotte Lennox, *The Female Quixote; or, The Adventures of Arabella* (London: Printed for A. Millar, 1752), 1:81.

59. Maslen, *Samuel Richardson of London*, 102, 304, 329.

60. Regina Martin, "Specters of Romance: *The Female Quixote* and Domestic Fiction," *Eighteenth-Century Novel* 8, no. 1 (2011): 147; Martin, "'High and Noble Adventures,'" 53.

61. Viele, "Plotting the Coquette," 203–204.

62. The *Novelist's Magazine* edition was part of a series that included *Tristram Shandy* (vol. 5), Tobias Smollett's translation of Miguel de Cervantes's *Don Quixote* (vol. 8), and Alonso Fernández de Avellaneda's continuation of *Don Quixote* (vol. 16).

63. Dorothee Birke, "Direction and Diversion: Chapter Titles in Three Mid-Century English Novels by Sarah Fielding, Henry Fielding, and Charlotte Lennox," *Studies in Eighteenth-Century Culture* 41 (2012): 224.

64. Eve Tavor Bannet, "Quixotes, Imitations, and Transatlantic Genres," *Eighteenth-Century Studies* 40, no. 4 (2007): 553–569.

65. Bannet, "Quixotes, Imitations, and Transatlantic Genres"; Scott Black, "Anachronism and the Uses of Form in *Joseph Andrews*," *Novel: A Forum on Fiction* 38, no. 2–3 (2005): 149.

66. David Marshall, *The Frame of Art: Fictions of Aesthetic Experience, 1750–1815* (Baltimore: Johns Hopkins University Press, 2005), 167; Subligny, *The Mock-Clelia*, 268.

67. Marshall, *The Frame of Art*, 166.

68. Ruth Perry, *Novel Relations: The Transformation of Kinship in English Literature and Culture, 1748–1818* (Cambridge: Cambridge University Press, 2004), 337.

69. Margaret Anne Doody, introduction to *The Female Quixote, or, The Adventures of Arabella*, by Charlotte Lennox, ed. Margaret Dalziel (Oxford: Oxford University Press, 1989), xx–xxi; Debra Malina, "Rereading the Patriarchal Text: *The Female Quixote, Northanger Abbey*, and the Trace of the Absent Mother," *Eighteenth-Century Fiction* 8, no. 2 (1996): 274; Anita Levy, "Reproductive Urges: Literacy, Sexuality, and Eighteenth-Century Englishness," in *Inventing Maternity: Politics, Science, and Literature, 1650–1865*, ed. Susan C. Greenfield and Carol Barash (Lexington: University Press of Kentucky, 1999), 195.

70. Patricia Meyer Spacks, *Desire and Truth: Functions of Plot in Eighteenth-Century English Novels* (Chicago: University of Chicago Press, 1990), 16.

71. Patricia L. Hamilton, "Arabella Unbound: Wit, Judgment, and the Cure of Lennox's *Female Quixote*," in *Masters of the Marketplace: British Women Novelists of the 1750s*, ed. Susan Carlile (Bethlehem, Pa.: Lehigh University Press, 2011), 110–112.

72. Malina, "Rereading the Patriarchal Text," 290.

73. Lennox, *The Lady's Museum*, 1:294.

74. Lennox, *The Lady's Museum*, 1:371.

75. Lennox, *The Lady's Museum*, 1:375.

76. Lennox, *The Lady's Museum*, 2:465.

77. Lennox, *The Lady's Museum*, 2:553.

78. This said, though Arabella's quixotism sets her in direct opposition to her father, there are also suggestions that her quixotic tendency is inherited from him. The Marquis, through

arranging his castle grounds to resemble an "Epitome of *Arcadia*," potentially retires from the world into fantasy (*FQ*, 6).

79. Lennox, *The Lady's Museum*, 1:370.
80. *Covent Garden Journal* 24 (March 24, 1752): n.p.
81. Susan Carlile identifies this as the first translation of *L'ami des femmes* (1758) into English. Lennox, *The Lady's Museum*, 1:13; Carlile, *Charlotte Lennox*, 197.
82. Judith Dorn, "Reading Women Reading History: The Philosophy of Periodical Form in Charlotte Lennox's *The Lady's Museum*," *Historical Reflections / Réflexions Historiques* 18, no. 3 (1992): 17; Manushag N. Powell, *Performing Authorship in Eighteenth-Century English Periodicals* (Lewisburg, Pa.: Bucknell University Press, 2012), 182. For a less didactic reading of *The Lady's Museum*, see Hall, "'All the Bright Eyes of the Kingdom.'"
83. Lennox, *The Lady's Museum*, 1:81.
84. Langbauer, *Women and Romance*, 90; Martin, "'High and Noble Adventures,'" 59.
85. Kate Levin, "'The Cure of Arabella's Mind': Charlotte Lennox and the Disciplining of the Female Reader," *Women's Writing* 2, no. 3 (1995): 276. For an extended reading of connections between *Clarissa* and *The Female Quixote*, see Joseph F. Bartolomeo, "Female Quixotism v. 'Feminine' Tragedy: Lennox's Comic Revision of *Clarissa*," in *New Essays on Samuel Richardson*, ed. Albert J. Rivero (New York: St. Martin's Press, 1996), 163–175.
86. Linda Hutcheon, *A Poetics of Postmodernism: History, Theory, Fiction* (London: Routledge, 1988), 18.
87. Charlotte Lennox, *Shakespear Illustrated: or The Novels and Histories, On which the Plays of Shakespear Are Founded, Collected and Translated from the Original Authors. With Critical Remarks* (London: Printed for A. Millar in the Strand, 1753), 1:89.
88. Margaret Anne Doody, "Shakespeare's Novels: Charlotte Lennox Illustrated," *Studies in the Novel* 19, no. 3 (1987): 302.
89. This theory was suggested by John Mitford, *Gentleman's Magazine*, no. 20 (August 1834): 132; *Gentleman's Magazine*, no. 21 (January 1844): 41. There is no external evidence to support it. See Duncan Isles, "Appendix: Johnson, Richardson, and *The Female Quixote*," in *The Female Quixote, or, The Adventures of Arabella*, by Charlotte Lennox, ed. Margaret Dalziel (1989; repr., Oxford: Oxford University Press, 2008), 419–428. More recently, O. M. Brack and Susan Carlile have demonstrated that Lennox wrote the whole novel. O. M. Brack and Susan Carlile, "Samuel Johnson's Contributions to Charlotte Lennox's *The Female Quixote*," *Yale University Library Gazette* 77, no. 3/4 (2003): 166–173. See also Schürer, *Charlotte Lennox*, xxxvi. Johnson, however, did author the book's dedication.
90. Marshall, *The Frame of Art*, 159.
91. Isles, "Appendix: Johnson, Richardson, and *The Female Quixote*," 424–427; Schürer, *Charlotte Lennox*, 29–31.
92. Carlile, *Charlotte Lennox*, 82–99.
93. Motooka, *The Age of Reasons*, 131.
94. Mack, "Quixotic Ethnography," 197–198; Clarke, *Dr Johnson's Women*, 96.
95. McKeon, *Origins*, 276; Mack "Quixotic Ethnography," 196.
96. Thompson, "Charlotte Lennox and the Agency of Romance," 95–100.
97. Thompson, "Charlotte Lennox and the Agency of Romance," 95–100.

CHAPTER 2 — PERFORMING PRINT IN *POLLY HONEYCOMBE, A DRAMATICK NOVEL OF ONE ACT*

1. The English Short Title Catalogue lists 669 titles with the exact phrase "As it is Acted" published between 1740 and 1770. English Short Title Catalogue, British Library, http://estc.bl.uk (accessed February 10, 2017).

2. David A. Brewer, "Appendix A: The Original Casts of the Plays," in *The Rivals and Polly Honeycombe*, by Richard Brinsley Sheridan and George Colman the Elder, ed. David A. Brewer (Peterborough, Ontario: Broadview Press, 2012), 260. Charles Churchill's satirical poem *The Rosciad* declaims, "Lo Y---s! [. . .] How vilely 'Hark'e! Hark'e!' grates the ear?" Charles Churchill, *The Rosciad* (London: Printed for the author, and sold by W. Flexney, near Gray's-Inn-Gate, 1761), 11.

3. Ros Ballaster, "Rivals for the Repertory: Theatre and Novel in Georgian London," *Restoration and Eighteenth-Century Theatre Research* 27, no. 1 (2012): 6.

4. Samuel Richardson, *The History of Sir Charles Grandison*, ed. Jocelyn Harris (London: Oxford University Press, 1972), 1:5.

5. David A. Brewer, "Print, Performance, Personhood, Polly Honeycombe," *Studies in Eighteenth-Century Culture* 41 (2012): 185–194; Ballaster, "Rivals for the Repertory." See also the Georgian Theatre and the Novel project of which Ballaster is part, which includes an electronic edition and a filmed performance of *Polly Honeycombe* (Oxford University, 2013). "Georgian Theatre and the Novel: 1714–1830—Rivals for the Repertory," https://georgiantheatrenovel.wordpress.com/ (accessed November 26, 2016).

6. See, for instance, Kate Rumbold, *Shakespeare and the Eighteenth-Century Novel: Cultures of Quotation from Samuel Richardson to Jane Austen* (Cambridge: Cambridge University Press, 2016); Francesca Saggini, *Backstage in the Novel: Frances Burney and the Theater Arts* (Charlottesville: University of Virginia Press, 2012); Francesca Saggini, *The Gothic Novel and the Stage: Romantic Appropriations* (London: Pickering and Chatto, 2015); Emily Hodgson Anderson, *Eighteenth-Century Authorship and the Play of Fiction: Novels and the Theater, Haywood to Austen* (New York: Routledge, 2009).

7. Anderson, *Eighteenth-Century Authorship and the Play of Fiction*, 3.

8. Ballaster, "Rivals for the Repertory," 22.

9. David A. Brewer, notes to *Polly Honeycombe*, in *The Rivals and Polly Honeycombe*, by Richard Brinsley Sheridan and George Colman the Elder, ed. David A. Brewer (Peterborough, Ontario: Broadview Press, 2012), 68n5.

10. Brewer, notes to *Polly Honeycombe*, 68n5.

11. The rest of the passage reads: "In all which, the Author is either allow'd to have no Faults at all, or accus'd of having run into more Errors than a Poet could possibly be guilty of." *An Essay on the New Species of Writing founded by Mr. Fielding: With a Word or Two upon the Modern State of Criticism* (London: Printed for W. Owen, near Temple-Bar, 1751), 11.

12. Julie Stone Peters, *Theatre of the Book, 1480–1880: Print, Text, and Performance in Europe* (Oxford: Oxford University Press, 2000), 50.

13. Brewer, "Print, Performance, Personhood, Polly Honeycombe," 192.

14. Richard Steele, *The Tender Husband* (London: Printed for Jacob Tonson, 1705), 26. An anonymous play, referencing Biddy in the title, *Angelica; or Quixote in Petticoats* (1758), describes in its preface how it was rejected by David Garrick on account of its using a subject already adeptly covered by Steele. *Angelica; or Quixote in Petticoats. A Comedy, in Two Acts* (London: Printed for the Author, and sold by the Booksellers of London and Westminster, 1758), iii. Female quixotism is also staged in countless other plays, including, famously, Richard Brinsley Sheridan's *The Rivals* (1775).

15. John Gay, *The Beggar's Opera*, in *Dramatic Works*, ed. John Fuller (Oxford: Clarendon Press, 1983), 2:21.

16. Gay, *The Beggar's Opera*, 2:19.

17. Brewer, "Print, Performance, Personhood, Polly Honeycombe," 186.

18. Its first performance was on December 5, 1760, in Drury Lane. George Winchester Stone Jr., ed., *The London Stage, 1660–1800; A Calendar of Plays, Entertainments and Afterpieces, Together with Casts, Box-Receipts and Contemporary Comment. Compiled from the*

Playbills, Newspapers and Theatrical Diaries of the Period, pt. 4, *1747–1776* (Carbondale: Southern Illinois University Press, 1962), 2:828.

19. Stone, *The London Stage*, pt. 4, 2:828.

20. James Boswell, for instance, enjoyed a performance of *Polly Honeycombe* following *King Lear*. James Boswell, *London Journal* (May 12, 1763), in *Boswell's London Journal, 1762–1763*, ed. Frederick A. Pottle (New Haven, Conn.: Yale University Press, 2004), 256–257. Other plays *Polly Honeycombe* was performed alongside included the Duke of Buckingham's comedy *The Rehearsal* (first performed 1671; first printed 1672) and Nicholas Rowe's tragedy *The Fair Penitent* (1703). Stone, *The London Stage*, pt. 4, 2:828–834.

21. Beyond the first London 1760 edition, there was a 1761 Corke edition, an Edinburgh 1761 edition, two different Dublin 1761 editions, a 1762 "third" London edition, and a "fourth" London edition 1778. Thomas Price argues that an unauthorized edition of *Polly Honeycombe* in Dublin prompted Thomas Becket to style his 1762 altered version of the farce "The THIRD EDITION" to avoid confusion with the Dublin edition. Thomas Price, introduction to *Polly Honeycombe*, in *Critical Edition of the Jealous Wife and Polly Honeycombe*, by George Colman the Elder, ed. Thomas Price (New York: Edwin Mellen Press, 1997), 184.

22. Devendra P. Varma, *The Evergreen Tree of Diabolical Knowledge* (Washington, D.C.: Consortium Press, 1972), 73. *Polly Honeycombe* is included in at least two undated mid-century catalogs of Thomas Lowndes's circulating library as well as catalogs well into the late eighteenth century.

23. Joseph Addison's *Cato* (1713) and John Gay's *The Beggar's Opera* (1728) were published over a hundred times during the eighteenth century. Peters, *Theatre of the Book*, 50, 345n62.

24. *London Magazine* 29 (December 1760): 672; *Edinburgh Magazine* 5 (January 1761): 55. A lengthy notice of *Polly Honeycombe* appeared soon after its first performance in both the *Public Ledger* and the *London Chronicle*. The notice, "*A letter from a young Lady to her friend, on the subject of the New Farce of* POLLY HONEYCOMB, *performed at* Drury-Lane *theatre*" contains such commendations as "never laughed so much in my life." *Public Ledger. Or, Daily Register of Commerce and Intelligence* 1, no. 284 (December 8, 1760): 1133; *The London Chronicle: or, Universal Evening Post* 8, no. 617 (December 6–9, 1760): 556. The *Public Ledger* followed this letter with another one from the same correspondent, further expounding on *Polly Honeycombe*'s merits. *Public Ledger* 1, no. 285 (December 9, 1760): 1137. A virulently negative letter followed in the *London Chronicle*, condemning the play. *The London Chronicle: or, Universal Evening Post* 9, no. 632 (January 10–13, 1761): 47. Milder reviews appeared in other periodicals. The *Monthly Review* reviewed the eight-volume, one-shilling Becket print edition: "Ridicules the fondness of our young Ladies for Novels and Romances. The piece is not ill written; and being well played, it met with a very good reception on the stage." *Monthly Review* 23 (December 1760): 524. Price writes that most critics "were favorably impressed by the new piece," with the major voice of dissent being Tobias Smollett. Price relates Smollett's criticism of *Polly Honeycombe* to Smollett's enmity with Garrick. Price, introduction to *Polly Honeycombe*, 182; Tobias Smollett, *Critical Review; or, Annals of Literature* 10 (December 1760): 486.

25. Ballaster, "Rivals for the Repertory," 10.

26. Smollett, *Critical Review* 10 (December 1760): 486.

27. *The Theatrical Review; or, New Companion to the Play-House* (London: Printed for S. Crowder, 1772), 1:249.

28. Clara Reeve, *The Progress of Romance, through Times, Countries, and Manners; with Remarks on the good and bad effects of them respectively* (Colchester: Printed for the Author by W. Keymer, 1785), 2:8.

29. *The London Chronicle: or, Universal Evening Post* 9, no. 632 (January 10–13, 1761): 47.

30. *The London Chronicle: or, Universal Evening Post* 9, no. 632 (January 10–13, 1761): 47.

31. There is a great body of mid-eighteenth-century writing on the continuities between drama and the novel. For instance, the anonymous *Essay on the New Species of Writing Founded by Mr. Fielding* writes that a novelist "must adhere pretty closely to the Manners of the Drama" (28–29). In the late seventeenth century, William Congreve, in his preface to *Incognita* (1692), also compares the two forms.

32. John Dryden, *Of Dramatick Poesie, an Essay*, in *Prose 1668–1691: An Essay of Dramatick Poesie and Shorter Works*, ed. Samuel Holt Monk, A. E. Wallace Maurer, and Vinton A. Dearing, vol. 17 of *The Works of John Dryden* (Berkeley and Los Angeles: University of California Press, 1971), 75.

33. George Colman the Elder, *Critical Reflections on the Old English Dramatick Writers; Intended as a Preface to the Works of Massinger. Addressed to David Garrick, Esq.* (London: Printed for T. Davies in Russel-Street, Covent-Garden, 1761), 7.

34. Colman, *Critical Reflections*, 6.

35. Colman, *Critical Reflections*, 12, 15.

36. Sarah Fielding and Jane Collier, *The Cry: A New Dramatic Fable*, ed. Carolyn Woodward (Lexington: University Press of Kentucky, 2018), 42.

37. Fielding and Collier, *The Cry*, 42–43.

38. Sarah Fielding, *Remarks on Clarissa, Addressed to the Author* (London: Printed for J. Robinson in Ludgate-Street, 1749), 35.

39. For a description of what it would be like to be an eighteenth-century theatergoer seeing *Polly Honeycombe*, see David A. Brewer, introduction to *The Rivals and Polly Honeycombe*, by Richard Brinsley Sheridan and George Colman the Elder, ed. David A. Brewer (Peterborough, Ontario: Broadview Press, 2012), 20–31.

40. George Colman the Elder and Bonnell Thornton, *The Connoisseur* 1, no. 43 (November 21, 1754), 254, 256.

41. Catherine Gallagher, *Nobody's Story: Gender, Property, and the Rise of the Novel* (Berkeley: University of California Press, 1999), 169–171.

42. Gallagher, *Nobody's Story*, 171.

43. Lisa Freeman, *Character's Theater: Genre and Identity on the Eighteenth-Century English Stage* (Philadelphia: University of Pennsylvania Press, 2002), 18–19.

44. Brewer, introduction to *The Rivals and Polly Honeycombe*, 26, 259.

45. Freeman, *Character's Theater*, 27.

46. Deidre Lynch, *The Economy of Character: Novels, Market Culture, and the Business of Inner Meaning* (Chicago: University of Chicago Press, 1998), 38; Deidre Lynch, "Personal Effects and Sentimental Fictions," *Eighteenth-Century Fiction* 12, no. 2–3 (2000): 345–368; Dror Wahrman, *The Making of the Modern Self: Identity and Culture in Eighteenth-Century England* (New Haven, Conn.: Yale University Press, 2006), 179.

47. Lynch, *The Economy of Character*, 7.

48. April Alliston, "Female Quixotism and the Novel: Character and Plausibility, Honesty and Fidelity," *The Eighteenth Century* 52, no. 3–4 (2011): 264.

49. Alliston's emphasis. Alliston, "Female Quixotism and the Novel," 265.

50. *Public Ledger* 1, no. 284 (December 8, 1760): 1136; *Public Ledger* 1, no. 285 (December 9, 1760): 1137.

51. *Public Ledger* 1, no. 285 (December 9, 1760): 1137.

52. *Public Ledger* 1, no. 285 (December 9, 1760): 1137.

53. Brewer, "Print, Performance, Personhood, Polly Honeycombe," 187.

54. Brewer, "Print, Performance, Personhood, Polly Honeycombe," 188.

55. Paul Goring, *The Rhetoric of Sensibility in Eighteenth-Century Culture* (Cambridge: Cambridge University Press, 2005), 2.

56. Peters, *Theatre of the Book*, 62.

57. Goring, *The Rhetoric of Sensibility*, 146.

58. Goring, *The Rhetoric of Sensibility*, 14.

59. Goring, *The Rhetoric of Sensibility*, 145.

60. Shearer West, *The Image of the Actor: Verbal and Visual Representation in the Age of Garrick and Kemble* (London: Pinter Publishers, 1991), 3.

61. Lynch, *The Economy of Character*, 72. Theories of oratory operated similarly. The prominent elocutionist Thomas Sheridan was interested in the extent affective impressions on the orator's body are legible to the audience. In *A Course of Lectures on Elocution* (1762), he argues that emoting/orating bodies are the surface on which "natural" signs are inscribed, which can be decoded like words. Thomas Sheridan, *A Course of Lectures on Elocution: Together with Two Dissertations on Language; And Some Other Tracts Relative to Those Subjects* (London: Printed by W. Strahan, 1762), 99.

62. Daniel Larlham, "The Felt Truth of Mimetic Experience: Motions of the Soul and the Kinetics of Passion in the Eighteenth-Century Theatre," *The Eighteenth Century* 53, no. 4 (2012): 435.

63. Aaron Hill, "The Art of Acting," in *The Works of the Late Aaron Hill* (London: Printed for the Benefit of the Family, 1753), 3:394; Joseph Roach, *The Player's Passion: Studies in the Science of Acting* (Newark: University of Delaware Press, 1985), 79–81.

64. Aaron Hill, *The Prompter*, no. 66 (June 27, 1735), n.p.

65. Aaron Hill, *An Essay on the Art of Acting*, in *The Works of the Late Aaron Hill* (London: Printed for the Benefit of the Family, 1753), 4:361.

66. Catherine Malabou, *The Future of Hegel: Plasticity, Temporality and Dialectic*, trans. Lisabeth During (London: Routledge, 2005), 8.

67. For example, Mark Akenside's *The Pleasures of the Imagination* (1744) and Joseph Warton's and William Duff's writings. James Engell, *The Creative Imagination: Enlightenment to Romanticism* (Cambridge, Mass.: Harvard University Press, 1981), 49, 85, 86.

68. Hill, "The Art of Acting," 3:408.

69. Hill, *An Essay on the Art of Acting*, 4:356.

70. Hill, *The Prompter*, no. 118 (December 26, 1735), n.p.

71. Hill, *An Essay on the Art of Acting*, 4:356.

72. John Hill, another acting theorist, describes Aaron Hill as "an author of allowed merit" who "requires to be studied as a classic." John Hill, *The Actor; or A Treatise on the Art of Playing, a New Work*, rev. ed. (London: Printed for R. Griffiths, at the Dunciad, 1755), 19.

73. Colman and Thornton, *The Connoisseur* 1, no. 34 (September 19, 1754), 200.

74. Robert Lloyd, *The Actor. A Poetical Epistle to Bonnell Thornton, Esq.* (London: Printed for R. and J. Dodsley, in Pall-Mall, 1760), 17, 20; Colman, *Critical Reflections*, 1.

75. Hill, *An Essay on the Art of Acting*, 4:368–370.

76. Hill, *An Essay on the Art of Acting*, 4:370.

77. William Scott, "George Colman's *Polly Honeycombe* and Circulating Library Fiction in 1760," *Notes and Queries* 15, no. 12 (1968): 465. Scott traced all the titles, except for *Spy on Mother Midnight, or F——'s Adventures*, which is held by the British Library.

78. Patrick Spedding, "Eliza Haywood, Writing (and) Pornography," in *Women Writing, 1550–1750*, ed. Jo Wallwork and Paul Salzman (Melbourne: Meridian, 2001), 241.

79. Peter Sabor, "The Censor Censured: Expurgating *Memoirs of a Woman of Pleasure*," in *'Tis Nature's Fault: Unauthorized Sexuality during the Enlightenment*, ed. Robert Purks Maccubbin (Cambridge: Cambridge University Press, 1988), 199–200.

80. Janet Ing Freeman, "Jack Harris and 'Honest Ranger': The Publication and Prosecution of Harris's *List of Covent-Garden Ladies*, 1760–95," *The Library: The Transactions of the Bibliographical Society* 13, no. 4 (2012): 423–456.

81. *Memoirs of the Celebrated Miss Fanny M[urray]* (London: J. Scott and M. Thrush, 1759), 98–102; Colman and Thornton, *The Connoisseur* 1, no. 49 (January 2, 1755), 294; Colman and Thornton, *The Connoisseur* 2, no. 91 (October 23, 1755), 549. I am indebted to Nicola Parsons for sharing her research on the early history of *Harris's List* with me.

82. *Harris's List of Covent-Garden Ladies; or, New Atalantis for the Year 1761* (London: Printed for H. Ranger, 1761).

83. Kitty Fisher's 1761 entry refers back to her entry in the 1760 edition. *Harris's List of Covent-Garden Ladies* (1761), 49–50. The "Extract" also lists the racy *New Atalantis* annuals for 1758, 1759, and 1760. The *New Atalantis* and *Harris's List* texts were frequently advertised together, and between 1761 and 1767 *Harris's List* went by the long title of *Harris's List of Covent-Garden Ladies; or, New Atalantis*. Freeman, "Jack Harris and 'Honest Ranger,'" 434. The 1764 edition of *Harris's List* advertises the *New Atalantis* for the years 1758, 1759, 1760, 1761, 1762, and 1763. *Harris's List of Covent-Garden Ladies; or, New Atalantis for the Year 1764* (London: Printed for H. Ranger, 1764), xxiv.

84. *Memoirs of the Celebrated Miss Fanny M[urray]*, 100. Another title in the "Extract," *Memoirs of the Shakspear's-Head* (1755), includes a portrayal of Jack Harris.

85. Emma Clery, *The Rise of Supernatural Fiction, 1762–1800* (Cambridge: Cambridge University Press, 1995), 97.

86. Bonnie Blackwell, "Corkscrews and Courtesans: Sex and Death in Circulation Novels," in *The Secret Life of Things: Animals, Objects, and It-Narratives in Eighteenth-Century England*, ed. Mark Blackwell (Lewisburg, Pa.: Bucknell University Press, 2007), 266.

87. Lynch, *The Economy of Character*, 41.

88. See Julie Park, *The Self and It: Novel Objects in Eighteenth-Century England* (Stanford, Calif.: Stanford University Press, 2010), xv.

89. Lothar Müller, *White Magic: The Age of Paper*, trans. Jessica Spengler (Cambridge: Polity Press, 2015), 46.

90. The title page of the first edition of William Guthrie's *The Friends. A Sentimental History* (1754), for instance, unlike the "Extract," places identical emphasis on "Sentimental" and "History." William Guthrie, *The Friends. A Sentimental History: Describing Love as a Virtue, as Well as a Passion* (London: Printed for T. Waller, 1754). Colman also chooses the italics for "Prostitutes of Quality, or Adultery a la Mode; being *authentic* and *genuine* Memoirs of several Persons of the *highest Quality*" (1757); the two existent editions' title pages emphasize "being" and "Memoirs," rather than "authentic," "genuine," and "highest Quality."

91. There appear to be no existing copies of *Clidanor and Cecilia*.

92. This title most likely refers to *The mother-in-Law; or, The innocent sufferer. Interspersed with the uncommon and entertaining adventures of Mr. Hervey Faulconer* (1757), an anonymous novel printed for John and Francis Noble's circulating libraries. Another possible text is a play by James Miller, *The mother-in-law; or, The doctor the disease* (1734). Given that the bulk of the texts in the list are from the 1750s, it is more likely a reference to the anonymous 1757 circulating library novel.

93. This title most likely refers to the anonymous circulating library published novel *The rival mother; or, The history of the Countess De Salens, and her two daughters. In two volumes* (1755).

94. Sarah Raff, *Jane Austen's Erotic Advice* (Oxford: Oxford University Press, 2014), 22.

95. John Locke, *The Clarendon Edition of the Works of John Locke: An Essay Concerning Human Understanding*, ed. Peter H. Nidditch (Oxford: Clarendon Press, 1975), 81.

96. Lynch, *The Economy of Character*, 85.

97. Park, *The Self and It*, xiv.

98. Sean Silver, *The Mind Is a Collection: Case Studies in Eighteenth-Century Thought* (Philadelphia: University of Pennsylvania Press, 2015), 1.

99. Extraction also evokes a reading practice that persisted into the eighteenth century, of selecting passages from the books read and transcribing them into separate notebooks, called commonplace books, for future reading and use. Eve Tavor Bannet, "History of Reading: The Long Eighteenth Century," *Literature Compass* 10, no. 2 (2013): 122–133.

100. Samuel Johnson, *A Dictionary of the English Language: In Which the Words Are Deduced from Their Originals, and Illustrated in Their Different Significations by Examples from the Best Writers*, 2nd ed., 2 vols. (London: Printed by W. Strahan, for J. and P. Knapton; T. and T. Longman; C. Hitch and L. Hawes; A. Millar; and R. and J. Dodsley, 1755–56), s.v. "extract."

101. Johnson, *Dictionary*, s.v. "extract."

102. Elizabeth W. Harries, *The Unfinished Manner: Essays on the Fragment in the Later Eighteenth Century* (Charlottesville: University Press of Virginia, 1994), 149.

103. Harries, *The Unfinished Manner*, 125. For a discussion of dilation, the female body, and textual copia, see Patricia Parker, *Literary Fat Ladies: Rhetoric, Gender, Property* (London: Methuen, 1987), 15, 32–33.

104. A series of "&c." also ends a possible precursor to the "Extract" identified by Price. A short list of titles under the heading "This Day is Published" appears in *The Connoisseur*. "Memoirs of *Lady Vainlove*; Adventures of *Tom Doughty*; *Jack Careless*; *Frank Easy*; *Dick Damnable*; *Molly Pierson*; &c. &c. &c. being a complete Collection of NOVELS for the Amusement of the present winter." With three rather than twenty, the list of "&c." in *The Connoisseur* is significantly shorter than the one in *Polly Honeycombe*. Colman and Thornton, *The Connoisseur* 1, no. 45 (December 5, 1754), 270; Price, introduction to *Polly Honeycombe*, 178.

105. Patrick Spedding and James Lambert, "Fanny Hill, Lord Fanny, and the Myth of Metonymy," *Studies in Philology* 108, no. 1 (2011): 123. Spedding and Lambert argue against Eric Rothstein's interpretation of Fielding's "&c." as vagina. Eric Rothstein, "The Framework of *Shamela*," *ELH* 35, no. 3 (1968): 381–402.

106. A 1693 comedy has "Et Caetera" defined as "a very Aenigmatical Word, and cannot be open'd till the Marriage-knot is ty'd." Roger Boyle, Earl of Orrery, *Guzman. A Comedy. Acted at the Theatre-Royal* (London: Printed for Francis Saunders at the Blue Anchor, 1693), 24; John Cleland's *Memoirs of a Woman of Pleasure* (1748–49) describes Fanny Hill being caressed on her "neck, breast, belly, thighs, and all the sweet *et cetera*, so dear to the imagination." John Cleland, *Memoirs of a Woman of Pleasure: Unexpurgated Text*, ed. Peter Sabor (1985; repr., Oxford: Oxford University Press, 2008), 168. In a parody of Hill's response to *Pamela*, in the preface to Henry Fielding's *Shamela*, Parson Tickletext remarks, "The Comprehensiveness of his [Richardson's] Imagination must be truly prodigious! It has stretched out this diminutive mere Grain of Mustard-seed (a poor Girl's little, &c.) into a Resemblance of that Heaven, which the best of good Books has compared it to." Henry Fielding, *An Apology for the Life of Mrs. Shamela Andrews* (1741), in *The Journal of a Voyage to Lisbon, Shamela, and Occasional Writings*, ed. Martin C. Battestin with Sheridan Warner Baker and Hugh Amory (Oxford: Clarendon Press, 2008), 156. Spedding and Lambert assert that "&c." in this context is deliberately oblique, yet I would suggest that the humor in part stems from the accuracy of Tickletext's description of the plot of *Pamela*, which centers on the accessibility of Pamela's vagina. Spedding and Lambert, "Fanny Hill, Lord Fanny, and the Myth of Metonymy," 123.

107. Scott, "George Colman's *Polly Honeycombe*," 465.

108. The prologue and epilogue were published alongside each other in the *London Chronicle*. *London Chronicle* 8, no. 618 (December 9–11, 1760): 568. The *London Magazine* published "A Humourous Scene" from *Polly Honeycombe* between commentary on Lord Clarendon and Methodism. *London Magazine* 29 (December 1760): 649–651.

109. There are titles in the "Extract" specifically printed for circulating libraries; for instance, *The Fair Citizen* (1757) and Edward Long's *Anti-Gallican, or The History and Adventures of Harry Cobham* (1757) were both printed for Lowndes's circulating library (*PH*, 64). Edward Jacobs, analyzing the 1766 circulating library catalog of Lowndes, shows that the library produced 12 percent of its total publications available. Edward Jacobs, "Eighteenth-Century British Circulating Libraries and Cultural Book History," *Book History* 6 (2003): 8.
110. *Gentleman's Magazine*, no. 37 (December 1767): 580–581.
111. Brewer, "Print, Performance, Personhood, Polly Honeycombe," 188.
112. Samuel Richardson, *Clarissa, or, The History of a Young Lady*, ed. Angus Ross (London: Penguin, 2004), 558.
113. Thomas Keymer, *Sterne, the Moderns and the Novel* (Oxford: Oxford University Press, 2002), 17.

CHAPTER 3 — PENETRATING READERS IN *TRISTRAM SHANDY*

1. Raymond Stephanson, *The Yard of Wit: Male Creativity and Sexuality, 1650–1750* (Philadelphia: University of Pennsylvania Press, 2004), 152.
2. Deidre Lynch, *The Economy of Character: Novels, Market Culture, and the Business of Inner Meaning* (Chicago: University of Chicago Press, 1998), 6.
3. Will Fisher, "Queer Money," *ELH* 66, no. 1 (1999): 9.
4. Jarred Wiehe, "No Penis? No Problem: Intersections of Queerness and Disability in Laurence Sterne's *The Life and Opinions of Tristram Shandy, Gentleman*," *The Eighteenth Century* 58, no. 2 (2017): 191.
5. Stephanson, *The Yard of Wit*, 72.
6. Stephanson, *The Yard of Wit*, 132.
7. Susan Staves, "Don Quixote in Eighteenth-Century England," *Comparative Literature* 24, no. 3 (1972): 202. See also Christopher Narozny and Diana de Armas Wilson, "Heroic Failure: Novelistic Impotence in *Don Quixote* and *Tristram Shandy*," in *The Cervantean Heritage: Reception and Influence of Cervantes in Britain*, ed. J.A.G. Ardila (London: Legenda, 2009), 148; J.A.G. Ardila, "The Influence and Reception of Cervantes in Britain, 1607–2005," in *The Cervantean Heritage: Reception and Influence of Cervantes in Britain*, ed. J.A.G. Ardila (London: Legenda, 2009), 14–15.
8. Wendy Motooka, *The Age of Reasons: Quixotism, Sentimentalism and Political Economy in Eighteenth-Century Britain* (London: Routledge, 1998), 174. See also Amelia Dale, "Gendering the Quixote in Eighteenth-Century England," *Studies in Eighteenth-Century Culture* 46 (2017): 12–15.
9. Leigh A. Ehlers argues for the importance of the Shandy women. Leigh A. Ehlers, "Mrs. Shandy's 'Lint and Basilicon': The Importance of Women in *Tristram Shandy*," *South Atlantic Review* 46, no. 1 (1981): 61–75. Other critics have argued that *Tristram Shandy* is thoroughly sexist; see, for example, Ruth Perry, "Words for Sex: The Verbal-Sexual Continuum in *Tristram Shandy*," *Studies in the Novel* 20 (1988): 24–34; Barbara M. Benedict, "'Dear Madam': Rhetoric, Cultural Politics and the Female Reader in Sterne's *Tristram Shandy*," *Studies in Philology* 89, no. 4 (1992): 485–498.
10. Juliet McMaster, *Reading the Body in the Eighteenth-Century Novel* (Basingstoke: Palgrave Macmillan, 2004), 213; Paula Loscocco, "Can't Live without 'Em: Walter Shandy and the Woman Within," *The Eighteenth Century* 32, no. 2 (1991): 169.
11. Elizabeth W. Harries, "Words, Sex, and Gender in Sterne's Novels," in *The Cambridge Companion to Laurence Sterne*, ed. Thomas Keymer (Cambridge: Cambridge University Press, 2009), 121.

12. For a compelling exception, see Michael Hardin, "'Is There a Straight Line in This Text?' The Homoerotics of *Tristram Shandy*," *Orbis Litterarum* 54, no. 3 (1999): 185–202.

13. Helen Ostovich, "Reader as Hobby-Horse in *Tristram Shandy*," *Philological Quarterly* 68 (1989): 326, 328.

14. Hardin, "'Is There a Straight Line in This Text?,'" 186.

15. Ostovich, "Reader as Hobby-Horse in *Tristram Shandy*," 326; Benedict, "'Dear Madam,'" 489–493.

16. In the records of a large provincial bookseller, *Tristram Shandy* was more popular with men than with women. Jane Fergus, *Provincial Readers in Eighteenth-Century England* (Oxford: Oxford University Press, 2006), 225.

17. The sexual connotations of the word "adventures" during the eighteenth century are used as a basis of comedy in Lennox's *The Female Quixote* (the focus of chapter 1), where Arabella uses it innocently to refer to exciting incidents. "Engaged in many Adventures, Madam! returned Miss *Glanville*, not liking the Phrase: I believe I have been engaged in as few as your Ladyship" (*FQ*, 87). David A. Brewer, "'Scholia' to the Florida *Tristram Shandy* Annotations," *Scriblerian* 30 (1997): 294–295.

18. Benedict, "'Dear Madam,'" 485.

19. Benedict, "'Dear Madam,'" 490.

20. Ostovich, "Reader as Hobby-Horse in *Tristram Shandy*," 330.

21. Hardin, "'Is There a Straight Line in This Text?,'" 186.

22. François, Rabelais, *The Works of Francis Rabelais*, ed. John Ozell, trans. Thomas Urquhart and Peter Motteux, rev. ed. (London: Printed by John Hart, for J. Brindley, 1750), 3:210; Melvyn New, Richard A. Davies, and W. G. Day, eds., *Tristram Shandy: The Notes*, vol. 3 of *The Florida Edition of the Works of Laurence Sterne* (Gainesville: University Presses of Florida, 1984), 240n28.23–25.

23. John Locke, *The Clarendon Edition of the Works of John Locke: An Essay Concerning Human Understanding*, ed. Peter H. Nidditch (Oxford: Clarendon Press, 1975), 363–364.

24. Locke, *An Essay Concerning Human Understanding*, 363.

25. Louis A. Landa, "The Shandean Homunculus: The Background of Sterne's 'Little Gentleman,'" in *Essays in Eighteenth-Century English Literature* (Princeton, N.J.: Princeton University Press, 1980), 140–159; Clara Pinto-Correia, *The Ovary of Eve: Egg and Sperm and Preformation* (Chicago: University of Chicago Press, 1998), 16–64.

26. Loscocco, "Can't Live without 'Em," 166.

27. Carol Kay, *Political Constructions: Defoe, Richardson, and Sterne in Relation to Hobbes, Hume, and Burke* (Ithaca, N.Y.: Cornell University Press, 1988), 232.

28. Susan Stanford Friedman, "Creativity and the Childbirth Metaphor: Gender Difference in Literary Discourse," *Feminist Studies* 13, no. 1 (1987): 52.

29. For an analysis of the glimpses we get of Mrs. Shandy's character, see Ruth Faurot, "Mrs. Shandy Observed," *Studies in English Literature, 1500–1900* 10, no. 3 (1970): 579–589.

30. The poem continues: "Matter too soft a lasting mark to bear." Alexander Pope, "Epistle II. To a Lady, Of the Characters of Women," in *Epistles to Several Persons (Moral Essays)*, ed. F. W. Bateson, vol. 3, pt. 2 of *The Twickenham Edition of the Poems of Alexander Pope*, ed. John Butt (London: Methuen, 1951), lines 2–3, p. 45.

31. Perry, "Words for Sex," 34.

32. Marilyn Francus, *Monstrous Motherhood: Eighteenth-Century Culture and the Ideology of Domesticity* (Baltimore: Johns Hopkins University Press, 2012), 43.

33. The notes to the Florida edition mention how the first successful caesarean, where the mother survived, took place in 1793, and "we may reasonably conclude that it was not an

operation that met with much favour." New, Davies, and Day, *Tristram Shandy: The Notes*, 203nn178.17–179.12.

34. *Tristram Shandy*'s use, and treatment, of Locke's theory of associationism has been the subject of a vast amount of criticism. See Darrell Jones, "Locke and Sterne: The History of a Critical Hobby-Horse," *The Shandean* 27 (2016): 83–111.

35. See Karen Harvey, "What Mary Toft Felt: Women's Voices, Pain, Power and the Body," *History Workshop Journal* 80 (2015): 33–51; Harvey, "Rabbits, Whigs and Hunters: Women and Protest in Mary Toft's Monstrous Births of 1726," *Past & Present* 238, no. 1 (2018): 43–83; Dennis Todd, *Imagining Monsters: Miscreations of the Self in Eighteenth-Century England* (Chicago: University of Chicago Press, 1995), 1–37; Lisa Cody, *Birthing the Nation: Sex, Science, and the Conception of Eighteenth-Century Britons* (Oxford: Oxford University Press, 2005), 129–132.

36. Jane Shaw, "Mary Toft, Religion and National Memory in Eighteenth-Century England," *Journal for Eighteenth-Century Studies* 32, no. 3 (2009): 321. See also Todd, *Imagining Monsters*, 38–63.

37. Bonnie Blackwell, "*Tristram Shandy* and the Theater of the Mechanical Mother," *ELH* 68, no. 1 (2001): 102.

38. For Sir Richard Manningham's role in both the Toft affair and the post-Toft satires that were published about the incident, see Todd, *Imagining Monsters*, 21–26, 67–68, 82–84.

39. Todd connects the Toft affair with *Tristram Shandy*, noting that Tristram's problems stem from the moment of his conception, when "the imaginations of his parents were disordered." Todd, *Imagining Monsters*, 105.

40. Donna Landry and Gerald MacLean, "Of Forceps, Patents, and Paternity: *Tristram Shandy*," *Eighteenth-Century Studies* 23, no. 4 (1990): 539; *Aristoteles Master-piece, Or The Secrets of Generation displayed in all the parts thereof* (London: Printed for J. How, 1684), 25–27.

41. Cody, *Birthing the Nation*, 133.

42. Wiehe, "No Penis? No Problem," 177–193.

43. J. Paul Hunter, "Clocks, Calendars, and Names: The Troubles of Tristram and the Aesthetics of Uncertainty," in *Rhetorics of Order / Ordering Rhetorics in English Neoclassical Literature*, ed. J. Douglas Canfield and J. Paul Hunter (Newark: University of Delaware Press, 1989), 184.

44. Adam Thirlwell, "Reproduction," *The Shandean* 21 (2010): 9–10; Hunter, "Clocks, Calendars, and Names," 182–196.

45. For other associations of the hobby-horse, particularly the Morris dance, see David Oakleaf, "Long Sticks, Morris Dancers, and Gentlemen: Associations of the Hobby-Horse in *Tristram Shandy*," *Eighteenth-Century Life* 11, no. 3 (1987): 62–76.

46. Alexander Pope, *An Essay on Man*, ed. Maynard Mack, vol. 3, pt. 1 of *The Twickenham Edition of the Poems of Alexander Pope*, ed. John Butt (London: Methuen, 1950), lines 141–142, p. 72.

47. George Cheyne, *The English Malady, or, A Treatise of Nervous Diseases of All Kinds* (London: G. Strahan and J. Leake, 1733), 181.

48. Carol Houlihan Flynn, "Running Out of Matter: The Body Exercised in Eighteenth-Century Fiction," in *The Languages of Psyche: Mind and Body in Enlightenment Thought*, ed. G. S. Rousseau (Berkeley: University of California Press, 1990), 149.

49. George Cheyne, *The Letters of Doctor George Cheyne to Samuel Richardson (1723–1743)*, ed. Charles F. Mullett (Columbia: University of Missouri, 1943), 60; Flynn, "Running Out of Matter," 148–149.

50. T. C. Duncan Eaves and Ben D. Kimpel, *Samuel Richardson: A Biography* (Oxford: Clarendon Press, 1971), 63–64.

51. William Mottolese, "Tristram Cyborg and Toby Toolmaker: Body, Tools, and Hobby-horse in *Tristram Shandy*," *Studies in English Literature, 1500–1900* 47, no. 3 (2007): 681; Ross King, "*Tristram Shandy* and the Wound of Language," *Studies in Philology* 92, no. 3 (1995): 294; Wiehe, "No Penis? No Problem," 178.

52. Frank Brady calls it "reverse impregnation." Frank Brady, "*Tristram Shandy*: Sexuality, Morality, and Sensibility," *Eighteenth-Century Studies* 4, no. 1 (1970): 42.

53. Mottolese, "Tristram Cyborg and Toby Toolmaker," 681–682.

54. Thomas Laqueur, *Making Sex: Body and Gender from the Greeks to Freud* (Cambridge, Mass.: Harvard University Press, 1992), 150. See also Anthony Fletcher, *Gender, Sex and Subordination in England 1500–1800* (New Haven, Conn.: Yale University Press, 1995), 33–42.

55. Miriam L. Wallace, "Gender Bending and Corporeal Limitations: The Modern Body in *Tristram Shandy*," *Studies in Eighteenth Century Culture* 26 (1997): 180.

56. Kay, *Political Constructions*, 232–233.

57. Kay, *Political Constructions*, 233. See also Carol Kay, "Canon, Ideology, and Gender: Mary Wollstonecraft's Critique of Adam Smith," *New Political Science* 15, no. 1 (1986): 63–76.

58. Especially in the sense to "tickle your toby." See, for instance, Thomas Otway's play *The Souldiers Fortune*, first performed in 1680, which contains the line "Tickle my Guts, you Mad-cap! I'll tickle your Toby if you do." Thomas Otway, *The Souldiers Fortune*, in *The Works of Thomas Otway*, vol. 2, *Plays, Poems, and Love-Letters*, ed. J. C. Ghosh (Oxford: Clarendon Press, 1932), 164. This sense continues across the century. See, for example, "There, that chair is charged with electric fluid; and; if any one touches that, a single turn of this handle will tickle their tobies." Thomas Dibdin, *Five Miles Off: or, The Finger Post; a Comedy, in Three Acts* (London: Printed and Published by Barker and Son, 1806), 35. See also Brady, "*Tristram Shandy*: Sexuality, Morality, and Sensibility," 42; Max Nänny, "Similarity and Contiguity in *Tristram Shandy*," *English Studies: A Journal of English Language and Literature* 60 (1979): 422–435; New, Davies, and Day, *Tristram Shandy: The Notes*, 94nn57.19–58.2.

59. Harries, "Words, Sex, and Gender in Sterne's Novels," 118.

60. Peter de Voogd, "*Tristram Shandy* as Aesthetic Object," *Word and Image: A Journal of Verbal/Visual Enquiry* 4, no. 1 (1988): 386–387.

61. Alex Wetmore, *Men of Feeling in Eighteenth-Century Literature: Touching Fiction* (Basingstoke: Palgrave Macmillan, 2013), 37.

62. William Holtz, "Typography, *Tristram Shandy*, the Aposiopesis, Etc.," in *The Winged Skull: Papers from the Laurence Sterne Bicentenary Conference*, ed. Arthur H. Cash and John M. Stedmond (London: Methuen, 1971), 252.

63. Narozny and Wilson, "Heroic Failure."

64. Sigurd Burckhardt notes that in *Tristram Shandy* the nose belongs "simultaneously to both the realm of words and that of things." It is at once a physical object, a bodily part, susceptible to mutilation, yet it also (through Walter's theory of its link with masculine potency and Slawkenbergius's story) comes to stand in as a sign for the penis. Sigurd Burckhardt, "*Tristram Shandy*'s Law of Gravity," *ELH* 28, no. 1 (1961): 83.

65. See also Motooka, *The Age of Reasons*, 196.

66. Wetmore, *Men of Feeling in Eighteenth-Century Literature*, 17.

67. Paul Goring, *The Rhetoric of Sensibility in Eighteenth-Century Culture* (Cambridge: Cambridge University Press, 2005), 201.

68. Pagination, with odd numbers on rectos, was "nearly universal" by the late sixteenth century. Michael F. Suarez, S.J., and H. R. Woudhuysen, eds., *The Oxford Companion to the Book* (Oxford: Oxford University Press, 2010), 2:994.

69. The Penguin edition of *Tristram Shandy* (2003), edited by Melvyn New and Joan New, follows the Florida edition in omitting ten pages, and the Oxford edition, edited by Ian Campbell Ross (1983), also skips ten pages. The Norton edition edited by Howard Ander-

son (1980) does not skip any pages. For a discussion of other examples of rendering the "chasm," see Nicholas D. Nace, "Unprinted Matter: Conceptual Writing and *Tristram Shandy*'s 'Chasm of Ten Pages,'" *The Shandean* 24 (2013): 31–58.

70. Ostovich, "Reader as Hobby-Horse in *Tristram Shandy*," 327.

71. Patricia Meyer Spacks notes "conflicts over control" between writer and reader in *Tristram Shandy*. Patricia Meyer Spacks, *Imagining a Self: Autobiography and Novel in Eighteenth-Century England* (Cambridge, Mass.: Harvard University Press, 1976), 129.

72. Staves, "Don Quixote in Eighteenth-Century England," 203.

73. Ian Campbell Ross, *Laurence Sterne: A Life* (Oxford: Oxford University Press, 2001), 282, 332–333, 405–407.

CHAPTER 4 — ENTHUSIASM, METHODISTS, AND METAPHORS IN *THE SPIRITUAL QUIXOTE*

1. Misty G. Anderson, *Imagining Methodism in Eighteenth-Century Britain: Enthusiasm, Belief and the Borders of the Self* (Baltimore: Johns Hopkins University Press, 2012), 146.

2. See, for example, Isaac Disraeli, *Miscellanies; or, Literary Recreations* (London: Printed for T. Cadell and W. Davies, 1796), 382.

3. Horace Walpole, *The Yale Edition of Horace Walpole's Correspondence*, ed. W. S. Lewis (New Haven, Conn.: Yale University Press, 1937–83), 20:81–82.

4. Samuel Foote, *The Minor, a Comedy* (London: Printed and sold by J. Coote, in Pater-Noster Row, 1760), 47.

5. A second edition was printed within the same year of its first publication (though dated 1774), and a third in 1783 and a fourth in 1792, as well as unauthorized printings in Dublin and the United States and a German and Dutch translation. All these editions were published anonymously, though Graves described himself on the title pages of his later works as "Editor of *The Spiritual Quixote*," capitalizing on the novel's success. Clarence Tracy, *A Portrait of Richard Graves* (Cambridge, U.K.: James Clarke, 1987), 128–129. *The Spiritual Quixote* (along with *The Female Quixote*) was included in Anna Letitia Barbauld's fifty-volume collection, *The British Novelists; With an Essay, and Prefaces Biographical and Critical, by Mrs. Barbauld* (London: F.C. and J. Rivington, 1810).

6. "Much indeed of his material came out of his own experience only slightly transmogrified in the process." Clarence Tracy, introduction to *The Spiritual Quixote, or The Summer's Ramble of Mr. Geoffry Wildgoose, a Comic Romance*, by Richard Graves, ed. Clarence Tracy (London: Oxford University Press, 1967), xix. See also Tracy, *A Portrait of Richard Graves*, 44.

7. Anderson, *Imagining Methodism*, 52.

8. Phyllis Mack, *Heart Religion in the British Enlightenment: Gender and Emotion in Early Methodism* (Cambridge: Cambridge University Press, 2008), 3.

9. Tracy, introduction to *The Spiritual Quixote*, xv; Anderson, *Imagining Methodism*, 220.

10. Dragoş Ivana, *Embattled Reason, Principled Sentiment and Political Radicalism: Quixotism in English Novels, 1742–1801* (Amsterdam: Rodopi, 2014), 229–230; Henry Fielding, *Joseph Andrews*, ed. Martin C. Battestin (Middletown, Conn.: Wesleyan University Press, 1966), 4.

11. The title *The Spiritual Quixote* had been used previously for a book by Pierre Quesnel, *The Spiritual Quixote; or The Entertaining History of Don Ignatius Loyola, founder of the Order of the Jesuits* (1755). J.A.G. Ardila argues that this text is quixotic only in title. J.A.G. Ardila, "The Influence and Reception of Cervantes in Britain, 1607–2005," in *The Cervantean Heritage: Reception and Influence of Cervantes in Britain*, ed. J.A.G. Ardila (London: Legenda, 2009), 23.

12. Voltaire, *Micromegas: A Comic Romance. Being a Severe Satire Upon the Philosophy, Ignorance, and Self-Conceit of Mankind. Together with a Detail of the Crusades: And a New Plan for the History of the Human Mind. Translated from the French of M. De Voltaire* (London: Printed for D. Wilson, and T. Durham, at Plato's Head, near Round-Court, in the Strand, 1753).

13. David Hempton, *Methodism: Empire of the Spirit* (New Haven, Conn.: Yale University Press, 2006), 33.

14. John Locke, *The Clarendon Edition of the Works of John Locke: An Essay Concerning Human Understanding*, ed. Peter H. Nidditch (Oxford: Clarendon Press, 1975), 699.

15. John Trenchard, *The Natural History of Superstition* (London: Sold by A. Baldwin at the Oxford Arms in Warwick Lane, 1709), 34.

16. For the publication dates of Hudibras, see Ashley Marshall, "The Aims of Butler's Satire in *Hudibras*," *Modern Philology* 105, no. 4 (2008): 637n2.

17. Don Quixote famously confused windmills with giants. Miguel de Cervantes, *The History and Adventures of the Renowned Don Quixote*, trans. Tobias Smollett (London: Printed for A. Millar, over against Catherine-Street, in the Strand, 1755), 1:37–38; George Lavington, *The Enthusiasm of Methodists and Papists Compared. In Three Parts* (London: Printed for J. and P. Knapton, in Ludgate-Street, 1754), 1:21.

18. *A Sovereign Remedy for the cure of Hypocrisy and Blind Zeal, Extracted from the Salutary Precepts of Jesus Christ* (London: Printed for T. Becket and P. A. de Hondt, near Surry-Street, in the Strand, 1764), 19.

19. Such sentiments are (with complex irony) reiterated by Henry Tilney in Jane Austen's *Northanger Abbey*: "Remember the country and the age in which we live. Remember that we are English, that we are Christians." Jane Austen, *Northanger Abbey*, ed. Barbara M. Benedict and Deirdre Le Faye (Cambridge: Cambridge University Press, 2006), 203.

20. Anderson, *Imagining Methodism*, 204, 30. In Graves's sermon "On Miracles," he describes miracles as occurring only when there is a dire need for social and religious reform, when "horrible practices" and "lewd and idolatrous worship" need to be curbed. Richard Graves, *Sermons* (Bath: Printed by R. Cruttwell; and sold by F. and C. Rivington, 1799), 66.

21. Conal Condren, *Argument and Authority in Early Modern England* (Cambridge: Cambridge University Press, 2006), 211.

22. Tracy identifies the books as Edward Fisher, *The Marrow of Divinity* (1645); Michael Sparke, *The Crumbs of Comfort* (6th ed., 1627); and John Price, *Honey out of the Rock* (1644). Clarence Tracy, notes to *The Spiritual Quixote, or The Summer's Ramble of Mr. Geoffry Wildgoose, a Comic Romance*, by Richard Graves, ed. Clarence Tracy (London: Oxford University Press, 1967), 477n19.

23. John Kersey's dictionary defines "collop" as a "slice of meat." John Kersey, *A New English Dictionary; or, A Compleat Collection of the Most Proper and Significant Words, and Terms of Art, Commonly Used in the Language*, 8th ed. (London: Printed for L. Hawes, 1772), s.v. "collop." In earlier centuries, "collop" could also refer to eggs with or without sliced meat. *Oxford English Dictionary Online*, s.v. "collop," accessed July 12, 2014, www.oed.com.

24. Condren, *Argument and Authority*, 211.

25. Anderson, *Imagining Methodism*, 27. Tillotson's nominalist Eucharist was part of a broad spectrum of Anglican beliefs in the Eucharist during the eighteenth century. Brian Douglas, *A Companion to Anglican Eucharistic Theology*, vol. 1, *The Reformation to the 19th Century* (Leiden: Brill, 2012), 293–294. The devotional manual *The Whole Duty of Man* (c. 1658), for instance, which Wildgoose dismisses as being as fanciful as "Jack the Giant-Killer" (*SQ*, 81), associates the consecrated bread and wine with the presence of Christ, linking the sign with the signified, but does not merge the two: Christ is present only in a spiritual sense, and the wafer does not become Christ's body. Douglas, *A Companion to Anglican*

Eucharistic Theology, 1:232–233. Wildgoose quotes Whitefield on Tillotson, "as knowing 'no more of Christianity than Mahomet.'" Tracy, notes to *The Spiritual Quixote*, 481n81.

26. See John Wesley, *The Works of the Late Reverend John Wesley, A.M.: From the Latest London Edition with the Last Corrections of the Author, Comprehending Also Numerous Translations, Notes, and an Original Preface, Etc.*, ed. John Emory (New York: Waugh and Mason, 1835), 5:400. Wesley refutes the insinuation of a belief in transubstantiation. Of course, these arguments were complicated by the contemporaneous controversy over what "spirit" and "matter" were, the precise role of the Trinity in the Eucharist, and the possibility of consubstantiation. David Butler, *Methodists and Papists: John Wesley and the Catholic Church in the Eighteenth Century* (London: Darton, Longman and Todd, 1995), 31.

27. *Critical Review* 16 (December 1763): 449.

28. Karin Littau, *Theories of Reading: Books, Bodies, and Bibliomania* (Cambridge, U.K.: Polity Press, 2006), 40–41. For another example, see the *Monthly Review*'s review of the novel *The History of the Miss Baltimores* (1783): "The mental imbecility which requires food of so very tender a nature, as is here set before us, is almost, if not entirely, past even the hope of cure!" *Monthly Review* 69 (November 1783): 439. James Beattie describes how, for people with lively imaginations, "[h]istory, philosophy, and simple nature suit not their taste: but those romances they greedily devour, which contain delusive pictures of happiness, or incredible exaggerations of calamity." James Beattie, *Dissertations Moral and Critical. On Memory and Imagination. On Dreaming. The Theory of Language. On Fable and Romance. On the Attachments of Kindred. Illustrations on Sublimity* (London: Printed for W. Strahan; and T. Cadell, in the Strand, 1783), 195.

29. For example, "This Drama [. . .] is a most unanswerable Satyr against the late Spirit of Enthusiasm." *Tatler*, no. 11 (May 3–5, 1709), n.p.

30. See also R. K. Webb, "Rational Piety," in *Enlightenment and Religion: Rational Dissent in Eighteenth-Century Britain*, ed. Knud Haakonssen (Cambridge: Cambridge University Press, 1996), 287–311. "[P]ractical piety," Jon Mee argues, "was not just the product of wisdom and learning, it was often defined by a modest restraint which kept its revelations to itself." Jon Mee, *Romanticism, Enthusiasm, and Regulation: Poetics and the Policing of Culture in the Romantic Period* (Oxford: Oxford University Press, 2003), 34. Arguably, during his life, Graves could be described as "reasonable" in his religion, and reserved when it came to discussing his religious views and experiences. Tracy, *A Portrait of Richard Graves*, 80–85.

31. Isabel Rivers, *Reason, Grace, and Sentiment: A Study of the Language of Religion and Ethics in England, 1600–1780* (Cambridge: Cambridge University Press, 1991), 1:216–217.

32. *The Spiritual Quixote*'s emphasis on the spiritual pleasures of the Christian heaven as opposed to the carnality of "other" religions echoes numerous eighteenth-century contrasts to the Christian heaven with conceptions of the Islamic paradise. Philip C. Almond, *Heaven and Hell in Enlightenment England* (Cambridge: Cambridge University Press, 1994), 105–106.

33. Richard Graves to James Dodsley, October 13, 1777, Letters, AL0287, Bath Record Office: Local Studies.

34. Tracy, introduction to *The Spiritual Quixote*, xxii.

35. See, for instance, the print *The Harlequin Methodist* (1750). The two hieroglyphic prints, *The Retort* (1760) and *Retort upon Retort* (1760), suggest a congruity between Foote's and Whitefield's discourse. For a comprehensive account of the "prickly connection" between Methodism and the theater, see Anderson, *Imagining Methodism*, 130–141.

36. Whitefield writes in his autobiography: "[T]aking a Play, to read a Passage out of it to a Friend, GOD struck my Heart with such Power, that I was obliged to lay it down again; and blessed be his Name, I have not read any such Book since." George Whitefield, *A Short Account of God's Dealings with the Reverend Mr. George Whitefield, A. B. Late of*

Pembroke-College, Oxford. From His Infancy, to the Time of His Entring into Holy Orders (London: Printed by W. Strahan, and sold by James Hutton, 1740), 25; Tracy, notes to *The Spiritual Quixote*, 487n244.

37. Goring notes that Graves holds quixotic fictions "*with* but *separately from* the most monumental of Richardson's works, suggesting his awareness that these represent different types of writing although they share the common feature of being instructive." Paul Goring, *The Rhetoric of Sensibility in Eighteenth-Century Culture* (Cambridge: Cambridge University Press, 2005), 83.

38. Anderson, *Imagining Methodism*, 224.

39. Henry Fielding's *Joseph Andrews*, another Cervantine influence on Graves, also offers a remasculinization of the quixotic subject. See Amelia Dale, "Gendering the Quixote in Eighteenth-Century England," *Studies in Eighteenth-Century Culture* 46 (2017): 9–12.

40. For Methodism and gender instability, see Anderson, *Imagining Methodism*, 71–72.

41. 1 Peter 2:2; Isaiah 66:11–13; Numbers 11:12. Citations are to the Authorized (King James) Version. Rachel Trubowitz, *Nation and Nurture in Seventeenth-Century English Literature* (Oxford: Oxford University Press, 2012), 122; Nicola Parsons, *Reading Gossip in Early Eighteenth-Century England* (Basingstoke: Palgrave Macmillan, 2009), 14. The metaphor of a monarch as a nurse persisted throughout the eighteenth century. The ministers and elders of Edinburgh are recorded as saying upon George II's accession to the throne, "[W]e shall find in your Majesty another nursing Father to our Church." *The Addresses to King George II. On His Accession to the Throne. To Which Is Added, an Exact and True List of the Present Parliament; Also His Majesty's First Speech, and the Addresses of the Lords and Commons* (London: Printed and sold by J. Cluer, in Bow Church-Yard; and by the booksellers of London and Westminster, 1727), 37.

42. Anderson, *Imagining Methodism*, 72.

43. "He brought me to the banqueting house, and his banner over me *was* love" (2:4).

44. The Aristotelian belief that breast milk was transformed blood was still existent in the late eighteenth century. Wesley himself describes how "blood forces its way" into the breasts of a pregnant woman, "till after the birth, they run with thick milk." John Wesley, *A Survey of the Wisdom of God in the Creation; or A Compendium of Natural Philosophy* (Bristol: Printed by William Pine, 1770), 1:60. Milk and blood's symbolic interchangeableness features in Methodist hymns, part of a tradition that stretches back to late medieval paintings of crucified Jesus, where his wound on his side spurts milk into his disciples' mouths. Mack, *Heart Religion in the British Enlightenment*, 214.

45. Marilyn Yalom, *A History of the Breast* (New York: Alfred A. Knopf, 1997), 106; Valerie Fildes, *Breasts, Bottles and Babies: A History of Infant Feeding* (Edinburgh: Edinburgh University Press, 1989), 99.

46. Tracy, notes to *The Spiritual Quixote*, 481n74(2); George Whitefield, *Christ the Best Husband; or An Earnest Invitation to Young Women to Come and See Christ. A Sermon Preached to a Society of Young Women, in Fetter-Lane* (London: C. Whitefield, 1740), 5.

47. G. J. Barker-Benfield, *The Culture of Sensibility: Sex and Society in Eighteenth-Century Britain* (Chicago: University of Chicago Press, 1992), 272.

48. Dennis Todd, *Imagining Monsters: Miscreations of the Self in Eighteenth-Century England* (Chicago: University of Chicago Press, 1995), 98.

49. Paula McDowell, "Mediating Media Past," in *This Is Enlightenment*, ed. Clifford Siskin and William Warner (Chicago: University of Chicago Press, 2010), 241. William Hogarth's painting *Sleeping Congregation* (c. 1735) provides a good illustration of the perceived dullness of the typical Anglican sermon, and can be contrasted to the gripping (if dangerous) theater described in Hogarth's *Enthusiasm Delineated* (1761).

50. Goring, *The Rhetoric of Sensibility*, 81–90.

51. In *A Discourse Concerning the Mechanical Operation of the Spirit* (1704), Jonathan Swift describes enthusiasm as a "launching out the Soul, as it is purely an Effect of Artifice and *Mechanick Operation.*" Jonathan Swift, *A Tale of a Tub and Other Works*, ed. Marcus Walsh (Cambridge: Cambridge University Press, 2010), 173.

52. Swift's *Mechanical Operation of the Spirit* is again potentially evoked: "[I]n Spiritual Harangues, the Disposition of the Words according to the Art of Grammar, hath not the least Use, but the Skill and Influence wholly lye in the Choice and Cadence of the Syllables." Swift, *Mechanical Operation of the Spirit*, 180.

53. Hempton, *Methodism: Empire of the Spirit*, 87.

54. Edmund Gibson, *Observations upon the Conduct and Behaviour of a Certain Sect, Usually Distinguished by the Name of Methodists*, 2nd ed. (London: E. Owen, 1744), 4.

55. Hempton, *Methodism: Empire of the Spirit*, 33.

56. Tracy, notes to *The Spiritual Quixote*, 475n2; William Warburton, *The Doctrine of Grace: or, the Office and Operations of the Holy Spirit Vindicated from the Insults of Infidelity, and the Abuses of Fanaticism* (London: Printed for A. Millar, and J. and R. Tonson, 1763), 2:169.

57. Vicesimus Knox, "On Novel Reading," in *Essays Moral and Literary*, rev. ed. (London: Charles Dilly, 1782), 1:70.

58. John Gregory, *A Father's Legacy to His Daughters*, 4th ed. (London: Printed for W. Strahan; T. Cadell, in the Strand; and J. Balfour, and W. Creech, at Edinburgh, 1774), 54.

59. Barker-Benfield, *The Culture of Sensibility*, 268.

60. Thomas Sheridan, *A Course of Lectures on Elocution: Together With Two Dissertations on Language; And Some other Tracts relative to those Subjects* (London: Printed by W. Strahan, 1762), 120.

61. Goring, *The Rhetoric of Sensibility*, 73.

62. Lavington, *The Enthusiasm of Methodists and Papists Compared*, 2:220.

63. The passage reads: "His spirit hath adorned the heavens, and his obstetric hand brought forth the winding serpent" (Job 26:13; Douay Version, first published 1609).

64. Alexander Pope, *The Dunciad*, ed. James Sutherland, in *The Twickenham Edition of the Poems of Alexander Pope*, ed. John Butt (London: Methuen, 1965), (B) IV, lines 386, 394, pp. 5:379–380; Adrian Wilson, *The Making of Man-Midwifery: Childbirth in England, 1660–1770* (Cambridge, Mass.: Harvard University Press, 1995), 86, 90n36.

65. Lisa Cody, *Birthing the Nation: Sex, Science, and the Conception of Eighteenth-Century Britons* (Oxford: Oxford University Press, 2005), 195.

66. *The Spiritual Quixote*'s connection between the Methodist new birth and the gender-bending man-midwife—and Dr. Slop in particular—is anticipated by a pamphlet purporting to be from Whitefield to Sterne (1760), and part of the same pamphlet war that produced *The Retort* and *Retort upon Retort*. In the letter, Dr. Slop is used to mock both the Methodist new birth and the literalism of Methodist discourse: "'Tis not Dr. *Slop* the man-midwife, 'tis not a papist quack that can by obstetric art, make you again enter your mother's womb, or come out of it again; Dr. Slop can never make you a child of election. There is but one man-midwife that can procure you a new birth, and that man-midwife is no other than the man J—s—s Ch—st." *A Letter from the Rev. George Whitfield, B.A. to the Rev. Laurence Sterne, M.A. The Supposed Author of a Book entitled the Life and Opinions of Tristram Shandy, Gentleman* (London: [n.p.], 1760), 15.

67. George Whitefield, *A Continuation of the Reverend Mr. Whitefield's Journal, from His Arrival at London, to His Departure from thence on his Way to Georgia*, 3rd ed. (London: Printed for James Hutton, at the Bible and Sun, 1739), 36; Tracy, notes to *The Spiritual Quixote*, 487n250.

68. Graves, *Sermons*, 29.

69. Warburton, *The Doctrine of Grace*, 1:103.

70. Arthur Robert Winnett, *Peter Browne: Provost, Bishop, Metaphysician* (London: S.P.C.K., 1974), 133. Wesley's belief in direct, unmediated experience of God was a split with Browne.

71. Peter Browne, *Things Divine and Supernatural Conceived by Analogy With Things Natural and Human* (London: Printed for William Innys and Richard Manby at the West-End of St. Paul's, 1733), 86.

72. Frederick A. Dreyer, *The Genesis of Methodism* (Cranbury, N.J.: Lehigh University Press, 1999), 84; David W. Bebbington, *Evangelicalism in Modern Britain: A History from the 1730s to the 1980s* (London: Routledge, 1989), 49–50.

73. Wesley, "The Circumcision of the Heart" in *Works*, 1:147.

74. Graves, *Sermons*, 28–29.

75. Influential defenses of theism on the grounds of design included Anthony Ashley Cooper, third Earl of Shaftesbury's *The Moralists* (1709) and Bishop George Berkeley's *Alciphron* (1732). For an overview of the argument by design and its variations, exponents, and opponents, see Dorothy Coleman, introduction to *Dialogues Concerning Natural Religion, and Other Writings*, by David Hume, ed. Dorothy Coleman (Cambridge: Cambridge University Press, 2007), xi–xli; A. M. Stewart, "Arguments for the Existence of God: The British Debate," in *The Cambridge History of Eighteenth-Century Philosophy*, ed. Knud Haakonssen (Cambridge: Cambridge University Press, 2006), 2:717–720.

76. Richard Graves, *The Love of Order: A Poetical Essay. In Three Cantos* (London: J. Dodsley, in Pall-Mall, 1773).

77. Graves included this description: "An handsome old Elm in the fore-ground, under which Wildgoose, with his hat on, harangues his first little audience [. . .] in the back ground a remarkable hill with a few trees about half a mile distant." Graves to James Dodsley, October 13, 1777, Letters, AL0287, Bath Record Office: Local Studies.

78. Graves to Dodsley, October 13, 1777, Letters, AL0287, Bath Record Office: Local Studies.

79. From John Milton, *Paradise Lost*, book 5, line 153. Wildgoose continues, reciting lines 154–159. The same quotation appears, in a similar context—admiring the view—in Charles Lucas's anti-Jacobin novel *The Infernal Quixote* (1801). Charles Lucas, *The Infernal Quixote: A Tale of the Day*, ed. M. O. Grenby (Peterborough, Ontario: Broadview Press, 2004), 302.

80. Milton was frequently cited in eighteenth-century paeans to nature, and the *Paradise Lost* passages set in Eden were especially popular. Malcolm Andrews, *The Search for the Picturesque: Landscape Aesthetics and Tourism in Britain, 1760–1800* (Stanford, Calif.: Stanford University Press, 1989), 12.

81. It is a clear shift from Graves's original plans for the frontispiece (figure 10). The first edition does not have illustrations.

82. Robert J. Mayhew, *Landscape, Literature and English Religious Culture, 1660–1800: Samuel Johnson and Languages of Natural Description* (Basingstoke: Palgrave Macmillan, 2004), 49; Wesley, *Works*, 4:463. Wesley records his first visit to Shenstone's gardens on Saturday, July 13, 1782, nine years after *The Spiritual Quixote* had been published. "I never was so surprised. I have seen nothing in all England to be compared with it. It is beautiful and elegant all over." Though Wildgoose accuses Shenstone's gardens of being idolatrous, Wesley stresses their lack of pretension: "[T]here is nothing grand, nothing costly; no temples, so called." Wesley, *Works*, 4:563.

83. Mee, *Romanticism, Enthusiasm, and Regulation*, 30.

CHAPTER 5 — CITATIONAL QUIXOTISM IN *MEMOIRS OF MODERN PHILOSOPHERS*

1. William Godwin, *The Enquirer. Reflections on Education, Manners, and Literature* (London: Printed for G. G. and J. Robinson, Paternoster-Row, 1797), 32.

2. Joe Bray, *The Female Reader in the English Novel: From Burney to Austen* (New York: Routledge, 2009), 72.
3. *Anti-Jacobin Review and Magazine* 7 (September 1800): 39.
4. A second and third edition of *Memoirs* was published during the first year of its publication, with the third having 1801 on the title page. They were followed by a fourth in 1804. Claire Grogan, *Politics and Genre in the Works of Elizabeth Hamilton, 1756–1816* (Farnham, U.K.: Ashgate, 2012), 52.
5. Simon Schaffer, "States of Mind: Enlightenment and Natural Philosophy," in *The Languages of Psyche: Mind and Body in Enlightenment Thought*, ed. G. S. Rousseau (Berkeley: University of California Press, 1990), 244.
6. See also Sarah Green's *The Reformist!!! A Serio-comic Political Novel* (1810) for another, later example of a reworking of Graves's *The Spiritual Quixote* with anti-Jacobin elements, also published by the Minerva Press.
7. Charles Lucas, *The Infernal Quixote: A Tale of the Day*, ed. M. O. Grenby (Peterborough, Ontario: Broadview Press, 2004), 160.
8. Lucas, *The Infernal Quixote*, 161.
9. *British Critic* 16 (October 1800): 439–440.
10. James Mosley, "The Technologies of Print," in *The Oxford Companion to the Book*, ed. Michael F. Suarez, S.J., and H. R. Woudhuysen (Oxford: Oxford University Press, 2010), 1:97.
11. Mosley, "The Technologies of Print," 1:97.
12. Richard De Ritter, *Imagining Women Readers, 1789–1820* (Manchester: Manchester University Press, 2014), 113.
13. Nicola J. Watson, *Revolution and the Form of the British Novel, 1790–1825: Intercepted Letters, Interrupted Seductions* (Oxford: Clarendon Press, 1994), 10.
14. That Harriet reads the notorious skeptic David Hume's *History of England* further demonstrates it is not what authors one reads but how one reads them that is at the forefront of *Memoirs'* concerns.
15. Patricia Parker, *Literary Fat Ladies: Rhetoric, Gender, Property* (London: Methuen, 1987), 9.
16. Parker, *Literary Fat Ladies*, 26.
17. Gary Kelly, *Women, Writing, and Revolution, 1790–1827* (Oxford: Clarendon Press, 1993), 153.
18. De Ritter's point about "germ" is again relevant. De Ritter, *Imagining Women Readers*, 113.
19. Ina Ferris, *The Achievement of Literary Authority: Gender, History, and the Waverley Novels* (Ithaca, N.Y.: Cornell University Press, 1991), 38. Some examples include: "Terrorist Novel Writing," in *The Spirit of the Public Journals for 1797. Being an Impartial Selection of the Most Exquisite Essays and Jeux D'esprits, Principally Prose, That Appear in Newspapers and Other Publications* (London: Printed for R. Phillips, 1798), 223; Mary Alcock, "A Receipt For Writing A Novel," in *Poems, &c. &c.* (London: Printed for C. Dilly, Poultry, 1799), 89–93.
20. W. M. Verhoeven, general introduction to *Anti-Jacobin Novels*, ed. W. M Verhoeven (London: Pickering and Chatto, 2005), 1:li. See also Kelly, *Women, Writing, and Revolution*, 157.
21. Lisa Wood, *Modes of Discipline: Women, Conservatism, and the Novel after the French Revolution* (Lewisburg, Pa.: Bucknell University Press, 2003), 94.
22. Susan B. Egenolf, *The Art of Political Fiction in Hamilton, Edgeworth, and Owenson* (Farnham, U.K.: Ashgate, 2009), 5.
23. For Hamilton's defense of her own writing as a woman, see *Letters of a Hindoo Rajah*, where a male character asks Charlotte Percy, Hamilton's own, slightly satiric self-portrait, "Why [. . .] should your mind, cultivated as it has been by education, and improved by listening to the conversation of the enlightened and the judicious; why should it not exert its powers, not only for your own entertainment, but for the instruction or innocent amusement of

others?" Elizabeth Hamilton, *Translation of the Letters of a Hindoo Rajah*, ed. Pamela Perkins and Shannon Russell (Peterborough, Ontario: Broadview Press, 2004), 302–303.

24. Kelly, *Women, Writing, and Revolution*, 157; Claire Grogan, introduction to *Memoirs of Modern Philosophers*, by Elizabeth Hamilton, ed. Claire Grogan (Peterborough, Ontario: Broadview Press, 2000), 24.

25. Kelly, *Women, Writing, and Revolution*, 157–158. Similarly, Graves connects Methodists' enthusiasm to that of Puritan rebels by citing *Hudibras* in *The Spiritual Quixote*. See chapter 4.

26. See, for instance, Claudia L. Johnson, *Jane Austen: Women, Politics, and the Novel* (Chicago: University of Chicago Press, 1988), xxi; Miriam L. Wallace, "Crossing from 'Jacobin' to 'Anti-Jacobin': Rethinking the Terms of English Jacobinism," in *Romantic Border Crossings*, ed. Jeffrey Cass and Larry Peer (Aldershot: Ashgate, 2008), 100–104; John Bugg, *Five Long Winters: The Trials of British Romanticism* (Stanford, Calif.: Stanford University Press, 2014), 109–111.

27. M. O. Grenby, *The Anti-Jacobin Novel: British Conservatism and the French Revolution* (Cambridge: Cambridge University Press, 2001), 4.

28. See chapters 2 and 3 of Grogan, *Politics and Genre*. The following critics class *Memoirs* as an anti-Jacobin novel, or Hamilton as an anti-Jacobin writer: Peter Garside, introduction to *Memoirs of Modern Philosophers*, by Elizabeth Hamilton, ed. Peter Garside (New York: Routledge, 1992), viii; Grenby, *The Anti-Jacobin Novel*, 26–27, 69–70; Wood, *Modes of Discipline*, 76–77; Nancy Johnson, "The 'French Threat' in Anti-Jacobin Novels of the 1790s," in *Illicit Sex: Identity Politics in Early Modern Culture*, ed. Thomas DiPiero and Pat Gill (Athens: University of Georgia Press, 1997), 184; Yi-Cheng Weng, "'She Had Recourse to Her Pen': Radical Voices in Elizabeth Hamilton's *Memoirs of Modern Philosophers*," *Romantic Textualities* 22 (2017): 36–51. The following critics query this classification: Janice Farrar Thaddeus, "Elizabeth Hamilton's Domestic Politics," *Studies in Eighteenth Century Culture* 23 (1994): 266–267; Miriam L. Wallace, *Revolutionary Subjects in the English "Jacobin" Novel, 1790–1805* (Lewisburg, Pa.: Bucknell University Press, 2009), 223–250; Eleanor Ty, "Female Philosophy Refunctioned: Elizabeth Hamilton's Parodic Novel," *Ariel* 22, no. 4 (1991): 111–129; Katherine Binhammer, "The Persistence of Reading: Governing Female Novel-Reading in *Memoirs of Emma Courtney* and *Memoirs of Modern Philosophers*," *Eighteenth-Century Life* 27, no. 2 (2003): 2–3.

29. Wallace, *Revolutionary Subjects*, 224–225.

30. Garside, introduction to *Memoirs of Modern Philosophers*, x.

31. *Anti-Jacobin Review and Magazine* 7 (September 1800): 39–66; *Anti-Jacobin Review and Magazine* 7 (December 1800): 369–376; *British Critic* 16 (October 1800): 439–440. That said, the classification was not unanimous. The *Scots Magazine*, for instance, wrote that *Memoirs* "was far from displaying here that violent spirit of *Anti Jacobinism*, conspicuous in many similar works [. . .]. There breathed through it, on the contrary, a very liberal spirit, and a zeal, within certain limits, for the freedom of philosophical inquiry." *Scots Magazine and Edinburgh Literary Miscellany* 78 (August 1816): 564.

32. Quoted in Grenby, *The Anti-Jacobin Novel*, 212–213n10; George Walker, *Le Vagabond, ou la rencontre de deux philosophes républicains; Roman philosophique, traduit de l'anglais de George Walker* (Paris: Hénée et Dumas, et al., 1807), v–vi.

33. Grenby, *The Anti-Jacobin Novel*, 184–185.

34. Grenby, *The Anti-Jacobin Novel*, 184–185; Ty, "Female Philosophy Refunctioned," 111–129; Johnson, *Jane Austen: Women, Politics, and the Novel*, 21.

35. Grenby, *The Anti-Jacobin Novel*, 10–11.

36. Grenby, *The Anti-Jacobin Novel*, 27, 20.
37. Jane West, *A Tale of the Times* (London: Printed for T. N. Longman and O. Rees, Paternoster-Row, 1799), 3:386–387. See also Jane West, *The Infidel Father* (London: Printed by A. Strahan, Printers-Street, for T. N. Longman, and O. Rees, Paternoster-Row, 1802), 1:ii. Similarly, George Walker writes in *The Vagabond* (1799), "[P]erhaps a *Novel* may gain attention, when arguments of the soundest sense and most perfect eloquence shall fail to arrest the feet of the *Trifler* from the specious paths of the new Philosophy. It is also an attempt to parry the Enemy with their own weapons; for no channel is deemed improper by them, which can introduce their sentiments." George Walker, *The Vagabond: A Novel*, ed. W. M. Verhoeven (Peterborough, Ontario: Broadview Press, 2004), 53.
38. To assert that anti-Jacobin novels are quixotic narratives, simultaneously reacting against and exploiting particular tropes, is not to deny that the quixotic narrative was used by "Jacobin" texts. Mary Wollstonecraft and Hays, for instance, were similarly concerned with the female, quixotic novel reader. See, for instance, Mary Hays, *Memoirs of Emma Courtney* (1796); Mary Wollstonecraft, *The Wrongs of Woman, or Maria* (1798).
39. Binhammer, "The Persistence of Reading," 3.
40. Ty, "Female Philosophy Refunctioned," 121; April London, "Novel and History in Anti-Jacobin Satire," *Yearbook of English Studies* 30 (2000): 77. See also Johnson, *Jane Austen: Women, Politics, and the Novel*, 6–7.
41. Linda Hutcheon, *A Theory of Parody: The Teachings of Twentieth-Century Art Forms* (London: Methuen, 1985), 6.
42. In Hays's own novel, Emma's transgressions are intimately connected with her reading of Rousseau, with Emma describing Harley as "the St Preux, the Emilius, of my sleeping and waking reveries." Mary Hays, *Memoirs of Emma Courtney*, ed. Eleanor Ty (1996; repr., Oxford: Oxford University Press, 2009), 59. See also Watson, *Revolution and the Form of the British Novel*, 85–86; Binhammer, "The Persistence of Reading," 8–9.
43. Claire Grogan, notes to *Memoirs of Modern Philosophers*, by Elizabeth Hamilton, ed. Claire Grogan (Peterborough, Ontario: Broadview Press, 2000), 310n30.
44. Lucas, *The Infernal Quixote*, 174n.
45. M. O. Grenby, introduction to *The Infernal Quixote: A Tale of the Day*, by Charles Lucas, ed. M. O. Grenby (Peterborough, Ontario: Broadview Press, 2004), 17.
46. Dragoş Ivana, *Embattled Reason, Principled Sentiment and Political Radicalism: Quixotism in English Novels, 1742–1801* (Amsterdam: Rodopi, 2014), 254.
47. Lucas, *The Infernal Quixote*, 127, 99.
48. Lucas, *The Infernal Quixote*, 75, 84.
49. Marilyn Butler, *Jane Austen and the War of Ideas* (Oxford: Oxford University Press, 1975), 118.
50. Lucas, *The Infernal Quixote*, 86.
51. Binhammer, "The Persistence of Reading," 15–16.
52. Hamilton herself was raised in a mixed religious household. Elizabeth Benger, *Memoirs of the Late Mrs. Elizabeth Hamilton; With a Selection from Her Correspondence, and Other Unpublished Writings* (London: Longman, Hurst, Rees, Orme, and Brown, 1818), 1:39–40.
53. See, for example, *Anti-Jacobin Review and Magazine* 1 (October 1798): 410; Lucas, *The Infernal Quixote*, 161–163.
54. Hamilton was not the only woman who was prompted, by her religion, to differ from the ultraconservative *Anti-Jacobin Review*. Hannah More was attacked by the *Anti-Jacobin Review* when she established a Sunday school in Mendips. See Anne Stott, "Hannah More and the Blagdon Controversy, 1799–1802," *Journal of Ecclesiastical History* 51, no. 2 (2000): 229–331.

55. *Memoirs* is not the only anti-Jacobin novel to deviate from this rule. In Lucas's *The Infernal Quixote*, Emily, who is seduced by the villainous Marauder, is allowed a happy marriage to Rattle after her repentance.

56. Grogan, *Politics and Genre*, 62.

57. Hamilton herself founded a House of Industry for indigent women. Pam Perkins, introduction to *The Cottagers of Glenburnie, and Other Educational Writing*, by Elizabeth Hamilton, ed. Pam Perkins (Glasgow: Association for Scottish Literary Studies, 2010), 13.

58. William Shenstone, *The Works in Verse and Prose, of William Shenstone, Esq; Most of which were never before printed* (London: Printed for R. and J. Dodsley in Pall-Mall, 1764), 1:99. This is the same William Shenstone who is represented in Graves's *The Spiritual Quixote*, discussed in the previous chapter.

59. Gary Kelly, *English Fiction of the Romantic Period, 1789–1830* (London: Longman, 1989), 149.

60. Jon Mee, "Anti-Jacobin Novels: Representation and Revolution," *Huntington Library Quarterly* 69, no. 4 (2006): 652. For instance, Godwin's statement that given the choice of who to save from a burning house, one should save the life that is more "valuable" (even if this means one's wife, mother, or benefactor dies) is cited in Walker's *The Vagabond*, when the anti-hero's mistress and her father are both trapped in a burning house. He cannot decide who will be the most use to society, so they both burn while he hesitates. William Godwin, *An Enquiry Concerning Political Justice*, ed. Mark Philp (Oxford: Oxford University Press, 2013), 53–54; Walker, *The Vagabond*, 84–86.

61. Kelly, *Women, Writing, and Revolution*, 148–149.

62. Elizabeth Hamilton, *Letters on the Elementary Principles of Education*, 3rd ed. (Bath: R. Crutwell, 1803), 2:34n, 2:34. First edition published as *Letters on Education* (1801).

63. For Hamilton's connections with Scottish "common sense" philosophy, see Pam Perkins, "Enlightening the Female Mind: Education, Sociability, and the Literary Woman in the Work of Elizabeth Hamilton," in *Women Writers and the Edinburgh Enlightenment*, Scottish Cultural Review of Language and Literature 15 (Amsterdam: Rodopi, 2010), 106; Fiona Price, "Democratizing Taste: Scottish Common Sense Philosophy and Elizabeth Hamilton," *Romanticism* 8, no. 2 (2002): 181–186; Rosalind Russell, "Elizabeth Hamilton: Enlightenment Educator," *Scottish Educational Review* 18, no. 1 (1986): 24–25.

64. Dugald Stewart, *Elements of the Philosophy of the Human Mind* (London: Printed for A. Strahan, and T. Cadell, 1792–1827), 1:405–406.

65. John Sutton, *Philosophy and Memory Traces: Descartes to Connectionism* (Cambridge: Cambridge University Press, 1998), 225.

66. For example, "Who also hath made us able ministers of the new testament; not of the letter, but of the spirit; for the letter killeth, but the spirit giveth life" (2 Corinthians 3:6 [Authorized (King James) Version]).

67. Elizabeth Hamilton, *Letters, Addressed to the Daughter of a Nobleman, on the Formation of Religious and Moral Principle*, facsimile of the second edition (1806), with an introduction by Gina Luria (New York: Garland Publishing, 1974), 2:111.

68. Hamilton, *Letters, Addressed to the Daughter of a Nobleman*, 2:124. For Hamilton's belief in the importance of an internalized piety, see her comments in her journal, on October 25, 1812: "The mode of worship, or the form in which my public prayers are offered up to God, I know to be a matter of indifference as to the *mere form*, so that they be *really* offered up 'in spirit and in truth.'" Benger, *Memoirs of the Late Mrs. Elizabeth Hamilton*, 1:264.

69. Hamilton, *Letters on the Elementary Principles of Education*, 1:111; Hannah More, *Strictures on the Modern System of Female Education*, 2nd ed. (London: T. Cadell Jun. and W. Davies, 1799), 2:193.

70. Benger, *Memoirs of the Late Mrs. Elizabeth Hamilton*, 2:195.
71. Elizabeth Hamilton, *The Cottagers of Glenburnie, and Other Educational Writing*, ed. Pam Perkins (Glasgow: Association for Scottish Literary Studies, 2010), 205, 202. See also Hamilton, *Letters on the Elementary Principles of Education*, 1:145.
72. Hamilton, *Letters, Addressed to the Daughter of a Nobleman*, 2:44. Similarly, in *Letters on the Elementary Principles of Education*, Hamilton writes, "[S]eek for the *general meaning* in the *general spirit* of the Gospel writers." Hamilton, *Letters on the Elementary Principles of Education*, 2:294.
73. Benger, *Memoirs of the Late Mrs. Elizabeth Hamilton*, 1:214.
74. Benger, *Memoirs of the Late Mrs. Elizabeth Hamilton*, 1:215.
75. The *Anti-Jacobin Review* reiterates this in its review of *Memoirs*: "Had the education of Julia been grounded on the doctrines of Christianity, instead of the vapid rules of modern honour," Julia would have been safe. *Anti-Jacobin Review and Magazine* 7 (December 1800): 375.
76. Lucas, *The Infernal Quixote*, 102.
77. *Anti-Jacobin Review and Magazine* 7 (September 1800): 41.
78. Adriana Craciun, *British Women Writers and the French Revolution: Citizens of the World* (Basingstoke: Palgrave Macmillan, 2005), 29.
79. Mee, "Anti-Jacobin Novels," 652.
80. Jane Rendall, "Hamilton and the *Memoirs of Agrippina*," in *Wollstonecraft's Daughters: Womanhood in England and France, 1780–1920*, ed. Clarissa Campbell Orr (Manchester: Manchester University Press, 1996), 90.
81. Grogan, *Politics and Genre*, 62.
82. Kelly, *Women, Writing, and Revolution*, 158.
83. Linda E. Merians, *Envisioning the Worst: Representations of "Hottentots" in Early-Modern England* (Newark: University of Delaware Press, 2001).
84. Grogan, *Politics and Genre*, 67–68.
85. Grogan, *Politics and Genre*, 68.
86. Grogan, *Politics and Genre*, 68–69.
87. Sara, Sarje, or Sarah Baartman is the subject of extensive scholarship. See, for instance, Natasha Gordon-Chipembere, ed., *Representation and Black Womanhood: The Legacy of Sarah Baartman* (Basingstoke: Palgrave Macmillan, 2011); Clifton Crais and Pamela Scully, *Sarah Baartman and the Hottentot Venus: A Ghost Story and a Biography* (Princeton, N.J.: Princeton University Press, 2009).
88. Crais and Scully, *Sarah Baartman and the Hottentot Venus*, 133.
89. Grogan, *Politics and Genre*, 71.
90. Erwin Panofsky, *Studies in Iconology: Humanistic Themes in the Art of the Renaissance* (New York: Harper and Row, 1962), 195. Jacob Huysmans's portrait of John Wilmot Rochester features the famous libertine poet crowning a monkey with a laurel wreath. Don-John Dugas argues that Rochester's interaction with the monkey involves Rochester acknowledging his base desires and embracing them. Don-John Dugas, "The Significance of 'Lord Rochester's Monkey,'" *Studia Neophilologica* 69, no. 1 (1997): 17.
91. *A New Dictionary of the Terms Ancient and Modern of the Canting Crew* defines "pug" as "Pugnasty, a meer Pug, a nasty Slut, a sorry Jade, of a Woman; also a Monkey." B.E., *A New Dictionary of the Terms Ancient and Modern of the Canting Crew* (London: W. Hawes, P. Gilbourne, W. Davis, 1699), s.v. "pug." In 1710, Thomas Ward wrote: "Whoever knew a Royal fancy / Stoop thus to such a Pug as *Nancy*." Thomas Ward, *England's Reformation from the Time of King Henry the VIIIth to the End of Oates's Plot* (Hambourgh [Saint-Omer]: [n.p.], 1710), 16.

92. Laura Brown, *Homeless Dogs and Melancholy Apes: Humans and Other Animals in the Modern Literary Imagination* (Ithaca, N.Y.: Cornell University Press, 2010), 105; Stephen Jay Gould, "The Hottentot Venus," *Natural History* 91, no. 10 (1982): 22; Georges Cuvier, "Extrait d'observations faites sur le cadavre d'une femme connue à Paris et à Londres sous le nom de Vénus Hottentotte," *Mémoires du Muséum d'histoire naturelle* 3 (1817): 259–274.

93. Jan Nederveen Pieterse, *White on Black: Images of Africa and Blacks in Western Popular Culture* (New Haven, Conn.: Yale University Press, 1995), 40–42.

94. Ingrid H. Tague, *Animal Companions: Pets and Social Change in Eighteenth-Century Britain* (University Park: Pennsylvania State University Press, 2015), 80–81.

95. Edward Long, *The History of Jamaica, or, General Survey of the Antient and Modern State of That Island* (London: Printed for T. Lowndes, 1774), 2:374–375.

96. Long, *The History of Jamaica*, 2:383.

97. Long, *The History of Jamaica*, 2:364.

98. Merians, *Envisioning the Worst*, 135. See also Mary L. Bellhouse, "Candide Shoots the Monkey Lovers: Representing Black Men in Eighteenth-Century French Visual Culture," *Political Theory* 34, no. 6 (2006): 741–784. For literary precedents, see Voltaire's *Candide* (1759). Voltaire, *Candide and Other Stories,* trans. Roger Pearson (Oxford: Oxford University Press, 2008), 37. The scene between the Hottentot female and the monkey is inverted in Jonathan Swift's *Gulliver's Travels* (1726), when a female Yahoo attacks Gulliver. Jonathan Swift, *Gulliver's Travels*, ed. David Womersley (Cambridge: Cambridge University Press, 2012), 266–267.

99. A similar scene occurs in Frances Burney's *Evelina* (1778), where Captain Mirvan plays a prank, confronting the foppish Mr. Lovel with a monkey introduced as Lovel's "twin-brother." Frances Burney, *Evelina, or, a Young Lady's Entrance into the World*, 2nd ed. (London: Printed for T. Lowndes, 1779), 3:250.

100. Brown, *Homeless Dogs and Melancholy Apes*, 27–63, 110.

101. Tague, *Animal Companions*, 56–57.

102. Edward Ward, *The Modern World Disrob'd; or, Both Sexes Stript of Their Pretended Vertue* (London: Printed for G.S. and sold by J. Woodward, 1708), 10.

103. Bellhouse, "Candide Shoots the Monkey Lovers," 746.

104. Ronald Paulson, "Emulative Consumption and Literacy: The Harlot, Moll Flanders, and Mrs. Slipslop," in *The Consumption of Culture, 1600–1800: Image, Object, Text*, ed. Ann Bermingham and John Brewer (London: Routledge, 1995), 384.

CONCLUSION

1. David Hartley, *Observations on Man, His Frame, His Duty, and His Expectations. In Two Parts* (London: Printed by S. Richardson, 1749), 1:12.

2. Alex Wetmore, *Men of Feeling in Eighteenth-Century Literature: Touching Fiction* (Basingstoke: Palgrave Macmillan, 2013), 54.

3. Hartley, *Observations on Man*, 1:77.

4. John Sutton, *Philosophy and Memory Traces: Descartes to Connectionism* (Cambridge: Cambridge University Press, 1998), 225.

5. Thomas Reid, *Essays on the Intellectual Powers of Man* (Edinburgh and London: Printed for John Bell and G.G.J. and J. Robinson, 1785), 102.

6. Sutton, *Philosophy and Memory Traces*, 262, 66.

7. Reid, *Essays on the Intellectual Powers of Man*, 31.

8. Samuel Taylor Coleridge, *Biographia Literaria*, ed. Adam Roberts (Edinburgh: Edinburgh University Press, 2014), 71.

9. Coleridge, *Biographia Literaria*, 73.

10. Sutton, *Philosophy and Memory Traces*, 225; Richard De Ritter, *Imagining Women Readers, 1789–1820* (Manchester: Manchester University Press, 2014), 29.

11. *Quarterly Review* 2, no. 3 (August 1809): 146.

12. M. O. Grenby argues that 1798–1805 was the high point of the anti-Jacobin novel. M. O. Grenby, *The Anti-Jacobin Novel: British Conservatism and the French Revolution* (Cambridge: Cambridge University Press, 2001), 10.

13. Sarah Green, *Romance Readers and Romance Writers (1810)*, ed. Christopher Goulding (London: Routledge, 2016), 99.

14. As well as Bridgetina and Julia in Elizabeth Hamilton's *Memoirs of Modern Philosophers* (1800, chapter 5), others include Sophia in Mary Charlton's *Rosella* (1799), Angelina in Maria Edgeworth's "Angelina; or, L'Amie Inconnue" (1801), and Corinna in E. M. Foster's *The Corinna of England* (1809).

15. Eaton Stannard Barrett, *The Heroine, or Adventures of a Fair Romance Reader*, ed. Avril Horner and Sue Zlosnik (Kansas City, Mo.: Valancourt Books, 2011), 287.

16. Barrett, *The Heroine*, 288.

17. For the crisis of sensibility, see G. J. Barker-Benfield, *The Culture of Sensibility: Sex and Society in Eighteenth-Century Britain* (Chicago: University of Chicago Press, 1992), 121; Claudia L. Johnson, *Equivocal Beings: Politics, Gender, and Sentimentality in the 1790s* (Chicago: University of Chicago Press, 1995).

18. Wetmore, *Men of Feeling in Eighteenth-Century Literature*, 153.

19. James Mosley, "The Technologies of Print," in *The Oxford Companion to the Book*, ed. Michael F. Suarez, S.J., and H. R. Woudhuysen (Oxford: Oxford University Press, 2010), 1:92.

20. Michael Suarez, S.J., and H. R. Woudhuysen, eds., *The Oxford Companion to the Book* (Oxford: Oxford University Press, 2010), 2:901.

21. Jane Austen, *Sense and Sensibility*, ed. Edward Copeland (Cambridge: Cambridge University Press, 2006), 7. Sarah Raff argues that within Marianne's quixotic narrative her (re-)education is suggestively aligned with a sexual fall rather than a reformation. Sarah Raff, *Jane Austen's Erotic Advice* (Oxford: Oxford University Press, 2014), 35–36.

22. Jane Austen, *Northanger Abbey*, ed. Barbara M. Benedict and Deirdre Le Faye (Cambridge: Cambridge University Press, 2006), 203.

23. Austen, *Northanger Abbey*, 256. For an extended discussion of how Austen inverts the conventions of a quixotic narrative in *Northanger Abbey*, see Raff, *Jane Austen's Erotic Advice*, 100–129.

24. Jane Austen, *Love and Freindship*, in *Juvenilia*, ed. Peter Sabor (Cambridge: Cambridge University Press, 2006), 108; Jane Austen, *Persuasion*, ed. Janet Todd and Antje Blank (Cambridge: Cambridge University Press, 2006), 108.

25. Jane Austen, *Sanditon*, in *Later Manuscripts*, ed. Janet Todd and Linda Bree (Cambridge: Cambridge University Press, 2008), 183.

26. Austen, *Sanditon*, 183.

27. Austen, *Sanditon*, 183.

28. Kate Flint, *The Woman Reader, 1837–1914* (Oxford: Oxford University Press, 1993), 251.

29. *Church of England Quarterly Review* 11 (April 1842): 287–288.

30. Flint, *The Woman Reader*, 252.

Addison, Joseph. *Dialogues Upon the Usefulness of Ancient Medals. Especially in Relation to the Latin and Greek Poets.* [N.p]: 1726.

The Addresses to King George II. On His Accession to the Throne. To Which Is Added, an Exact and True List of the Present Parliament; Also His Majesty's First Speech, and the Addresses of the Lords and Commons. London: Printed and sold by J. Cluer, in Bow Church-Yard; and by the booksellers of London and Westminster, 1727.

Ahmed, Sara. *The Cultural Politics of Emotion.* Edinburgh: Edinburgh University Press, 2004.

Alcock, Mary. *Poems, &c. &c.* London: Printed for C. Dilly, Poultry, 1799.

Allestree, Richard. *The Ladies Calling.* 2nd ed. 2 vols. Oxford: Printed at the Theater, 1673.

Alliston, April. "Female Quixotism and the Novel: Character and Plausibility, Honesty and Fidelity." *The Eighteenth Century* 52, no. 3–4 (2011): 249–269.

Almond, Philip C. *Heaven and Hell in Enlightenment England.* Cambridge: Cambridge University Press, 1994.

Anderson, Emily Hodgson. *Eighteenth-Century Authorship and the Play of Fiction: Novels and the Theater, Haywood to Austen.* New York: Routledge, 2009.

Anderson, Misty G. *Imagining Methodism in Eighteenth-Century Britain: Enthusiasm, Belief and the Borders of the Self.* Baltimore: Johns Hopkins University Press, 2012.

Andrews, Malcolm. *The Search for the Picturesque: Landscape Aesthetics and Tourism in Britain, 1760–1800.* Stanford, Calif.: Stanford University Press, 1989.

Angelica; or Quixote in Petticoats. A Comedy, in Two Acts. London: Printed for the Author, and sold by the Booksellers of London and Westminster, 1758.

Anti-Jacobin Review and Magazine. 1798–1800.

Ardila, J.A.G., ed. *The Cervantean Heritage: Reception and Influence of Cervantes in Britain.* London: Legenda, 2009.

———. "The Influence and Reception of Cervantes in Britain, 1607–2005." In *The Cervantean Heritage: Reception and Influence of Cervantes in Britain,* edited by J.A.G. Ardila, 2–31. London: Legenda, 2009.

Aristoteles Master-piece, Or The Secrets of Generation displayed in all the parts thereof. London: Printed for J. How, 1684.

Aristotle. *Complete Works of Aristotle: The Revised Oxford Translation.* Edited by Jonathan Barnes. Princeton, N.J.: Princeton University Press, 2014. Vol. 1.

Austen, Jane. *Love and Freindship.* In *Juvenilia,* edited by Peter Sabor, 101–141. Cambridge: Cambridge University Press, 2006.

———. *Northanger Abbey.* Edited by Barbara M. Benedict and Deirdre Le Faye. Cambridge: Cambridge University Press, 2006.

———. *Persuasion.* Edited by Janet Todd and Antje Blank. Cambridge: Cambridge University Press, 2006.

———. *Sanditon.* In *Later Manuscripts,* edited by Janet Todd and Linda Bree, 137–209. Cambridge: Cambridge University Press, 2008.

————. *Sense and Sensibility*. Edited by Edward Copeland. Cambridge: Cambridge University Press, 2006.

Bacon, Francis. *The Instauratio Magna Part II: Novum Organum and Associated Texts*. Edited by Graham Rees and Maria Wakely. Vol. 11 of *The Oxford Francis Bacon*. Oxford: Oxford University Press, 2004.

————. *The Instauratio Magna Part III: Historia Naturalis et Experimentalis: Historia Ventorum and Historia Vitæ & Mortis*. Edited by Graham Rees and Maria Wakely. Vol. 12 of *The Oxford Francis Bacon*. Oxford: Oxford University Press, 2007.

Ballaster, Ros. "Rivals for the Repertory: Theatre and Novel in Georgian London." *Restoration and Eighteenth-Century Theatre Research* 27, no. 1 (2012): 5–24.

Bannet, Eve Tavor. "History of Reading: The Long Eighteenth Century." *Literature Compass* 10, no. 2 (2013): 122–133.

————. "Quixotes, Imitations, and Transatlantic Genres." *Eighteenth-Century Studies* 40, no. 4 (2007): 553–569.

Barbauld, Anna Letitia. *The British Novelists; with an Essay, and Prefaces Biographical and Critical, by Mrs. Barbauld*. 50 vols. London: F.C. and J. Rivington, 1810.

Barchas, Janine. *Graphic Design, Print Culture, and the Eighteenth-Century Novel*. Cambridge: Cambridge University Press, 2003.

Barker, Jane. *The Lining of the Patch-Work Screen; Design'd for the Farther Entertainment of the Ladies*. London: Printed for A. Bettesworth, at the Red Lion in Pater-Noster Row, 1726.

Barker-Benfield, G. J. *The Culture of Sensibility: Sex and Society in Eighteenth-Century Britain*. Chicago: University of Chicago Press, 1992.

Barrett, Eaton Stannard. *The Heroine, or Adventures of a Fair Romance Reader*. Edited by Avril Horner and Sue Zlosnik. Kansas City, Mo.: Valancourt Books, 2011.

Bartolomeo, Joseph F. "Female Quixotism v. 'Feminine' Tragedy: Lennox's Comic Revision of *Clarissa*." In *New Essays on Samuel Richardson*, edited by Albert J. Rivero, 163–175. New York: St. Martin's Press, 1996.

Beattie, James. *Dissertations Moral and Critical. On Memory and Imagination. On Dreaming. The Theory of Language. On Fable and Romance. On the Attachments of Kindred. Illustrations on Sublimity*. London: Printed for W. Strahan; and T. Cadell, in the Strand, 1783.

Bebbington, David W. *Evangelicalism in Modern Britain: A History from the 1730s to the 1980s*. London: Routledge, 1989.

Bellhouse, Mary L. "Candide Shoots the Monkey Lovers: Representing Black Men in Eighteenth-Century French Visual Culture." *Political Theory* 34, no. 6 (2006): 741–784.

Benedict, Barbara M. "'Dear Madam': Rhetoric, Cultural Politics and the Female Reader in Sterne's *Tristram Shandy*." *Studies in Philology* 89, no. 4 (1992): 485–498.

Benger, Elizabeth. *Memoirs of the Late Mrs. Elizabeth Hamilton; With a Selection from Her Correspondence, and Other Unpublished Writings*. 2 vols. London: Longman, Hurst, Rees, Orme, and Brown, 1818.

Bermingham, Ann, and John Brewer, eds. *The Consumption of Culture, 1600–1800: Image, Object, Text*. London: Routledge, 1995.

Binhammer, Katherine. "The Persistence of Reading: Governing Female Novel-Reading in *Memoirs of Emma Courtney* and *Memoirs of Modern Philosophers*." *Eighteenth-Century Life* 27, no. 2 (2003): 1–22.

Birke, Dorothee. "Direction and Diversion: Chapter Titles in Three Mid-Century English Novels by Sarah Fielding, Henry Fielding, and Charlotte Lennox." *Studies in Eighteenth-Century Culture* 41 (2012): 211–232.

Black, Scott. "Anachronism and the Uses of Form in *Joseph Andrews*." *Novel: A Forum on Fiction* 38, no. 2–3 (2005): 147–164.

Blackwell, Bonnie. "Corkscrews and Courtesans: Sex and Death in Circulation Novels." In *The Secret Life of Things: Animals, Objects, and It-Narratives in Eighteenth-Century England*, edited by Mark Blackwell, 262–291. Lewisburg, Pa.: Bucknell University Press, 2007.

———. "*Tristram Shandy* and the Theater of the Mechanical Mother." *ELH* 68, no. 1 (2001): 81–133.

Boswell, James. *Boswell's London Journal, 1762–1763*. Edited by Frederick A. Pottle. New Haven, Conn.: Yale University Press, 2004.

Boyle, Roger, Earl of Orrery. *Guzman. A Comedy. Acted at the Theatre-Royal*. London: Printed for Francis Saunders at the Blue Anchor, 1693.

Brack, O. M., and Susan Carlile. "Samuel Johnson's Contributions to Charlotte Lennox's *The Female Quixote*." *Yale University Library Gazette* 77, no. 3/4 (2003): 166–173.

Brady, Frank. "*Tristram Shandy*: Sexuality, Morality, and Sensibility." *Eighteenth-Century Studies* 4, no. 1 (1970): 41–56.

Bray, Joe. *The Female Reader in the English Novel: From Burney to Austen*. New York: Routledge, 2009.

Brewer, David A. *The Afterlife of Character, 1726–1825*. Philadelphia: University of Pennsylvania Press, 2005.

———. "Appendix A: The Original Casts of the Plays." In *The Rivals and Polly Honeycombe*, by Richard Brinsley Sheridan and George Colman the Elder, 255–260. Edited by David A. Brewer. Peterborough, Ontario: Broadview Press, 2012.

———. Introduction to *The Rivals and Polly Honeycombe*, by Richard Brinsley Sheridan and George Colman the Elder, 11–55. Edited by David A. Brewer. Peterborough, Ontario: Broadview Press, 2012.

———. "Print, Performance, Personhood, Polly Honeycombe." *Studies in Eighteenth-Century Culture* 41 (2012): 185–194.

———. "'Scholia' to the Florida *Tristram Shandy* Annotations." *Scriblerian* 30 (1997): 294–295.

Brewer, John. *The Pleasures of the Imagination: English Culture in the Eighteenth Century*. London: HarperCollins, 1997.

British Critic. 1800.

Brooks, Douglas A., ed. *Printing and Parenting in Early Modern England*. Aldershot: Ashgate, 2005.

Brown, Laura. *Homeless Dogs and Melancholy Apes: Humans and Other Animals in the Modern Literary Imagination*. Ithaca, N.Y.: Cornell University Press, 2010.

Browne, Peter. *Things Divine and Supernatural Conceived by Analogy With Things Natural and Human*. London: Printed for William Innys and Richard Manby at the West-End of St. Paul's, 1733.

Bugg, John. *Five Long Winters: The Trials of British Romanticism*. Stanford, Calif.: Stanford University Press, 2014.

Buickerood, James G. "Clarification of Some Matters Pertinent to the Authorship of *Two Dissertations Concerning Sense, and the Imagination, with an Essay on Consciousness (1728)*." *Notes and Queries* 48, no. 4 (2001): 406–409.

Burckhardt, Sigurd. "*Tristram Shandy*'s Law of Gravity." *ELH* 28, no. 1 (1961): 70–88.

Burney, Frances. *Evelina, or, a Young Lady's Entrance into the World*. 2nd ed. 3 vols. London: Printed for T. Lowndes, 1779.

Butler, David. *Methodists and Papists: John Wesley and the Catholic Church in the Eighteenth Century*. London: Darton, Longman and Todd, 1995.

Butler, Marilyn. *Jane Austen and the War of Ideas*. Oxford: Oxford University Press, 1975.

Canfield, J. Douglas, and J. Paul Hunter, eds. *Rhetorics of Order / Ordering Rhetorics in English Neoclassical Literature*. Newark: University of Delaware Press, 1989.

Carlile, Susan. *Charlotte Lennox: An Independent Mind.* Toronto: University of Toronto Press, 2018.
———, ed. *Masters of the Marketplace: British Women Novelists of the 1750s.* Bethlehem, Pa.: Lehigh University Press, 2011.
Cash, Arthur H., and John M. Stedmond, eds. *The Winged Skull: Papers from the Laurence Sterne Bicentenary Conference.* London: Methuen, 1971.
Cass, Jeffrey, and Larry Peer, eds. *Romantic Border Crossings.* Aldershot: Ashgate, 2008.
Cervantes, Miguel de. *The History and Adventures of the Renowned Don Quixote.* Translated by Tobias Smollett. 2 vols. London: Printed for A. Millar, over against Catherine-Street, in the Strand, 1755.
Cheyne, George. *The English Malady, or, A Treatise of Nervous Diseases of All Kinds.* London: G. Strahan and J. Leake, 1733.
———. *The Letters of Doctor George Cheyne to Samuel Richardson (1723–1743).* Edited by Charles F. Mullett. Columbia: University of Missouri, 1943.
Church of England Quarterly Review. 1842.
Churchill, Charles. *The Rosciad.* London: Printed for the author, and sold by W. Flexney, near Gray's-Inn-Gate, 1761.
Clarke, Norma. *Dr Johnson's Women.* London: Hambledon and London, 2000.
Cleland, John. *Memoirs of a Woman of Pleasure: Unexpurgated Text.* Edited by Peter Sabor. 1985. Reprint, Oxford: Oxford University Press, 2008.
Clery, Emma. *The Feminization Debate in Eighteenth-Century England.* Basingstoke: Palgrave Macmillan, 2004.
———. *The Rise of Supernatural Fiction, 1762–1800.* Cambridge: Cambridge University Press, 1995.
Cody, Lisa. *Birthing the Nation: Sex, Science, and the Conception of Eighteenth-Century Britons.* Oxford: Oxford University Press, 2005.
Coleman, Dorothy. Introduction to *Dialogues Concerning Natural Religion, and Other Writings,* by David Hume, xi–xli. Edited by Dorothy Coleman. Cambridge: Cambridge University Press, 2007.
Coleridge, Samuel Taylor. *Biographia Literaria.* Edited by Adam Roberts. Edinburgh: Edinburgh University Press, 2014.
Colman, George, the Elder. *Critical Reflections on the Old English Dramatick Writers; Intended as a Preface to the Works of Massinger. Addressed to David Garrick, Esq.* London: Printed for T. Davies in Russel-Street, Covent-Garden, 1761.
———. *Polly Honeycombe.* In *The Rivals and Polly Honeycombe,* by Richard Brinsley Sheridan and George Colman the Elder, 59–110. Edited by David A. Brewer. Peterborough, Ontario: Broadview Press, 2012.
Colman, George, the Elder, and Bonnell Thornton. *The Connoisseur. By Mr. Town, Critic and Censor-General.* 2 vols. London: Printed for R. Baldwin, at the Rose in Pater-Noster Row, 1754–55.
Condren, Conal. *Argument and Authority in Early Modern England.* Cambridge: Cambridge University Press, 2006.
Covent Garden Journal. 1752.
Craciun, Adriana. *British Women Writers and the French Revolution: Citizens of the World.* Basingstoke: Palgrave Macmillan, 2005.
Crais, Clifton, and Pamela Scully. *Sarah Baartman and the Hottentot Venus: A Ghost Story and a Biography.* Princeton, N.J.: Princeton University Press, 2009.
Critical Review; or, Annals of Literature. 1760–63.
Cuvier, Georges. "Extrait d'observations faites sur le cadavre d'une femme connue à Paris et à Londres sous le nom de Vénus Hottentotte." *Mémoires du Muséum d'histoire naturelle* 3 (1817): 269–274.

Dale, Amelia. "Gendering the Quixote in Eighteenth-Century England." *Studies in Eighteenth-Century Culture* 46 (2017): 5–19.

de Grazia, Margreta. "Imprints: Shakespeare, Gutenberg, and Descartes." In *Printing and Parenting in Early Modern England*, edited by Douglas A. Brooks, 29–58. Aldershot: Ashgate, 2005.

De Ritter, Richard. *Imagining Women Readers, 1789–1820*. Manchester: Manchester University Press, 2014.

Derrida, Jacques. *Writing and Difference*. Translated by Alan Bass. 1978. Reprint, London: Routledge, 2001.

Descartes, René. *The Philosophical Writings of Descartes*. Translated by John Cottingham, Robert Stoothoff, Dugald Murdoch, and Anthony Kenny. 3 vols. Cambridge: Cambridge University Press, 1985–91.

Dibdin, Thomas. *Five Miles Off: or, The Finger Post; a Comedy, in Three Acts*. London: Printed and Published by Barker and Son, 1806.

DiPiero, Thomas, and Pat Gill, eds. *Illicit Sex: Identity Politics in Early Modern Culture*. Athens: University of Georgia Press, 1997.

Disraeli, Isaac. *Miscellanies; or, Literary Recreations*. London: Printed for T. Cadell and W. Davies, 1796.

Doody, Margaret Anne. Introduction to *The Female Quixote, or, The Adventures of Arabella*, by Charlotte Lennox, xi–xxxii. Edited by Margaret Dalziel. 1989. Reprint, Oxford: Oxford University Press, 2008.

———. "Shakespeare's Novels: Charlotte Lennox Illustrated." *Studies in the Novel* 19, no. 3 (1987): 296–310.

Dorn, Judith. "Reading Women Reading History: The Philosophy of Periodical Form in Charlotte Lennox's *The Lady's Museum*." *Historical Reflections / Réflexions Historiques* 18, no. 3 (1992): 7–27.

Douglas, Brian. *A Companion to Anglican Eucharistic Theology*. Vol. 1, *The Reformation to the 19th Century*. Leiden: Brill, 2012.

Draaisma, Douwe. *Metaphors of Memory: A History of Ideas about the Mind*. Translated by Paul Vincent. Cambridge: Cambridge University Press, 2000.

Dreyer, Frederick A. *The Genesis of Methodism*. Cranbury, N.J.: Lehigh University Press, 1999.

Dryden, John. *Of Dramatick Poesie, an Essay*. In *Prose 1668–1691: An Essay of Dramatick Poesie and Shorter Works*, edited by Samuel Holt Monk, A. E. Wallace Maurer, and Vinton A. Dearing, 2–81. Vol. 17 of *The Works of John Dryden*. Berkeley and Los Angeles: University of California Press, 1971.

Du Bosc, Jacques. *The Accomplish'd Woman. Written in French by M. Du Boscq*. 2 vols. London: Printed by and for J. Watts, 1753.

Dugas, Don-John. "The Significance of 'Lord Rochester's Monkey.'" *Studia Neophilologica* 69, no. 1 (1997): 11–20.

E., B. *A New Dictionary of the Terms Ancient and Modern of the Canting Crew*. London: W. Hawes, P. Gilbourne, W. Davis, 1699.

Eaves, T. C. Duncan, and Ben D. Kimpel. *Samuel Richardson: A Biography*. Oxford: Clarendon Press, 1971.

Edinburgh Magazine. 1761.

Egenolf, Susan B. *The Art of Political Fiction in Hamilton, Edgeworth, and Owenson*. Farnham, U.K.: Ashgate, 2009.

Ehlers, Leigh A. "Mrs. Shandy's 'Lint and Basilicon': The Importance of Women in *Tristram Shandy*." *South Atlantic Review* 46, no. 1 (1981): 61–75.

Engell, James. *The Creative Imagination: Enlightenment to Romanticism*. Cambridge, Mass.: Harvard University Press, 1981.

Esquire, A. G. *The Impetuous Lover, or The Guiltless Parricide, Shewing, to What Lengths Love May Run, and the Extream Folly of Forming Schemes for Futurity. Written under the Instructions, and at the Request of One of the Interested Partys*. London: Printed for E. Ross, at his circulating Library, 1757.

An Essay on the New Species of Writing founded by Mr. Fielding: With a Word or Two upon the Modern State of Criticism. London: Printed for W. Owen, near Temple-Bar, 1751.

Faurot, Ruth. "Mrs. Shandy Observed." *Studies in English Literature, 1500–1900* 10, no. 3 (1970): 579–589.

Fergus, Jane. *Provincial Readers in Eighteenth-Century England*. Oxford: Oxford University Press, 2006.

Ferris, Ina. *The Achievement of Literary Authority: Gender, History, and the Waverley Novels*. Ithaca, N.Y.: Cornell University Press, 1991.

Fielding, Henry. *An Apology for the Life of Mrs. Shamela Andrews* (1741). In *The Journal of a Voyage to Lisbon, Shamela, and Occasional Writings*, edited by Martin C. Battestin with Sheridan Warner Baker and Hugh Amory, 147–195. Oxford: Clarendon Press, 2008.

———. *Joseph Andrews*. Edited by Martin C. Battestin. Middletown, Conn.: Wesleyan University Press, 1966.

Fielding, Sarah. *Remarks on Clarissa, Addressed to the Author*. London: Printed for J. Robinson in Ludgate-Street, 1749.

Fielding, Sarah, and Jane Collier. *The Cry: A New Dramatic Fable*. Edited by Carolyn Woodward. Lexington: University Press of Kentucky, 2018.

Fildes, Valerie. *Breasts, Bottles and Babies: A History of Infant Feeding*. Edinburgh: Edinburgh University Press, 1989.

Fisher, Will. "Queer Money." *ELH* 66, no. 1 (1999): 1–23.

Fletcher, Anthony. *Gender, Sex and Subordination in England 1500–1800*. New Haven, Conn.: Yale University Press, 1995.

Flint, Kate. *The Woman Reader, 1837–1914*. Oxford: Oxford University Press, 1993.

Flynn, Carol Houlihan. "Running Out of Matter: The Body Exercised in Eighteenth-Century Fiction." In *The Languages of Psyche: Mind and Body in Enlightenment Thought*, edited by G. S. Rousseau, 147–185. Berkeley: University of California Press, 1990.

Foote, Samuel. *The Minor, a Comedy*. London: Printed and sold by J. Coote, in Pater-Noster Row, 1760.

Francus, Marilyn. *Monstrous Motherhood: Eighteenth-Century Culture and the Ideology of Domesticity*. Baltimore: Johns Hopkins University Press, 2012.

Freeman, Janet Ing. "Jack Harris and 'Honest Ranger': The Publication and Prosecution of *Harris's List of Covent-Garden Ladies*, 1760–95." *The Library: The Transactions of the Bibliographical Society* 13, no. 4 (2012): 423–456.

Freeman, Lisa. *Character's Theater: Genre and Identity on the Eighteenth-Century English Stage*. Philadelphia: University of Pennsylvania Press, 2002.

Freud, Sigmund. "A Note Upon the 'Mystic Writing-Pad.'" Translated by James Strachey. In *The Standard Edition of the Complete Psychological works of Sigmund Freud*, 19:227–232. 1961. Reprint, London: Vintage Books, 2001.

Friedman, Susan Stanford. "Creativity and the Childbirth Metaphor: Gender Difference in Literary Discourse." *Feminist Studies* 13, no. 1 (1987): 49–82.

Gallagher, Catherine. *Nobody's Story: Gender, Property, and the Rise of the Novel*. Berkeley: University of California Press, 1999.

Garside, Peter. Introduction to *Memoirs of Modern Philosophers*, by Elizabeth Hamilton, v–xvii. Edited by Peter Garside. New York: Routledge, 1992.

Gay, John. *The Beggar's Opera*. In *Dramatic Works*, edited by John Fuller, 2:1–66. Oxford: Clarendon Press, 1983.

Gentleman's Magazine. 1767–1844.

Gibson, Edmund. *Observations upon the Conduct and Behaviour of a Certain Sect, Usually Distinguished by the Name of Methodists*. 2nd ed. London: E. Owen, 1744.

Gilmartin, Kevin. *Writing against Revolution*. Cambridge: Cambridge University Press, 2006.

Godwin, William. *Caleb Williams*. Edited by Pamela Clemit. Oxford: Oxford University Press, 2009.

———. *The Enquirer. Reflections on Education, Manners, and Literature*. London: Printed for G. G. and J. Robinson, Paternoster-Row, 1797.

———. *An Enquiry Concerning Political Justice*. Edited by Mark Philp. Oxford: Oxford University Press, 2013.

Gordon, Scott Paul. *The Practice of Quixotism: Postmodern Theory and Eighteenth-Century Women's Writing*. Basingstoke: Palgrave Macmillan, 2006.

Gordon-Chipembere, Natasha, ed. *Representation and Black Womanhood: The Legacy of Sarah Baartman*. Basingstoke: Palgrave Macmillan, 2011.

Goring, Paul. *The Rhetoric of Sensibility in Eighteenth-Century Culture*. Cambridge: Cambridge University Press, 2005.

Gould, Stephen Jay. "The Hottentot Venus." *Natural History* 91, no. 10 (1982): 20–27.

Graves, Richard. Letters. Bath Record Office: Local Studies.

———. *The Love of Order: A Poetical Essay. In Three Cantos*. London: J. Dodsley, in Pall-Mall, 1773.

———. *Sermons*. Bath: Printed by R. Cruttwell; and sold by F. and C. Rivington, 1799.

———. *The Spiritual Quixote, or The Summer's Ramble of Mr. Geoffry Wildgoose, a Comic Romance*. Edited by Clarence Tracy. London: Oxford University Press, 1967.

Green, Sarah. *Romance Readers and Romance Writers (1810)*. Edited by Christopher Goulding. London: Routledge, 2016.

Greenfield, Susan C., and Carol Barash, eds. *Inventing Maternity: Politics, Science, and Literature, 1650–1865*. Lexington: University Press of Kentucky, 1999.

Gregory, John. *A Father's Legacy to His Daughters*. 4th ed. London: Printed for W. Strahan; T. Cadell, in the Strand; and J. Balfour, and W. Creech, at Edinburgh, 1774.

Grenby, M. O. *The Anti-Jacobin Novel: British Conservatism and the French Revolution*. Cambridge: Cambridge University Press, 2001.

———. Introduction to *The Infernal Quixote: A Tale of the Day*, by Charles Lucas, 9–31. Edited by M. O. Grenby. Peterborough, Ontario: Broadview Press, 2004.

Grogan, Claire. Introduction to *Memoirs of Modern Philosophers*, by Elizabeth Hamilton, 9–26. Edited by Claire Grogan. Peterborough, Ontario: Broadview Press, 2000.

———. *Politics and Genre in the Works of Elizabeth Hamilton, 1756–1816*. Farnham, U.K.: Ashgate, 2012.

Grosz, Elizabeth. *Volatile Bodies*. St. Leonards, N.S.W.: Allen and Unwin, 1994.

Guthrie, William. *The Friends. A Sentimental History: Describing Love as a Virtue, as Well as a Passion*. London: Printed for T. Waller, 1754.

Haakonssen, Knud, ed. *The Cambridge History of Eighteenth-Century Philosophy*. 2 vols. Cambridge: Cambridge University Press, 2006.

———, ed. *Enlightenment and Religion: Rational Dissent in Eighteenth-Century Britain*. Cambridge: Cambridge University Press, 1996.

Hall, S. Cailey. "'All the Bright Eyes of the Kingdom': Charlotte Lennox's Discursive Communities." *Eighteenth-Century Life* 41, no. 2 (2017): 89–104.

Hamilton, Elizabeth. *The Cottagers of Glenburnie, and Other Educational Writing*. Edited by Pam Perkins. Glasgow: Association for Scottish Literary Studies, 2010.

———. *Letters, Addressed to the Daughter of a Nobleman, on the Formation of Religious and Moral Principle*. 1806. Facsimile of the second edition, with an introduction by Gina Luria. 2 vols. New York: Garland Publishing, 1974.

————. *Letters on the Elementary Principles of Education.* 3rd ed. 2 vols. Bath: R. Crutwell, 1803.

————. *Memoirs of Modern Philosophers.* Edited by Claire Grogan. Peterborough, Ontario: Broadview Press, 2000.

————. *Translation of the Letters of a Hindoo Rajah.* Edited by Pamela Perkins and Shannon Russell. Peterborough, Ontario: Broadview Press, 2004.

Hamilton, Patricia L. "Arabella Unbound: Wit, Judgment, and the Cure of Lennox's *Female Quixote.*" In *Masters of the Marketplace: British Women Novelists of the 1750s,* edited by Susan Carlile, 108–127. Bethlehem, Pa.: Lehigh University Press, 2011.

Hanlon, Aaron R. "Maids, Mistresses, and 'Monstrous Doubles': Gender-Class Kyriarchy in *The Female Quixote* and *Female Quixotism.*" *The Eighteenth Century* 55, no. 1 (2014): 77–96.

————. "Quixotism as Global Heuristic: Atlantic and Pacific Diasporas." *Studies in Eighteenth-Century Culture* 46 (2017): 49–62.

————. "Toward a Counter-Poetics of Quixotism." *Studies in the Novel* 46, no. 2 (2014): 141–158.

Hardin, Michael. "'Is There a Straight Line in This Text?' The Homoerotics of *Tristram Shandy.*" *Orbis Litterarum* 54, no. 3 (1999): 185–202.

Harries, Elizabeth W. *The Unfinished Manner: Essays on the Fragment in the Later Eighteenth Century.* Charlottesville: University Press of Virginia, 1994.

————. "Words, Sex, and Gender in Sterne's Novels." In *The Cambridge Companion to Laurence Sterne,* edited by Thomas Keymer, 111–124. Cambridge: Cambridge University Press, 2009.

Harris's List of Covent-Garden Ladies; or, New Atalantis for the Year 1761. London: Printed for H. Ranger, 1761.

Harris's List of Covent-Garden Ladies; or, New Atalantis for the Year 1764. London: Printed for H. Ranger, 1764.

Hartley, David. *Observations on Man, His Frame, His Duty, and His Expectations. In Two Parts.* 2 vols. London: Printed by S. Richardson, 1749.

Harvey, Karen. "Rabbits, Whigs and Hunters: Women and Protest in Mary Toft's Monstrous Births of 1726." *Past & Present* 238, no. 1 (2018): 43–83.

————. "What Mary Toft Felt: Women's Voices, Pain, Power and the Body." *History Workshop Journal* 80 (2015): 33–51.

Hays, Mary. *Memoirs of Emma Courtney.* Edited by Eleanor Ty. 1996. Reprint, Oxford: Oxford University Press, 2009.

Hempton, David. *Methodism: Empire of the Spirit.* New Haven, Conn.: Yale University Press, 2006.

Hill, Aaron. *The Works of the Late Aaron Hill.* 4 vols. London: Printed for the Benefit of the Family, 1753.

Hill, John. *The Actor; or A Treatise on the Art of Playing, a New Work.* Rev. ed. London: Printed for R. Griffiths, at the Dunciad, 1755.

Hobbes, Thomas. *Leviathan: The English and Latin Texts.* Edited by Noel Malcolm. Vols. 4 and 5 of *The Clarendon Edition of the Works of Thomas Hobbes.* Oxford: Clarendon Press, 2012.

Holtz, William. "Typography, *Tristram Shandy,* the Aposiopesis, Etc." In *The Winged Skull: Papers from the Laurence Sterne Bicentenary Conference,* edited by Arthur H. Cash and John M. Stedmond, 247–257. London: Methuen, 1971.

Huet, Marie-Hélène. *Monstrous Imagination.* Cambridge, Mass.: Harvard University Press, 1993.

Hume, David. *An Enquiry Concerning Human Understanding.* Edited by Tom L. Beauchamp. Oxford: Oxford University Press, 2000.

————. "Of the Study of History." In *Essays, Moral and Political,* 53–59. 3rd ed. London: Printed for A. Millar, over against Catharine Street in the Strand; and A. Kincaid in Edinburgh, 1748.

———. *A Treatise of Human Nature*. Edited by David Fate Norton and Mary J. Norton. 2 vols. Oxford: Oxford University Press, 2007.

Hunter, J. Paul. "Clocks, Calendars, and Names: The Troubles of Tristram and the Aesthetics of Uncertainty." In *Rhetorics of Order / Ordering Rhetorics in English Neoclassical Literature*, edited by J. Douglas Canfield and J. Paul Hunter, 173–198. Newark: University of Delaware Press, 1989.

Hutcheon, Linda. *A Poetics of Postmodernism: History, Theory, Fiction*. London: Routledge, 1988.

———. *A Theory of Parody: The Teachings of Twentieth-Century Art Forms*. London: Methuen, 1985.

Ingrassia, Catherine. *Authorship, Commerce, and Gender in Early Eighteenth-Century England: A Culture of Paper Credit*. Cambridge: Cambridge University Press, 1998.

Iser, Wolfgang. *The Fictive and the Imaginary: Charting Literary Anthropology*. Baltimore: Johns Hopkins University Press, 1993.

Isles, Duncan. "Appendix: Johnson, Richardson, and *The Female Quixote*." In *The Female Quixote, or, The Adventures of Arabella*, by Charlotte Lennox, 419–428. Edited by Margaret Dalziel. 1989. Reprint, Oxford: Oxford University Press, 2008.

———. "The Lennox Collection (Part One)." *Harvard Library Bulletin* 18, no. 4 (1970): 317–344.

Ivana, Dragoş. *Embattled Reason, Principled Sentiment and Political Radicalism: Quixotism in English Novels, 1742–1801*. Amsterdam: Rodopi, 2014.

Jacobs, Edward. "Eighteenth-Century British Circulating Libraries and Cultural Book History." *Book History* 6 (2003): 1–22.

Johns, Adrian. *The Nature of the Book: Print and Knowledge in the Making*. Chicago: University of Chicago Press, 1998.

Johnson, Claudia L. *Equivocal Beings: Politics, Gender, and Sentimentality in the 1790s*. Chicago: University of Chicago Press, 1995.

———. *Jane Austen: Women, Politics, and the Novel*. Chicago: University of Chicago Press, 1988.

Johnson, Nancy. "The 'French Threat' in Anti-Jacobin Novels of the 1790s." In *Illicit Sex: Identity Politics in Early Modern Culture*, edited by Thomas DiPiero and Pat Gill, 181–202. Athens: University of Georgia Press, 1997.

Johnson, Samuel. *A Dictionary of the English Language: In Which the Words Are Deduced from Their Originals, and Illustrated in Their Different Significations by Examples from the Best Writers*. 2nd ed. 2 vols. London: Printed by W. Strahan, for J. and P. Knapton; T. and T. Longman; C. Hitch and L. Hawes; A. Millar; and R. and J. Dodsley, 1755–56.

Jones, Darrell. "Locke and Sterne: The History of a Critical Hobby-Horse." *The Shandean* 27 (2016): 83–111.

Kay, Carol. "Canon, Ideology, and Gender: Mary Wollstonecraft's Critique of Adam Smith." *New Political Science* 15, no. 1 (1986): 63–76.

———. *Political Constructions: Defoe, Richardson, and Sterne in Relation to Hobbes, Hume, and Burke*. Ithaca, N.Y.: Cornell University Press, 1988.

Kelly, Gary. *English Fiction of the Romantic Period, 1789–1830*. London: Longman, 1989.

———. *Women, Writing, and Revolution, 1790–1827*. Oxford: Clarendon Press, 1993.

Kersey, John. *A New English Dictionary; or, A Compleat Collection of the Most Proper and Significant Words, and Terms of Art, Commonly Used in the Language*. 8th ed. London: Printed for L. Hawes, 1772.

Keymer, Thomas, ed. *The Cambridge Companion to Laurence Sterne*. Cambridge: Cambridge University Press, 2009.

———. *Sterne, the Moderns and the Novel*. Oxford: Oxford University Press, 2002.

King, Ross. "*Tristram Shandy* and the Wound of Language." *Studies in Philology* 92, no. 3 (1995): 291–310.

Knox, Vicesimus. *Essays Moral and Literary.* Rev. ed. 2 vols. London: Charles Dilly, 1782.

Kvande, Marta. "Reading Female Readers: *The Female Quixote* and *Female Quixotism.*" In *Masters of the Marketplace: British Women Novelists of the 1750s,* edited by Susan Carlile, 219–241. Bethlehem, Pa.: Lehigh University Press, 2011.

Landa, Louis A. "The Shandean Homunculus: The Background of Sterne's 'Little Gentleman.'" In *Essays in Eighteenth-Century English Literature,* 140–159. Princeton, N.J.: Princeton University Press, 1980.

Landry, Donna, and Gerald MacLean. "Of Forceps, Patents, and Paternity: *Tristram Shandy.*" *Eighteenth-Century Studies* 23, no. 4 (1990): 522–543.

Langbauer, Laurie. *Women and Romance: The Consolations of Gender in the English Novel.* Ithaca, N.Y.: Cornell University Press, 1990.

Laqueur, Thomas. *Making Sex: Body and Gender from the Greeks to Freud.* Cambridge, Mass.: Harvard University Press, 1992.

———. *Solitary Sex: A Cultural History of Masturbation.* New York: Zone Books, 2004.

Larlham, Daniel. "The Felt Truth of Mimetic Experience: Motions of the Soul and the Kinetics of Passion in the Eighteenth-Century Theatre." *The Eighteenth Century* 53, no. 4 (2012): 432–454.

Lavington, George. *The Enthusiasm of Methodists and Papists Compared. In Three Parts.* 2 vols. London: Printed for J. and P. Knapton, in Ludgate-Street, 1754.

Lennox, Charlotte. *The Female Quixote, or, The Adventures of Arabella.* Edited by Margaret Dalziel, introduction by Margaret Anne Doody, chronology and appendix by Duncan Isles. 1989. Reprint, Oxford: Oxford University Press, 2008.

———. *The Female Quixote; or, The Adventures of Arabella.* 2 vols. London: Printed for A. Millar, 1752.

———. *The Lady's Museum.* 2 vols. London: J. Newbery in St. Paul's Church-Yard, 1760–61.

———. *Shakespear Illustrated: or The Novels and Histories, On which the Plays of Shakespear Are Founded, Collected and Translated from the Original Authors. With Critical Remarks.* 2 vols. London: Printed for A. Millar in the Strand, 1753.

A Letter from the Rev. George Whitfield, B.A. to the Rev. Laurence Sterne, M.A. The Supposed Author of a Book entitled the Life and Opinions of Tristram Shandy, Gentleman. London: [n.p.], 1760.

Levin, Kate. "'The Cure of Arabella's Mind': Charlotte Lennox and the Disciplining of the Female Reader." *Women's Writing* 2, no. 3 (1995): 271–290.

Levy, Anita. "Reproductive Urges: Literacy, Sexuality, and Eighteenth-Century Englishness." In *Inventing Maternity: Politics, Science, and Literature, 1650–1865,* edited by Susan C. Greenfield and Carol Barash, 193–214. Lexington: University Press of Kentucky, 1999.

Littau, Karin. *Theories of Reading: Books, Bodies, and Bibliomania.* Cambridge, U.K.: Polity Press, 2006.

Lloyd, Robert. *The Actor. A Poetical Epistle to Bonnell Thornton, Esq.* London: Printed for R. and J. Dodsley, in Pall-Mall, 1760.

Locke, John. *The Clarendon Edition of the Works of John Locke: An Essay Concerning Human Understanding.* Edited by Peter H. Nidditch. Oxford: Clarendon Press, 1975.

London, April. "Novel and History in Anti-Jacobin Satire." *Yearbook of English Studies* 30 (2000): 71–81.

The London Chronicle: or, Universal Evening Post. 1760–61.

London Magazine. 1760–61.

Long, Edward. *The History of Jamaica, or, General Survey of the Antient and Modern State of That Island.* 3 vols. London: Printed for T. Lowndes, 1774.

Loscocco, Paula. "Can't Live without 'Em: Walter Shandy and the Woman Within." *The Eighteenth Century* 32, no. 2 (1991): 166–179.

Lucas, Charles. *The Infernal Quixote. A Tale of the Day*. London: Minerva Press, 1801.

———. *The Infernal Quixote: A Tale of the Day*. Edited by M. O. Grenby. Peterborough, Ontario: Broadview Press, 2004.

Lupton, Christina. *Knowing Books: The Consciousness of Mediation in Eighteenth-Century Britain*. Philadelphia: University of Pennsylvania Press, 2012.

Lynch, Deidre. *The Economy of Character: Novels, Market Culture, and the Business of Inner Meaning*. Chicago: University of Chicago Press, 1998.

———. "Personal Effects and Sentimental Fictions." *Eighteenth-Century Fiction* 12, no. 2–3 (2000): 345–368.

Maccubbin, Robert Purks, ed. *'Tis Nature's Fault: Unauthorized Sexuality during the Enlightenment*. Cambridge: Cambridge University Press, 1988.

Mack, Phyllis. *Heart Religion in the British Enlightenment: Gender and Emotion in Early Methodism*. Cambridge: Cambridge University Press, 2008.

Mack, Ruth. "Quixotic Ethnography: Charlotte Lennox and the Dilemma of Cultural Observation." *Novel: A Forum on Fiction* 38, no. 2–3 (2005): 193–213.

Malabou, Catherine. *The Future of Hegel: Plasticity, Temporality and Dialectic*. Translated by Lisabeth During. London: Routledge, 2005.

Malina, Debra. "Rereading the Patriarchal Text: *The Female Quixote, Northanger Abbey*, and the Trace of the Absent Mother." *Eighteenth-Century Fiction* 8, no. 2 (1996): 271–292.

Marshall, Ashley. "The Aims of Butler's Satire in *Hudibras*." *Modern Philology* 105, no. 4 (2008): 637–665.

Marshall, David. *The Frame of Art: Fictions of Aesthetic Experience, 1750–1815*. Baltimore: Johns Hopkins University Press, 2005.

Martin, Mary Patricia. "'High and Noble Adventures': Reading the Novel in *The Female Quixote*." *Novel: A Forum on Fiction* 31, no. 1 (1997): 45–62.

Martin, Regina. "Specters of Romance: *The Female Quixote* and Domestic Fiction." *Eighteenth-Century Novel* 8, no. 1 (2011): 147–166.

Maslen, Keith. *Samuel Richardson of London, Printer: A Study of His Printing Based on Ornament Use and Business Accounts*. Christchurch, New Zealand: University of Otago, 2001.

Mayhew, Robert J. *Landscape, Literature and English Religious Culture, 1660–1800: Samuel Johnson and Languages of Natural Description*. Basingstoke: Palgrave Macmillan, 2004.

Mayne, Zachary. *Two Dissertations Concerning Sense, and the Imagination. With an Essay on Consciousness*. London: Printed for J. Tonson in the Strand, 1728.

McDowell, Paula. "Mediating Media Past." In *This Is Enlightenment*, edited by Clifford Siskin and William Warner, 229–246. Chicago: University of Chicago Press, 2010.

McKeon, Michael. *The Origins of the English Novel, 1600–1740*. 1987. Reprint, Baltimore: Johns Hopkins University Press, 2002.

———. *The Secret History of Domesticity: Public, Private, and the Division of Knowledge*. Baltimore: Johns Hopkins University Press, 2005.

McMaster, Juliet. *Reading the Body in the Eighteenth-Century Novel*. Basingstoke: Palgrave Macmillan, 2004.

Mee, Jon. "Anti-Jacobin Novels: Representation and Revolution." *Huntington Library Quarterly* 69, no. 4 (2006): 649–653.

———. *Romanticism, Enthusiasm, and Regulation: Poetics and the Policing of Culture in the Romantic Period*. Oxford: Oxford University Press, 2003.

Memoirs of the Celebrated Miss Fanny M[urray]. London: J. Scott and M. Thrush, 1759.

Merians, Linda E. *Envisioning the Worst: Representations of "Hottentots" in Early-Modern England*. Newark: University of Delaware Press, 2001.

Monthly Review. 1760–83.

More, Hannah. *Strictures on the Modern System of Female Education.* 2nd ed. 2 vols. London: T. Cadell Jun. and W. Davies, 1799.

Mosley, James. "The Technologies of Print." In *The Oxford Companion to the Book,* edited by Michael F. Suarez, S.J., and H. R. Woudhuysen, 1:89–104. Oxford: Oxford University Press, 2010.

Motooka, Wendy. *The Age of Reasons: Quixotism, Sentimentalism and Political Economy in Eighteenth-Century Britain.* London: Routledge, 1998.

Mottolese, William. "Tristram Cyborg and Toby Toolmaker: Body, Tools, and Hobbyhorse in *Tristram Shandy.*" *Studies in English Literature, 1500–1900* 47, no. 3 (2007): 679–701.

Mullan, John. *Sentiment and Sociability: The Language of Feeling in the Eighteenth Century.* Oxford: Clarendon Press, 1990.

Müller, Lothar. *White Magic: The Age of Paper.* Translated by Jessica Spengler. Cambridge, U.K.: Polity Press, 2015.

Nace, Nicholas D. "Unprinted Matter: Conceptual Writing and *Tristram Shandy*'s 'Chasm of Ten Pages.'" *The Shandean* 24 (2013): 31–58.

Nänny, Max. "Similarity and Contiguity in *Tristram Shandy.*" *English Studies: A Journal of English Language and Literature* 60 (1979): 422–435.

Narozny, Christopher, and Diana de Armas Wilson. "Heroic Failure: Novelistic Impotence in *Don Quixote* and *Tristram Shandy.*" In *The Cervantean Heritage: Reception and Influence of Cervantes in Britain,* edited by J.A.G. Ardila, 142–150. London: Legenda, 2009.

Nederveen Pieterse, Jan. *White on Black: Images of Africa and Blacks in Western Popular Culture.* New Haven, Conn.: Yale University Press, 1995.

New, Melvyn, Richard A. Davies, and W. G. Day, eds. *Tristram Shandy: The Notes.* Vol. 3 of *The Florida Edition of the Works of Laurence Sterne.* Gainesville: University Presses of Florida, 1984.

Oakleaf, David. "Long Sticks, Morris Dancers, and Gentlemen: Associations of the Hobby-Horse in *Tristram Shandy.*" *Eighteenth-Century Life* 11, no. 3 (1987): 62–76.

Onania; or, The Heinous Sin of Self-Pollution, and All Its Frightful Consequences, in Both Sexes, Considerd, with Spiritual and Physical Advice to those, who have already injur'd themselves by this abominable Practice. And seasonable Admonition to the Youth of the Nation, (of Both Sexes) and those whose Tuition They are under, whether Parents, Guardians, Masters, or Mistresses. 8th ed. London: Printed by Eliz. Rumball, for Thomas Crouch, 1723.

Orr, Clarissa Campbell. "Cross Channel Perspectives." In *Wollstonecraft's Daughters: Womanhood in England and France, 1780–1920,* edited by Clarissa Campbell Orr, 1–42. Manchester: Manchester University Press, 1996.

———, ed. *Wollstonecraft's Daughters: Womanhood in England and France, 1780–1920.* Manchester: Manchester University Press, 1996.

Ostovich, Helen. "Reader as Hobby-Horse in *Tristram Shandy.*" *Philological Quarterly* 68 (1989): 325–342.

Otway, Thomas. *The Souldiers Fortune.* In *Plays, Poems, and Love-Letters,* edited by J. C. Ghosh, 89–196. Vol. 2 of *The Works of Thomas Otway.* Oxford: Clarendon Press, 1932.

Paige, Nicholas. *Before Fiction: The Ancien Régime of the Novel.* Philadelphia: University of Pennsylvania Press, 2011.

Panofsky, Erwin. *Studies in Iconology: Humanistic Themes in the Art of the Renaissance.* New York: Harper and Row, 1962.

Park, Julie. *The Self and It: Novel Objects in Eighteenth-Century England.* Stanford, Calif.: Stanford University Press, 2010.

Parker, Patricia. *Literary Fat Ladies: Rhetoric, Gender, Property.* London: Methuen, 1987.

Parsons, Nicola. *Reading Gossip in Early Eighteenth-Century England*. Basingstoke: Palgrave Macmillan, 2009.

Pasanek, Brad. *Metaphors of Mind: An Eighteenth-Century Dictionary*. Baltimore: Johns Hopkins University Press, 2015.

Paulson, Ronald. *Don Quixote in England: The Aesthetics of Laughter*. Baltimore: Johns Hopkins University Press, 1998.

———. "Emulative Consumption and Literacy. The Harlot, Moll Flanders, and Mrs. Slipslop." In *The Consumption of Culture, 1600–1800: Image, Object, Text*, edited by Ann Bermingham and John Brewer, 383–400. London: Routledge, 1995.

Pearson, David. "Bookbinding." In *The Oxford Companion to the Book*, edited by Michael F. Suarez, S.J., and H. R. Woudhuysen, 1:147–155. Oxford: Oxford University Press, 2010.

Pearson, Jacqueline. *Women's Reading in Britain, 1750–1835: A Dangerous Recreation*. Cambridge: Cambridge University Press, 1999.

Perkins, Pam. "Enlightening the Female Mind: Education, Sociability, and the Literary Woman in the Work of Elizabeth Hamilton." In *Women Writers and the Edinburgh Enlightenment*, 55–134. Scottish Cultural Review of Language and Literature 15. Amsterdam: Rodopi, 2010.

———. Introduction to *The Cottagers of Glenburnie, and Other Educational Writing*, by Elizabeth Hamilton, 1–44. Edited by Pam Perkins. Glasgow: Association for Scottish Literary Studies, 2010.

Perovic, Sanja. *The Calendar in Revolutionary France*. Cambridge: Cambridge University Press, 2012.

Perry, Ruth. *Novel Relations: The Transformation of Kinship in English Literature and Culture, 1748–1818*. Cambridge: Cambridge University Press, 2004.

———. "Words for Sex: The Verbal-Sexual Continuum in *Tristram Shandy*." *Studies in the Novel* 20 (1988): 27–42.

Peters, Julie Stone. *Theatre of the Book, 1480–1880: Print, Text, and Performance in Europe*. Oxford: Oxford University Press, 2000.

Pinto-Correia, Clara. *The Ovary of Eve: Egg and Sperm and Preformation*. Chicago: University of Chicago Press, 1998.

Plato. *Complete Works*. Edited by John M. Cooper. Indianapolis: Hackett Publishing Company, 1997.

Pope, Alexander. *Letters of Mr Pope, and Several Eminent Persons, From the Year 1705, to 1735*. Vol. 1. London: Printed for T. Cooper, at the Globe in Pater-Noster-Row, 1735.

———. *The Twickenham Edition of the Poems of Alexander Pope*. Edited by John Butt. 11 vols. London: Methuen, 1938–68.

Powell, Manushag N. *Performing Authorship in Eighteenth-Century English Periodicals*. Lewisburg, Pa.: Bucknell University Press, 2012.

———. "See No Evil, Hear No Evil, Speak No Evil: Spectation and the Eighteenth-Century Public Sphere." *Eighteenth-Century Studies* 45, no. 2 (2012): 255–276.

Price, Fiona. "Democratizing Taste: Scottish Common Sense Philosophy and Elizabeth Hamilton." *Romanticism* 8, no. 2 (2002): 179–196.

Price, Thomas. Introduction to *Polly Honeycombe*. In *Critical Edition of the Jealous Wife and Polly Honeycombe*, by George Colman the Elder, 175–188. Edited by Thomas Price. New York: Edwin Mellen Press, 1997.

Priestley, Joseph. *Hartley's Theory Of The Human Mind, on the Principle of the Association of Ideas; With Essays Relating To The Subject Of It*. London: J. Johnson, 1775.

The Prompter. 1735.

Public Ledger. Or, Daily Register of Commerce and Intelligence. 1760.

Quarterly Review. 1809.

Rabelais, François. *The Works of Francis Rabelais*. Edited by John Ozell. Translated by Thomas Urquhart and Peter Motteux. Rev. ed. 5 vols. London: Printed by John Hart, for J. Brindley, 1750.

Raff, Sarah. *Jane Austen's Erotic Advice*. Oxford: Oxford University Press, 2014.

Reeve, Clara. *The Progress of Romance, through Times, Countries, and Manners; with Remarks on the good and bad effects of them respectively.* 2 vols. Colchester: Printed for the Author by W. Keymer, 1785.

Reid, Thomas. *Essays on the Intellectual Powers of Man*. Edinburgh and London: Printed for John Bell and G.G.J. and J. Robinson, 1785.

Rendall, Jane. "Hamilton and the *Memoirs of Agrippina*." In *Wollstonecraft's Daughters: Womanhood in England and France, 1780–1920*, edited by Clarissa Campbell Orr, 79–93. Manchester: Manchester University Press, 1996.

Richardson, Samuel. *Clarissa, or, The History of a Young Lady*. Edited by Angus Ross. London: Penguin, 2004.

———. *The History of Sir Charles Grandison*. Edited by Jocelyn Harris. 3 vols. London: Oxford University Press, 1972.

Rivero, Albert J., ed. *New Essays on Samuel Richardson*. New York: St. Martin's Press, 1996.

Rivers, Isabel. *Reason, Grace, and Sentiment: A Study of the Language of Religion and Ethics in England, 1600–1780*. 2 vols. Cambridge: Cambridge University Press, 1991.

Roach, Joseph. *The Player's Passion: Studies in the Science of Acting*. Newark: University of Delaware Press, 1985.

Rorty, Richard. *Philosophy and the Mirror of Nature*. 1979. Reprint, Princeton, N.J.: Princeton University Press, 2009.

Ross, Ian Campbell. *Laurence Sterne: A Life*. Oxford: Oxford University Press, 2001.

Rothstein, Eric. "The Framework of *Shamela*." *ELH* 35, no. 3 (1968): 381–402.

Rousseau, G. S., ed. *The Languages of Psyche: Mind and Body in Enlightenment Thought*. Berkeley: University of California Press, 1990.

Rumbold, Kate. *Shakespeare and the Eighteenth-Century Novel: Cultures of Quotation from Samuel Richardson to Jane Austen*. Cambridge: Cambridge University Press, 2016.

Russell, Rosalind. "Elizabeth Hamilton: Enlightenment Educator." *Scottish Educational Review* 18, no. 1 (1986): 23–30.

Sabor, Peter. "The Censor Censured: Expurgating *Memoirs of a Woman of Pleasure*." In *'Tis Nature's Fault: Unauthorized Sexuality during the Enlightenment*, edited by Robert Purks Maccubbin, 192–201. Cambridge: Cambridge University Press, 1988.

Saggini, Francesca. *Backstage in the Novel: Frances Burney and the Theater Arts*. Charlottesville: University of Virginia Press, 2012.

———. *The Gothic Novel and the Stage: Romantic Appropriations*. London: Pickering and Chatto, 2015.

Sale, William M. *Samuel Richardson: Master Printer*. Ithaca, N.Y.: Cornell University Press, 1950.

Schaffer, Simon. "States of Mind: Enlightenment and Natural Philosophy." In *The Languages of Psyche: Mind and Body in Enlightenment Thought*, edited by G. S. Rousseau, 233–290. Berkeley: University of California Press, 1990.

Schürer, Norbert, ed. *Charlotte Lennox: Correspondence and Miscellaneous Documents*. Lewisburg, Pa.: Bucknell University Press, 2012.

Scots Magazine and Edinburgh Literary Miscellany. 1816.

Scott, William. "George Colman's *Polly Honeycombe* and Circulating Library Fiction in 1760." *Notes and Queries* 15, no. 12 (1968): 465–467.

Shaw, Jane. "Mary Toft, Religion and National Memory in Eighteenth-Century England." *Journal for Eighteenth-Century Studies* 32, no. 3 (2009): 321–338.

Shenstone, William. *The Works in Verse and Prose, of William Shenstone, Esq; Most of which were never before printed*. 2 vols. London: Printed for R. and J. Dodsley in Pall-Mall, 1764.

Sheridan, Thomas. *A Course of Lectures on Elocution: Together With Two Dissertations on Language; And Some other Tracts relative to those Subjects*. London: Printed by W. Strahan, 1762.

Silver, Sean. *The Mind Is a Collection: Case Studies in Eighteenth-Century Thought*. Philadelphia: University of Pennsylvania Press, 2015.

Siskin, Clifford, and William Warner, eds. *This Is Enlightenment*. Chicago: University of Chicago Press, 2010.

A Sovereign Remedy for the cure of Hypocrisy and Blind Zeal, Extracted from the Salutary Precepts of Jesus Christ. London: Printed for T. Becket and P. A. de Hondt, near Surry-Street, in the Strand, 1764.

Spacks, Patricia Meyer. *Desire and Truth: Functions of Plot in Eighteenth-Century English Novels*. Chicago: University of Chicago Press, 1990.

———. *Imagining a Self: Autobiography and Novel in Eighteenth-Century England*. Cambridge, Mass.: Harvard University Press, 1976.

Spedding, Patrick. "Eliza Haywood, Writing (and) Pornography." In *Women Writing, 1550–1750*, edited by Jo Wallwork and Paul Salzman, 237–251. Melbourne: Meridian, 2001.

Spedding, Patrick, and James Lambert. "Fanny Hill, Lord Fanny, and the Myth of Metonymy." *Studies in Philology* 108, no. 1 (2011): 108–132.

The Spirit of the Public Journals for 1797. Being an Impartial Selection of the Most Exquisite Essays and Jeux D'esprits, Principally Prose, That Appear in Newspapers and Other Publications. London: Printed for R. Phillips, 1798.

St. Clair, William. *The Reading Nation in the Romantic Period*. Cambridge: Cambridge University Press, 2004.

Staves, Susan. "Don Quixote in Eighteenth-Century England." *Comparative Literature* 24, no. 3 (1972): 193–215.

Steele, Richard. *The Tender Husband*. London: Printed for Jacob Tonson, 1705.

Stephanson, Raymond. *The Yard of Wit: Male Creativity and Sexuality, 1650–1750*. Philadelphia: University of Pennsylvania Press, 2004.

Sterne, Laurence. *The Life and Opinions of Tristram Shandy, Gentleman*. Vols. 1 and 2 of *The Florida Edition of the Works of Laurence Sterne*. Edited by Melvyn New and Joan New. Gainesville: University Presses of Florida, 1978.

Stewart, A. M. "Arguments for the Existence of God: The British Debate." In *The Cambridge History of Eighteenth-Century Philosophy*, edited by Knud Haakonssen, 2:710–730. Cambridge: Cambridge University Press, 2006.

Stewart, Dugald. *Elements of the Philosophy of the Human Mind*. 3 vols. London: Printed for A. Strahan, and T. Cadell, 1792–1827.

Stone, George Winchester, Jr., ed. *The London Stage, 1660–1800; A Calendar of Plays, Entertainments and Afterpieces, Together with Casts, Box-Receipts and Contemporary Comment. Compiled from the Playbills, Newspapers and Theatrical Diaries of the Period. Part 4: 1747–1776*. 3 vols. Carbondale: Southern Illinois University Press, 1962.

Stott, Anne. "Hannah More and the Blagdon Controversy, 1799–1802." *Journal of Ecclesiastical History* 51, no. 2 (2000): 319–346.

Suarez, Michael F., S.J., and H. R. Woudhuysen, eds. *The Oxford Companion to the Book*. 2 vols. Oxford: Oxford University Press, 2010.

Subligny, Adrien-Thomas Perdou de. *The Mock-Clelia: Being A Comical History of French Gallantries, and Novels, in Imitation of Dom Quixote*. London: Printed for L.C., 1678.

Sutton, John. *Philosophy and Memory Traces: Descartes to Connectionism*. Cambridge: Cambridge University Press, 1998.

Swift, Johnathan. *Gulliver's Travels*. Edited by David Womersley. Cambridge: Cambridge University Press, 2012.

———. *A Tale of a Tub and Other Works*. Edited by Marcus Walsh. Cambridge: Cambridge University Press, 2010.

Tague, Ingrid H. *Animal Companions: Pets and Social Change in Eighteenth-Century Britain*. University Park: Pennsylvania State University Press, 2015.

Tatler. 1709.

Tenney, Tabitha Gilman. *Female Quixotism: Exhibited in the Romantic Opinions and Extravagant Adventures of Dorcasina Sheldon*. Edited by Jean Nienkamp and Andrea Collins. Oxford: Oxford University Press, 1992.

Thaddeus, Janice Farrar. "Elizabeth Hamilton's Domestic Politics." *Studies in Eighteenth Century Culture* 23 (1994): 265–284.

The Theatrical Review; or, New Companion to the Play-House. 2 vols. London: Printed for S. Crowder, 1772.

Thirlwell, Adam. "Reproduction." *The Shandean* 21 (2010): 9–34.

Thompson, Helen. "Charlotte Lennox and the Agency of Romance." *The Eighteenth Century* 43, no. 2 (2002): 91–114.

Tierney-Hynes, Rebecca. *Novel Minds: Philosophers and Romance Readers, 1680–1740*. Basingstoke: Palgrave Macmillan, 2012.

Todd, Dennis. *Imagining Monsters: Miscreations of the Self in Eighteenth-Century England*. Chicago: University of Chicago Press, 1995.

Toor, Kiran. "'Offspring of His Genius': Coleridge's Pregnant Metaphors and Metamorphic Pregnancies." *Romanticism* 13, no. 3 (2007): 257–270.

Tracy, Clarence. Introduction to *The Spiritual Quixote, or The Summer's Ramble of Mr. Geoffry Wildgoose, a Comic Romance*, by Richard Graves, iii–xxv. Edited by Clarence Tracy. London: Oxford University Press, 1967.

———. *A Portrait of Richard Graves*. Cambridge, U.K.: James Clarke, 1987.

Trenchard, John. *The Natural History of Superstition*. London: Sold by A. Baldwin at the Oxford Arms in Warwick Lane, 1709.

Trubowitz, Rachel. *Nation and Nurture in Seventeenth-Century English Literature*. Oxford: Oxford University Press, 2012.

Ty, Eleanor. "Female Philosophy Refunctioned: Elizabeth Hamilton's Parodic Novel." *Ariel* 22, no. 4 (1991): 111–129.

Varma, Devendra P. *The Evergreen Tree of Diabolical Knowledge*. Washington, D.C.: Consortium Press, 1972.

Verhoeven, W. M. General introduction to *Anti-Jacobin Novels*. Edited by W. M. Verhoeven, 1:vii–lxxv. London: Pickering and Chatto, 2005.

Viele, Anna. "Plotting the Coquette: Gender and Genre in the Eighteenth-Century British Cultural Imagination." PhD diss., University of California, Santa Barbara, 2007.

Voltaire. *Candide and Other Stories*. Translated by Roger Pearson. Oxford: Oxford University Press, 2008.

———. *Micromegas: A Comic Romance. Being a Severe Satire Upon the Philosophy, Ignorance, and Self-Conceit of Mankind. Together with a Detail of the Crusades: And a New Plan for the History of the Human Mind. Translated from the French of M. De Voltaire*. London: Printed for D. Wilson, and T. Durham, at Plato's Head, near Round-Court, in the Strand, 1753.

Voogd, Peter de. "*Tristram Shandy* as Aesthetic Object." *Word and Image: A Journal of Verbal/Visual Enquiry* 4, no. 1 (1988): 383–392.

Wahrman, Dror. *The Making of the Modern Self: Identity and Culture in Eighteenth-Century England*. New Haven, Conn.: Yale University Press, 2006.

Walker, George. *Le Vagabond, ou la rencontre de deux philosophes républicains; Roman philosophique, traduit de l'anglais de George Walker.* Paris: Hénée et Dumas, et al., 1807.

———. *The Vagabond: A Novel.* Edited by W. M. Verhoeven. Peterborough, Ontario: Broadview Press, 2004.

Wall, Wendy. *The Imprint of Gender: Authorship and Publication in the English Renaissance.* Ithaca, N.Y.: Cornell University Press, 1993.

Wallace, Miriam L. "Crossing from 'Jacobin' to 'Anti-Jacobin': Rethinking the Terms of English Jacobinism." In *Romantic Border Crossings*, edited by Jeffrey Cass and Larry Peer, 99–112. Aldershot: Ashgate, 2008.

———. "Gender Bending and Corporeal Limitations: The Modern Body in *Tristram Shandy*." *Studies in Eighteenth Century Culture* 26 (1997): 175–194.

———. *Revolutionary Subjects in the English "Jacobin" Novel, 1790–1805.* Lewisburg, Pa.: Bucknell University Press, 2009.

Wallwork, Jo, and Paul Salzman, eds. *Women Writing, 1550–1750.* Melbourne: Meridian, 2001.

Walpole, Horace. *The Yale Edition of Horace Walpole's Correspondence.* Edited by W. S. Lewis. 48 vols. New Haven, Conn.: Yale University Press, 1937–83.

Warburton, William. *The Doctrine of Grace: or, the Office and Operations of the Holy Spirit Vindicated from the Insults of Infidelity, and the Abuses of Fanaticism.* 2 vols. London: Printed for A. Millar, and J. and R. Tonson, 1763.

Ward, Edward. *The Modern World Disrob'd; or, Both Sexes Stript of Their Pretended Vertue.* London: Printed for G.S. and sold by J. Woodward, 1708.

Ward, Thomas. *England's Reformation from the Time of King Henry the VIIIth to the End of Oates's Plot.* Hambourgh [Saint-Omer]: [n.p.], 1710.

Warner, William. *Licensing Entertainment: The Elevation of Novel Reading in Britain, 1684–1750.* Berkeley: University of California Press, 1998.

———. "Staging Readers Reading." *Eighteenth-Century Fiction* 12, no. 2–3 (2000): 391–416.

Watson, Nicola J. *Revolution and the Form of the British Novel, 1790–1825: Intercepted Letters, Interrupted Seductions.* Oxford: Clarendon Press, 1994.

Webb, R. K. "Rational Piety." In *Enlightenment and Religion: Rational Dissent in Eighteenth-Century Britain*, edited by Knud Haakonssen, 287–311. Cambridge: Cambridge University Press, 1996.

Weng, Yi-Cheng. "'She Had Recourse to Her Pen': Radical Voices in Elizabeth Hamilton's *Memoirs of Modern Philosophers*." *Romantic Textualities* 22 (2017): 36–51.

Wesley, John. *A Survey of the Wisdom of God in the Creation; or A Compendium of Natural Philosophy.* 2nd ed. 3 vols. Bristol: Printed by William Pine, 1770.

———. *The Works of the Late Reverend John Wesley, A.M.: From the Latest London Edition with the Last Corrections of the Author, Comprehending Also Numerous Translations, Notes, and an Original Preface, Etc.* Edited by John Emory. 7 vols. New York: Waugh and Mason, 1835.

West, Jane. *The Infidel Father.* 3 vols. London: Printed by A. Strahan, Printers-Street, for T. N. Longman, and O. Rees, Paternoster-Row, 1802.

———. *A Tale of the Times.* 3 vols. London: Printed for T. N. Longman and O. Rees, Paternoster-Row, 1799.

West, Shearer. *The Image of the Actor: Verbal and Visual Representation in the Age of Garrick and Kemble.* London: Pinter Publishers, 1991.

Wetmore, Alex. *Men of Feeling in Eighteenth-Century Literature: Touching Fiction.* Basingstoke: Palgrave Macmillan, 2013.

Whitefield, George. *Christ the Best Husband; or An Earnest Invitation to Young Women to Come and See Christ. A Sermon Preached to a Society of Young Women, in Fetter-Lane.* London: C. Whitefield, 1740.

———. *A Continuation of the Reverend Mr. Whitefield's Journal, from His Arrival at London, to His Departure from thence on his Way to Georgia.* 3rd ed. London: Printed for James Hutton, at the Bible and Sun, 1739.

———. *A Short Account of God's Dealings with the Reverend Mr. George Whitefield, A. B. Late of Pembroke-College, Oxford. From His Infancy, to the Time of His Entring into Holy Orders.* London: Printed by W. Strahan, and sold by James Hutton, 1740.

Wiehe, Jarred. "No Penis? No Problem: Intersections of Queerness and Disability in Laurence Sterne's *The Life and Opinions of Tristram Shandy, Gentleman.*" *The Eighteenth Century* 58, no. 2 (2017): 177–193.

Wilson, Adrian. *The Making of Man-Midwifery: Childbirth in England, 1660–1770.* Cambridge, Mass.: Harvard University Press, 1995.

Winnett, Arthur Robert. *Peter Browne: Provost, Bishop, Metaphysician.* London: S.P.C.K., 1974.

Wood, Lisa. *Modes of Discipline: Women, Conservatism, and the Novel after the French Revolution.* Lewisburg, Pa.: Bucknell University Press, 2003.

The World. 1754.

Wyett, Jodi L. "Female Quixotism Refashioned: *Northanger Abbey*, the Engaged Reader, and the Woman Writer." *The Eighteenth Century* 56, no. 2 (2015): 261–276.

———. "Quixotic Legacy: *The Female Quixote* and the Professional Woman Writer." *Authorship* 4, no. 1 (2015): 1–19.

Yalom, Marilyn. *A History of the Breast.* New York: Alfred A. Knopf, 1997.

Page numbers in italics refer to figures.

ruin (sexual). *See* "fallen" women
ruling passions, 81, 88. *See also*
  hobby-horses

satire, 94–95, 105, 133
Scheming Triumvirate, The, 100, *101*
Scots Magazine, 182n31
Scudéry, Madeleine de, *Clélie*, 12, 19, 25,
  33, 41
secularism, 96–97, 98–99, 113, 133, 136,
  140–141
Sedan, 60
self-consciousness, 11, 16, 26, 31, 67
sensibility: and the body, 11, 54–55, 83,
  85–86, 109–111, 127–128, 150–151; and
  class, 54; and masculinity, 83, 85–86; and
  Methodism, 109–110; politicization of,
  11–12, 16, 126, 127, 140, 150–151; and
  quixotism, 13, 54–55, 109–110, 126, 152
sentimentalism. *See* sensibility; sentimental
  literature
sentimental literature: and affective display,
  11, 41–42, 48, 52–55, 151; and the
  book-object, 11, 151; parodied, 48, 52–54,
  128, 133; and quixotism, 48, 63, 152; and
  romance, 41–42
sermons: and enthusiasm, 106–109, 178n49;
  as mass entertainment, 100–101, 178n49;
  and novels, 100–103; and quixotism,
  102, 108
servants, 12–13, 31, 40, 106, 127, 147, 159n46;
  Lucy (*The Female Quixote*), 31, 40;
  Tugwell (*The Spiritual Quixote*), 94, 96,
  104, 118, *119*
sex, one-sex model, 83
Shaftesbury, 3rd Earl of (Anthony Ashley
  Cooper), *The Moralists*, 180n75
Shakespeare, William, 38, 49, 57
Shenstone, William: gardens, 116, 180n82;
  poetry, 136; in *The Spiritual Quixote*, 116,
  118
Sheridan, Richard Brinsley, 165n14
Sheridan, Thomas, 110, 168n61
signification, 52–53, 91, 107–108, 118–120,
  124, 137–140, 148, 176–177n25
Silver, Sean, 15, 16, 63
sketches, 116, *117*
skin, 2, 8, 11, 40, 147
slave to the letter, 135–140, 184n66
smell, 21

Smollett, Tobias, 166n24; *Critical Review*,
  48, 166n24; translation of *Don Quixote*,
  163n62; *Roderick Random*, 160n1
snuff, 125–126
sodomy, 70, 83, 86–87
softness, 12–13, 35, 76, 149, 150, 172n30
souls, 3, 9, 56, 78, 82, 83, 106, 114–115, 116,
  179n51
sound, 21, 149; of language, 91, 110, 121, 124,
  137–140
*Sovereign Remedy for the cure of Hypocrisy
  and Blind Zeal, A*, 96
Spacks, Patricia Meyer, 35, 175n71
Spedding, Patrick, 59, 65, 170nn105–106
sperm, 75, 76–77
spots, 7, 9–10, 40
Staël, Germaine de, *Delphine*, 150
stage. *See* theater
St. André, Nathanael, 79–80
Staves, Susan, 71, 88
Steele, Richard, *The Tender Husband*, 46, 67,
  162n33, 165n14
Stephanson, Raymond, 69, 71
stereotypes (printing), 125, 142, 147
Sterne Laurence, 89, 100–101; Shandean
  body, 69–72, 84; *Tristram Shandy*, 9–10,
  17, 25–26, 34, 63–90, 100–101, 105, 106,
  107, 111–112, 113, 137, 163n62, 171n9,
  172n16, 173n34, 173n39, 174n64,
  174–175n69, 175n71, 179n66
Stewart, Dugald, 138
subject, the, 2–4, 7, 9–10, 13, 15–16, 20–24,
  26, 41, 62–64, 76, 103, 124, 130, 147–148,
  149–153
Subligny, Adrien-Thomas Perdou de, *La
  fausse Clélie*, 25, 33, 37, 162n34
surface, 2–4, 7, 12, 15, 40–41, 50–52, 55, 67,
  70–71, 86, 152, 168n61
Swift, Johnathan: *A Discourse Concerning
  the Mechanical Operation of the
  Spirit*, 179nn51–52; *Gulliver's Travels*,
  186n98
swooning, 41–42
sympathy: and history writing, 22–23; and
  the novel, 49–50; performance of, 53–55;
  and romance, 22–23; and the theater,
  49–50, 55

tabula rasa, 63, 67. *See also* blank page
Tatler, 177n29

ABOUT THE AUTHOR

AMELIA DALE is a lecturer in the School of Languages and Literature at Shanghai University of International Business and Economics.

TRANSITS:
LITERATURE, THOUGHT & CULTURE, 1650–1850